WILD WOMEN
∽of the Old West∽

WILD WOMEN
~of the Old West~

Edited by

Glenda Riley & Richard W. Etulain

Fulcrum Publishing
GOLDEN, COLORADO

Library of Congress Cataloging-in-Publication Data

Wild women of the Old West / edited by Glenda Riley and Richard W. Etulain.
    p. cm. — (Notable westerners)
Includes bibliographical references and index.
  ISBN 1-55591-295-8 (pbk. : alk. paper)
  1. Women pioneers—West (U.S.)—Biography. 2. Women—West (U.S.)—Biography. 3. Frontier and pioneer life—West (U.S.) 4. West (U.S.)—Biography. I. Riley, Glenda, 1938- II. Etulain, Richard W. III. Series.
  F596 .W5798 2003
  978'.02'0922—dc21

                              2002154877

Printed in the United States of America
0 9 8 7 6 5 4 3 2 1

Editorial: Don Graydon, Daniel Forrest-Bank
Cover design: Jennifer LaRock-Shontz
Interior design: Anne Clark
Cover art: Calamity Jane, copyright © Thom Ross,
    Ravenwork Studio, Seattle, Washington.
    Collection of Denise Meyers, Palm Springs, California.
Back cover photo: Calamity Jane in buckskins; the Wild West
    woman as performer. Courtesy of American Heritage
    Center, University of Wyoming.

Fulcrum Publishing
16100 Table Mountain Parkway, Suite 300
Golden, Colorado 80403
(800) 992-2908 • (303) 277-1623
www.fulcrum-books.com

Contents

Series Preface

Fulcrum Publishing is proud to be the publisher of the Notable Westerners series. The volumes in this series explore the real stories behind the personalities and events that continue to shape our national character.

The American West — land of myth, epitome of the independent American spirit. When we think of the men and women who shaped the West, we tend to think in terms of caricatures, of larger-than-life heroes and heroines. Notable men and women have always loomed large on the open and wide landscapes of the American West. From the earliest Native American leaders to more recent westerners, these influential people have attracted the attention of travelers, historians, and writers. Often, such visitors focus on how these heroes and heroines of the region were important in shaping and reshaping images of the West.

Books in the Notable Westerners series explore the personalities and influences of such outstanding western characters. Editors Glenda Riley and Richard W. Etulain draw on their long experience in western history and their wide associations with western historians of varied racial, ethnic, gender, and social backgrounds. To these volumes, contributors bring expertise in their fields, knowledge of significant individuals, and lucid writing styles.

The result is a variety of essays providing insight into the movers and shakers of a unique region of the United States. The American West not only helped shape the American national character, but provides a continuing source of fascination for Americans and non-Americans alike.

Acknowledgments

The editors appreciate the help and support of several people and organizations in creating this book. We are especially indebted to the contributors for taking the time from their full schedules to write essays for this collection, as well as for their professionalism and insightful analyses.

Glenda Riley expresses gratitude to Ball State University, especially to the Alexander M. Bracken Fund, to the Department of History at Ball State, and to research assistant Deborah L. Rogers. Additionally, Riley would like to thank the following for their cooperation, comments, and information: Oleta Mae Nelson, a great-niece of Sadie Orchard, who lives in Tacoma, Washington; Gloria J. Anders, curator of the Black Range Museum in Hillsboro, New Mexico; LaRena Miller and Ann Welborn at the Geronimo Springs Museum in Truth or Consequences, New Mexico; Edward Montoya of Hillsboro and Truth or Consequences; the Sierra County Clerk's office, the District Court Clerk's office, and Carol Kirikos of French Mortuary, all in Truth or Consequences, New Mexico; and director Susan Berry and the staff of the Silver City Museum, Silver City, New Mexico.

Richard W. Etulain is much indebted to James McLaird and William Whiteside for reading an earlier draft of his essay on Calamity Jane and for providing references to valuable, obscure sources. David Key also read and commented on the essay, with Cindy Tyson helping in preparing the piece. In addition, he is indebted to the Research Allocations Committee and the Center for the American West at the University of New Mexico for research support of his essay and this volume. He likewise wishes to thank Chuck Rankin (formerly director of publications at the Montana Historical Society), David Holtby and the University of New Mexico Press, and Marlene Blessing and editors at Fulcrum Publishing for permission to use parts of previous publications on Calamity Jane for his essay in this collection.

Finally, the editors wish to indicate their appreciation for encouragement and aid from the staff at Fulcrum Publishing, notably Marlene Blessing and Daniel Forrest-Bank.

GLENDA RILEY   RICHARD W. ETULAIN
Ball State University   University of New Mexico

Introduction
What Is a Wild Woman?

GLENDA RILEY

The phrase "wild woman" conjures up all types of images. For the late nineteenth- and early twentieth-century West, wild women included rebellious daughters, dance-hall girls, cowgirls, and female outlaws, all of who gambol through the following pages. For the purposes of this collection, wild women are defined as individuals who deviated from their culture's and their era's expectations of a "proper" woman. Their lives encompassed unusual escapades and often involved quests for freedom, notoriety, or wealth. Some wild women had sensational lives, full of drama and adventure. Other women's lives were filled with achievement, while less fortunate ones faced privation or violence.

Due to their exploits, many wild women's names have entered the lexicon of western myth and legend. A few are less well-known. Even though some of these women's stories may have been overlooked, the following essays demonstrate that they should be writ large in the history of the American West—and of the United States. After all, the West's wild women also contributed to the development of national character, folklore, and images of women. More recently, some have served as models for young women who also want to try different roads.

As with "wild" western men, such women's lives have been romanticized and idealized until truth lies hidden behind myth. Moreover, restaurants and businesses are named after them, monuments have been erected to commemorate them, and a few towns even bear their names. As outrageous as these women might have been, however, a closer look usually reveals less glamor and more devotion to feminine ideals than one might expect. The essays that follow reveal both sides of a particular woman's story, the mythological and whatever "facts" can be established.

The articles in section one, "Errant Daughters," indicate that a number of wild women left home and challenged their upbringing. Their reasons were diverse. Perhaps, like many men, they sought wealth or a freer way of life. Others sought causes worthy of their life energies. The latter was true of the

Sarah Winnemucca, as she appeared in 1908 in General O. O. Howard, Famous Indian Chiefs I Have Known *(New York, Century). (Courtesy of Glenda Riley.)*

Paiute leader Sarah Winnemucca. Although her life story is not included among the essays, a brief glimpse of Winnemucca here in the introduction demonstrates many of the qualities that characterized wild women.

Sarah—or Thoc-me-tony (Shell-Flower in Paiute)—was born around 1844 to a traditional Paiute family. Even though Anglos had already begun to penetrate the Paiutes' homeland near the Humboldt River of present-day Nevada, Sarah's family hoped for the best. Earlier in the nineteenth century, Sarah's grandfather, Chief Winnemucca I, widely known as Captain Truckee, had led Captain John Frémont and his party across the Great Basin to California. Similarly, Sarah's father, Chief Winnemucca II, tried to befriend Anglo settlers. In fact, it was when Chief Winnemucca visited Anglo families in California and later placed Sarah for a year with the family of William Ormsby near Genoa, Nevada, that Sarah resolved her fear of Anglos and began to learn English. She later mastered not only English, but Spanish and several Indian dialects as well.

As a young woman, Sarah led a chaotic life. In 1860, she witnessed the horrors of the Paiute War and, afterward, experienced the destitution of life on a Paiute reservation at Pyramid Lake near Reno. Between 1868 to 1871, when Sarah acted as a translator at Camp McDermott in northeastern Nevada, she saw firsthand how corruption among politicians and Indian agents cost her people food, supplies, and even education. Sarah also watched her mother and sister die from, in her view, abuses by Indian agents.

It is said that in 1878 Sarah fought in the Bannock War, where she proved a tireless warrior for the Americans against the Bannocks. Records show, however, that after risking her own life to locate her father, Sarah served as General O. O. Howard's aide, scout, and interpreter. The U.S. government repaid such loyalty by force-marching a large group of Paiutes in mid-winter to the Malheur reservation in southeastern Oregon.

It was at Malheur that the Paiutes elected Sarah Winnemucca as their chief. In this role, she spoke and wrote about the wrongs her people endured. Wearing Indian clothing, Chief Sarah crisscrossed the country making speeches that especially blamed Indian agents. In 1880, she met with President Rutherford B. Hayes, exacting promises that were never fulfilled. In 1883, Sarah's book, *Life Among the Piutes: Their Wrongs and Claims*, was privately published and subsequently sold at her lectures to help defray costs. During the late 1880s, Sarah finally saw some results of her public crusades. Those Paiutes who had managed to survive the deplorable conditions at Malheur were allowed to return to Nevada. Meanwhile, Sarah established a Paiute school in Nevada.

In her personal life, Sarah fared less well. In a time when "proper" women married, Sarah refused to remain in a destructive relationship. She ended her 1871 marriage to an army officer after a year because of his alleged intemperance. Similarly, she left an Indian husband for abuse. In 1881, Sarah married Lieutenant L. H. Hopkins, who died of tuberculosis five years later. The couple had no children. Sarah's health and spirit were broken, and in 1891, she also died of tuberculosis.

Clearly, Sarah Winnemucca qualifies as a wild woman. Although she had not been raised as a fighter, Sarah fought every day of her adult life. She struggled to stay alive, to protect her people, to combat corruption. Insubordination became her stock in trade. Also, in an era when a woman's appearance on a theater stage was still controversial, Sarah became a performer—one with a cause. Rather than becoming a pariah, Sarah was a heroine. The town of Winnemucca, Nevada, as well as the Winnemucca Indian Reservation, honored Sarah Winnemucca by taking her name. In Nevada, historical marker #143 reminds modern-day Americans that Sarah "worked tirelessly to remedy injustice and to advocate peace." Farther away, in New York state, the National Women's Hall of Fame inducted Sarah as an honoree.

In addition to Sarah Winnemucca, numerous other daughters not only left home, but became alien and curious to the very parents who raised them. In the first section of essays, the reader meets Elizabeth Bonduel McCord, better known as Baby Doe Tabor. Because Baby Doe was a reputed beauty, she was able to marry above her social class. Her husband took her to Colorado, where a family gold mine promised the couple riches. When that husband and that plan failed to work out, Baby Doe took matters into her own hands, rocking the nation with scandal. The historian of western women, author Glenda Riley, argues that Baby Doe's immersion in the Victorian "culture of beauty" served her well in some ways, while destroying her in others. Nonetheless, after her death Baby Doe became famous, with an opera, a museum, and a doll of her own.

The second errant daughter was a free black woman, Emily D. West (Morgan), better known to history as the Yellow Rose of Texas. According to the Texan journalist Carmen Goldthwaite, Emily left her home in New Haven, Connecticut, during the mid-1830s for New York City. In 1835, she sailed from New York to Texas, not knowing that Texas tottered on the brink of war with Mexico. At the Battle of San Jacinto, Emily reportedly saved Texas by diverting the attention of the Mexican general Antonio López de Santa Anna. Gently and with good humor, Goldthwaite turns what she calls "history's lamp" on the Yellow Rose, one of Texas's most loved legends.

The third chapter focuses on Polly Bemis, supposedly a Chinese prostitute won in a poker game by Idaho saloon-keeper Charlie Bemis. The independent historian and historical archeologist Priscilla Wegars skillfully probes Polly's legend to show that Polly was a concubine, or a secondary wife with a recognized status whose children were considered legitimate. How Polly got to Warren, Idaho, and her meeting and eventual marriage to Charlie Bemis remain enigmatic, however. Wegars aptly concludes that, despite Polly's "questionable" reputation, based mostly on a fantasy often applied to Chinese women, Polly was a highly significant pioneer woman in the Pacific Northwest.

The second set of essays, "Sellers of Sex," focuses on a very different type of wild women; those who exchanged for money—or who were reported to exchange for money—their companionship and sexual favors. Because of racial prejudice, certain types of women were often assumed to be prostitutes, even when their actual lives proved otherwise. African American and Chinese women were especially branded unfairly. Of course, dance hall girls, prostitutes, and madams did include a few women of color. Along with Anglo women, they usually led difficult lives. The time they spent in brothels, in saloons, in small buildings called cribs, or as streetwalkers often involved hard work, low status, danger, and violence. Yet western prostitution, at least that which occurred in relatively safe brothels, has been glorified. As a result, life in western bawdy houses appears amusing and even enjoyable.

Western daughters may have dressed "properly," but many went where they pleased. This Arizona woman daringly reveals her petticoat in the Grand Canyon in 1903. (Courtesy of the Arizona Historical Society, Tucson, AHS #63547.)

Today, Americans commemorate the West's "bad" women in all sorts of unexpected ways. In Georgetown, Colorado, for example, famous madam Mattie Silks is not forgotten. Once a "roaring" gold camp, Georgetown now offers tourists trendy boutiques, one of which is Mattie Silks antiques and collectibles shop. In Denver, Silks's home base, the Mattie Silks Restaurant keeps Mattie's name alive. More recently, Denver's infamous House of Mirrors, originally a "parlor house" built in 1889 on Market Street by madam Jennie Rogers, had a facelift. The original House of Mirrors was built to— and did—provide competition for Mattie Silks, who eventually bought the business and operated it until 1915. In 2001, the refurbished House of Mirrors opened as a sophisticated restaurant with a gourmet menu.

Why Americans of the twenty-first century cling to, and perpetuate, inaccurate memories of prostitutes and madams is an enigma. In their own time, such women led little more than half-lives. Pushed into prostitution by poverty, force, or chicanery, many hated what they did to earn a living. Even women who chose prostitution as one of the most well-paid jobs open to women sometimes regretted their choices. Also, because prostitutes were anathemas to "good" women, they found themselves restricted to "tenderloin" or "red-light" districts. When prostitutes and madams interacted with local citizens, it was usually on a cash-for-sex basis. Or they might meet the local constabulary during police raids or have the chance to talk to a town's no-gooders during a stint in jail. At the same time, "good" women put pressure on local officials to enforce anti-prostitution laws and to drive lawbreakers out of the county.

Whether they be madams or prostitutes, these women often pined for three things: respectability, personal safety, and families. Although some had families, the existence of a husband and children did not gain a prostitute respect or freedom from violence. Like other women, single and married prostitutes and madams often yearned for commonplace domesticity. They would have gladly exchanged for a banal existence the possibility of personal assault, being cheated or robbed of hard-earned money, or ending up in jail.

Even Laura Evans, a successful madam first in Denver and later in Leadville, admitted that her business had its dark side. Always ebullient, Evans reveled in high times and gaiety. Yet, she also noted that suicides or suicide-attempts among "her girls" took a heavy toll on her. Moreover, in order to cash in on a gold or other mineral strike, she had to follow the miners from place to place. If a town's "good" women failed to push Evans out, the playing out of a mine eventually did so.

At the same time, life as a soiled dove had its attractions. In some houses, prostitutes wore fine clothes and jewels (most of which belonged to the proprietor of the house). Some madams encouraged "fun," notably dancing and drinking, which caused male clients to spend considerable amounts of money during the course of an evening. Often, prostitutes found friends among their colleagues; they watched out for each other and helped one another when they were down. In addition, some prostitutes caught the fancy of one particular man, who would "buy" all their time. Occasionally, a woman even struck it lucky, marrying a man of means and leaving "the life" behind her.

Of course, these are the aspects of the "sporting life" that stick in people's minds. The color and romance overshadows the boredom and abuse. Prostitutes and madams who operated in the "wild" West now appear spicy, daring, and colorful. They were women unafraid to grab their chances and live to the fullest. The fact that they violated society's moral codes can be explained away by the unusual nature of the frontier. In addition, the fabulous money they supposedly earned makes prostitution an economic issue rather than a moral one.

In reality, each individual woman made her own accommodations—or her own escape. Although some women gave their entire lives to the profession, others left it behind as soon as they could. They may have been forced by circumstances

In the late 1920s, dressy outfits and impractical shoes did not stop these Arizona women from enjoying the wide open spaces. (Courtesy of the Arizona Historical Society, Tucson, AHS #70350.)

into prostitution, yet they did not accept their status as a life-long fate. Some married out of prostitution, while others, with the aid of women's reform societies, obtained enough education and skills to land other jobs.

The diverse experiences and responses of such women provide the theme for Part Two. By presenting a composite picture of three prostitutes, the western historian Anne M. Butler demonstrates that the West offered a wide range of job opportunities to women, including prostitution, but that the latter also involved greater risks than most other occupations. More specifically, Butler deftly chronicles the adversities faced by Denver madams Mattie Silks and Katie Fulton, both white, and Ida Jones, an African American. Butler explores the influence of race in shaping prostitutes' lives, and also explains that the "ribald excitement" associated with western prostitution is what makes it so entrancing and, well, so western.

The next piece reports on Sadie Orchard, a legendary prostitute and madam in gold- and silver-rush New Mexico. Although Orchard started out in Kingston, she spent most of her life and career in Hillsboro. The author Glenda Riley shows the dangers associated with prostitution and how Orchard attempted to escape through marriage and by establishing a "respectable" hotel. After the marriage became a disaster, Orchard was again on her own. As a

divorced woman who always called herself a widow, Orchard kept the legiti-
mate hotel, but turned a hotel around the corner into a brothel. Unlike Mattie
Silks, Kate Fulton, and Ida Jones, however, Orchard projected the image of a
Victorian lady, thus becoming one of Hillsboro's local characters.

The third group of essays, "Showtime Cowgirls," showcases a very different type of wild women. These women captured public attention not only by
riding horses—often astride rather than sidesaddle—but employed lariats or
even firearms to make a living. A brief sketch of the first cowgirl, Annie
Oakley, reveals what readers might expect of the women who followed in
Oakley's footsteps. Although many commentators identify Lucille Mulhall as
the nation's first cowgirl, neither the concept nor the image of the cowgirl
originated with rodeo. In 1885, the year of Lucile Mulhall's birth, Annie
Oakley joined Buffalo Bill's Wild West and became America's first cowgirl.

Without Oakley challenging what she identified as "prejudice" in the
arena, such early rodeo stars as Annie Shaffer of Arkansas and Lucille
Mulhall of Oklahoma would have encountered disbelieving audiences and
hostile journalists. Annie won over audiences and journalists alike. She
projected an image so feminine, ladylike, Victorian, and appealing that most
people thought of cowgirls as charming. With her flowing hair, calf-length

*Properly attired western women also handled weapons and hunted. Here a Utah woman
poses with a bird she shot in 1901. (Courtesy of the Utah State Historical Society,
917.8, #27287.)*

MISS ANNIE OAKLEY,
THE PEERLESS LADY WING-SHOT.

Annie Oakley, "The Peerless Lady Wing-Shot," in an advertisement for Buffalo Bill's Wild West Show, circa 1890. (Courtesy of Glenda Riley)

skirts, and modest behavior, Annie made it acceptable and even admirable for women to appear first in wild-west—and soon in rodeo—arenas.

When Annie joined Buffalo Bill's company in 1885, she had no intention of helping Cody create a genre of western women called the cowgirl. Annie was an Ohio farm girl who had been shooting such small game as rabbits and wild turkeys since she was ten or so, and had later participated in occasional shooting competitions in southwestern Ohio. After defeating professional shooter Frank Butler in a match, and then marrying him, Annie performed in vaudeville and the circus arena as part of the team "Butler and Oakley."

Beginning in 1885, Annie and Frank, who acted as her manager and publicity agent, accepted her new image as the model western woman. Cody, however, was treading on unfamiliar terrain. At the time, popular writers, poets, and artists included women in their work, but they tended to present them as victims. As a result, Cody hired during the mid- and late 1880s a number of actresses to enact victims in such sketches as "The Burning of the Settlers' Cabin" and "The Attack on the Deadwood Stage." At the same time, he added "strong" women who performed as riders and shooters. As early as 1886, the Wild West's program included Georgia Duffy of Wyoming and Dell Ferrel of Colorado, as well as sharp-shooter Lillian Smith, billed as "The California Girl."

By the 1890s, the Wild West advertised cowgirls and "prairie girls," meaning women who rode horses in complicated drills, performed tricks bareback, rode broncos, and participated in the Virginia Reel on horseback. During her early years with Cody, Annie Oakley not only shot, but took part in the Virginia Reel and rode bucking-horses. In 1887, she trained a horse named Gypsy to follow her everywhere, including up flights of stairs and into a theater's freight elevator. About the same time, when Annie drew as her mount in a horse race what a journalist called a "small, sleepy-looking buck-skin," he credited her with turning the animal into a "wide-awake little horse" that won that race, as well as every other race it ran.

As Oakley's fame grew during the 1890s, other women followed her example. May Lillie, who had grown up in Philadelphia and attended Smith College, became a rider and shooter with Pawnee Bill's troupe and star of the show's "Beautiful Daring Western Girls." May once declared that being a wild-west performer gave a woman far more enjoyment that "any pink tea or theater party or ballroom ever yielded."

During the late 1890s and early 1900s, many other cowgirls modeled themselves after Annie Oakley's feminine cowgirl. Most wild-west and rodeo cowgirls continued to wear dresses or skirts and bodices, gloves, and hats with turned-up brims. When Lucille Mulhall made her debut in 1897 at age thirteen, she, like Annie, dressed primly. Similarly, even though Bertha Blancett of Wyoming, rode broncs in competition and worked as a stunt-rider for Bison Moving Picture Company, she dressed "properly."

When Annie, who had retired from Cody's company in 1901, returned to the wild-west arena between 1911 and 1913, she wore her usual conservative clothing and acted like a Victorian lady. Again, what athlete and performer Annie Oakley achieved in the wild-west arena had a decided impact on rodeo. Florence Reynolds, who went into rodeo during the 1910s, said that she "watched the early day Wild West show change into today's rodeo." It is little wonder, then, that Oakley's cowgirl continued to appeal to a number of other cowgirls, including Vera McGinnis, who rode side-saddle, and trick-rider Tad Lucas, who made all her own costumes, feminine in style.

Since her death in 1926, Annie Oakley has been memorialized in many ways. For example, the city of Greenville, Ohio, where Annie died has an Annie Oakley Park featuring a splendid bronze statue of Oakley. On July 28, 2001, a historical marker was added to the park. Greenville is also the home of the Annie Oakley Foundation, the Garst Museum with its Annie Oakley room, and an annual Annie Oakley festival.

Even though Annie is well remembered as the nation's first cowgirl, other women institutionalized the cowgirl image in rodeo. Two of the most notable rodeo competitors of the early 1900s are depicted here. The first is Lucille Mulhall by the western writer and editor Candy Moulton. In her lively essay, Moulton presents Mulhall as rodeo's first cowgirl. Mulhall enlarged on Annie Oakley's feats by becoming a champion rider and roper. Wearing a prim white shirtwaist and dark skirt, Mulhall could bring a steer to the ground and tie it in seconds. Mulhall was from the "true" West—Oklahoma— whereas Annie Oakley was from Ohio. Thus, Mulhall learned her skills on the family ranch and parlayed them into a profession that deviated from women's usual duties, keeping her in the arena and the spotlight for most of her life.

The second rodeo cowgirl was Bertha Kaepernik Blancett, adroitly por- trayed by M. J. Van Deventer, editor, author, and director of publications for the National Cowboy and Western Heritage Museum in Oklahoma City. Van Deventer persuasively suggests that Bertha's path to rodeo began when she was five years old and her father put her on the back of a horse with instruc- tions to watch a herd of cattle and to "stay aboard." Like Mulhall, this Colorado ranch girl learned to ride and rope in the course of daily life. As a

Female hunters, who still wore skirts, went after bigger game as well. Here a Montana woman poses with the coyote she shot near Eagle Rock on the Montana West Fork River, after 1900. (Courtesy of the Montana Historical Society, Helena, MHS #35.)

Belle Starr at Fort Smith, Arkansas, in 1887. (Courtesy of the Western History Collection, University of Oklahoma Libraries.)

teenager, she entered local rodeos along with her male peers. According to Van Deventer, throughout Bertha's renowned career as a bronc rider, she always fulfilled her father's instruction to stay aboard.

Lastly, the essays in Part Four, "Almost Outlaws," explore the lives of female Wild Bill Hickoks and Billy the Kids. Of all the women who gained fame as outlaws, Belle Starr was, and continues to be, the most well-known. Her life is especially interesting because it offers many clues as to what forces shaped a wild woman. For one thing, Belle Starr chose to live on the edge, both of the law and of women's culture. For another, the media enlarged her story almost to the point of being unrecognizable. Called by journalists and dime novelists the "bandit queen," Belle Starr was supposedly a rough-riding, hard-shooting, mean-mouthed outlaw. Yet she began life as a traditional southern woman.

In 1848, Belle was born Myra Maybelle Shirley near Modoc, Missouri. In 1855, her parents enrolled Belle in the Carthage Female Seminary, where she learned to play the piano and was supposed to acquire other social graces expected of well-bred women of the era. But Myra clearly preferred the outdoors and the company of her brother Bud. It was he who taught Myra how to use firearms, to ride every horse in their father's stable, and to view life as an adventure. When the Civil War started, Bud volunteered. Myra assisted him by relaying information and carrying intelligence across the lines. After Bud was killed in June of 1864, Myra reportedly strapped on two revolvers and swore to avenge his death.

Before Myra could act, however, her father relocated the family in Scyene, south of Dallas, Texas. Shortly after the move, the James brothers and four of their band traded on Cole Younger's acquaintance with the Shirleys back in Missouri by seeking brief refuge with the family. Although Myra supposedly fell in love with Cole Younger and was pregnant with his child by the time the group departed, no evidence supports this contention. On November 1, 1866, eighteen-year-old Myra married twenty-year-old James C. Reed. Like Bud, Jim was handsome and dashing, handy with weapons, an expert rider, and a risk-taker.

Even though Myra tried to be a good wife and a devoted mother to the Reeds' two children, odds seemed against her. Charged with theft and passing counterfeit money, Jim ran from the law until 1873, when he was shot dead. For Myra, other troublesome liaisons followed. For a time, she lived with Bruce Younger, half-brother to Cole Younger's father. Next, in 1880, she married Cherokee Sam Starr. She also lopped five years off her age and renamed herself Belle—Belle Starr.

Belle, who hoped to escape her past, was discouraged to learn how difficult it would be to reform her image. According to her, "it soon became nosed around that I was a woman of some notoriety from Texas, and from that time on my home and actions have been severely criticized." Belle herself contributed to her growing infamy. When wanted-criminal Jesse James found Belle's cabin, she allowed him to remain in her home for three weeks. She also played fast and loose with other people's property, notably their horses. In July of 1882, the U.S. Commissioner's Court in Fort Smith put out an arrest order for Belle and Sam, charging that the pair had stolen an $80 horse. Belle was sentenced to two six-month terms and Sam to one year in the House of Corrections in Detroit, Michigan.

Journalists inflated the trial and its outcome far beyond its original proportions. According to one, "the very idea of a woman being charged with an offense of this kind and that she was the leader of a band of horse thieves and wielding a power over them as their queen and guiding spirit, was sufficient to fill the courtroom with spectators." In addition, rumors flew across Indian Territory and beyond. Belle's "gang" grew beyond believable proportions, and her supposed exploits exceeded the capability of one person. Gradually,

Belle seemed to accept her image and even to play to it. She wore large gold earrings with a man's sombrero and called her Colt .45 pistol "my baby."

After their release from the workhouse, Belle and Sam found themselves again in trouble with the law. Sam was implicated in several robberies; Belle was charged with horse-stealing and being a "gang leader" in a recent robbery. Belle seemed to realize that in most people's eyes she would never be anything more than a female outlaw. She even consented to pose for a photograph with the notorious criminal Blue Duck. Shortly afterward, juries exonerated Belle of all charges. A deputy sheriff pursuing Sam shot him to death.

Once again, Belle selected as her companion a young, dashing, devil-may-care kind of fellow who was a liquor-runner and horse-thief. After Belle invited a Cherokee named Bill July to live with her as her de facto husband, he kept the couple embroiled in legal problems. On February 2, 1889, Belle rode with July into Fort Smith to respond to a federal charge of horse theft against him. The next day, Belle headed home alone. As she rode toward her cabin on Sunday, February 3, 1889, an unknown assailant gunned her down. Three days later, Belle was buried with her favorite revolver in her hands.

The following year, when the U.S. Bureau of the Census declared the frontier "closed" by virtue of its population, Belle Starr provided a perfect subject for people anxious to idealize and romanticize the waning West. She soon became a daring and glamorous female gunslinger, called the "queen of the bandits." The name of Belle Starr is still widely known, but it does not stand alone. Such women as Cattle Kate, Calamity Jane, the Rose of Cimarron, and Pearl Hart gained similar ignominy. Of these, the infamous Cattle Kate and Calamity Jane constitute Part Four.

Cattle Kate, presented by the western writer and independent historian Lori Van Pelt, had the dubious distinction of being the only woman ever hanged in Wyoming. Also known as Ella Watson, Cattle Kate earned her living through prostitution and cattle rustling. As a divorcee who claimed homestead land, Kate put herself squarely in the middle of the contretemps between homesteaders and ranchers during the 1870s and 1880s. Long after her lynching in 1889, Kate became a folk hero. Like Baby Doe Tabor, Kate's life was chronicled in an opera. Today, an upscale line of western clothing carries her name. Van Pelt effectively reasons that Kate may have been a rustler—or not—but that her story has so much drama that fans of the Old West will not let it fade away.

The final chapter concerns Martha Canary, more widely known as Calamity Jane. The noted western historian Richard W. Etulain explores

Other women adopted clothing more suitable to their work, such as Feliz Ruelas at the A Ranch in Arizona's Box Canyon in the Santa Rita Mountains during the 1920s. (Courtesy of the Arizona Historical Society, Tucson, AHS #79440.)

how this particular western woman became one of the West's most enduring legends. He persuasively argues that Martha became Jane during the three years between 1875 and 1878, when she insisted on accompanying military and other expeditions on their quests for Black Hills gold. Calamity Jane caught and held the public imagination, appearing in stage shows and as the protagonist of almost twenty dime novels, all in her own lifetime. After her death in 1903, the myth of Calamity Jane grew, eventually providing material for several Hollywood films. Etulain insightfully concludes that the development of Jane's image, like those of the other women in this volume, demonstrated Americans' desire to hold on to—and magnify—figures of the vanishing American frontier.

Today, during the early twenty-first century, Americans are still fascinated with wild women, all of whom possessed one or more engaging characteristics. Some wild women were insubordinate, refusing to meet gender expectations or speaking out in public. Others were disobedient, going against family teachings or societal morality. Yet others were courageous, endangering their very lives to achieve their goals. Many were underdogs who triumphed, or competitors who won against tough odds. A few even broke the law, sometimes following male desperados, sometimes acting on their own.

Whatever their style, these women are fondly remembered. Because the West's wild women were bold and courageous, willing to take chances, and seldom bothered by what other folks might think, they stand as symbols to modern Americans who fear they have lost those very qualities. The women's stories persisted throughout the twentieth century; they will most likely weather the twenty-first as well.

Part One

Errant Daughters

Baby Doe Tabor

The Culture of Beauty

GLENDA RILEY

E lizabeth McCourt, also known as Baby Doe Tabor, lived during the late Victorian era when society judged white women largely on three attributes: family lineage and social standing, physical attractiveness, and the ability to work. The McCourt family pedigree was solid yet unimpressive. Fortunately for Elizabeth, she possessed such unusual comeliness that no one expected her to earn her own way in the world. In a culture that esteemed beauty, McCourt's looks would get her whatever she wanted. She did not disappoint. She married above her social class and, after a divorce, eventually became the paramour and second wife of the Colorado silver magnate Horace Austin Warner Tabor.

Along the way, McCourt discovered that the currency of beauty was difficult to spend wisely. She occasionally alienated her father and siblings, as well as setting herself at odds with her church. She also found herself defying Victorian gender expectations, becoming the subject of gossip, and isolating herself from the company of other women. Although Baby Doe got much of what she wanted, she ended up spending some thirty years of her later life as a destitute recluse, imposing little penances upon herself for her earlier vanity and hoping that her great silver fortune would return. Yet the tormented woman who came to be known as Baby Doe Tabor had then, and has yet today, a reputation as one of the most beautiful, flamboyant, and alluring women in the mining West. As a result, Baby Doe's life is shrouded by myth and hearsay, but its central outline can be reconstructed.

The Making of Baby Doe

No one would have predicted her future when Elizabeth Nellis McCourt came into the world in 1854, in Oshkosh, Wisconsin. She was the fourth out of eleven surviving children of Irish immigrants Peter McCourt and Elizabeth Nellis McCourt. Legend has it that, perhaps because of the confusion of

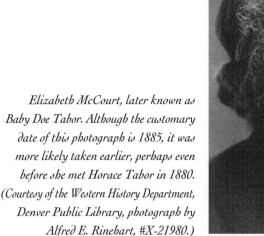

Elizabeth McCourt, later known as Baby Doe Tabor. Although the customary date of this photograph is 1885, it was more likely taken earlier, perhaps even before she met Horace Tabor in 1880. (Courtesy of the Western History Department, Denver Public Library, photograph by Alfred E. Rinehart, #X-21980.)

names, the younger Elizabeth later changed her middle name from Nellis to Bonduel after Father Bonduel, missionary to the Menominee Indians and a good friend of her parents. Other sources maintain that her original middle name was Bonduel rather than Nellis. The exact day of Elizabeth's birth is also uncertain because Oshkosh's fires destroyed the courthouse and its records. A recently retrieved document, however, shows the date as May 5, 1854. A baptismal certificate says she was christened on October 7, 1854. In a sense, the details of her birth seem rather inconsequential because Elizabeth revised her birthday, lopping six years off her age by changing the date from 1854 to 1860. Apparently even her great attractiveness could not free her from the era's emphasis on having youth as well as beauty.

As she was growing up, life was good for young Lizzie, as Elizabeth was called. Her mother was a full-time wife and mother, her father a partner in the clothing and tailoring shop of McCourt and Cameron. Her family lived in a substantial two-story home with white columns and a picket fence and employed a maid. As for the town, Lizzie would remember Oshkosh as an up-and-coming part of the lumber frontier, with whirring sawmills, shingle mills, and planing mills that made fortunes for some men and employed others who seemed, at least to Lizzie, romantic and intensely masculine. She absorbed a

3

frontier spirit of enterprise, as well as admiration for men who took risks, financial and otherwise.

In addition, Lizzie came to think of herself as a local beauty, supposedly dubbed the Belle of Oshkosh. The most frequent praise came from her mother, who told Lizzie she was not only too lovely to work, but had within her reach all the things her mother felt she had missed. Although Lizzie helped care for the younger children, she was free of most other domestic tasks, for her mother wanted her daughter to keep unimpaired the smooth skin of her hands and arms. In addition, whatever Lizzie wanted, even to become an actress, was fine with her mother.

Lizzie's father took a different view. He chided his wife for taking Lizzie to matinees at the Harding Opera House and for staying up nights sewing Lizzie striking outfits. Rather than arguing with his wife and daughter, however, McCourt left the house for long walks, sometimes stopping at St. Peter's Catholic Church to pray. Perhaps he harbored a measure of responsibility for the situation, in that he had owned Oshkosh's first theater, McCourt Hall, which preceded the Harding Opera House. To him, McCourt Hall had been a source of income, but to his young daughter, the building and its players suggested an exciting way of life and a potential career.

Despite his worries regarding Lizzie, McCourt allowed her to hang around his shop, admiring the fashionable buggies and carriages that stopped in front, often driven by attractive, wealthy men who seldom failed to compliment McCourt on his comely daughter. Perhaps McCourt thought he could watch over Lizzie, giving her some of the chaperonage that he accused his wife of neglecting. The result was that instead of making friends with girls her own age, Lizzie spent her spare time in a world of self-assured and well-to-do men.

At age sixteen, Lizzie had reached her adult height of five feet, four inches and was girlishly chubby. She was well aware of her white teeth, exquisite smile, and blond hair. Her frantic social life included dances, "sociables," the theater, buggy rides, and yachting parties on Lake Winnebago. As Lizzie honed her social skills and slimmed a bit—but still remained fashionably plump—she and her mother believed that anything was possible, from a career as an actress to marriage with a wealthy husband.

Unfortunately, the women's dreams took hard hits in 1874 and again in 1875, when sweeping fires consumed much of Oshkosh. In 1874, the McCourt home and clothing shop went. In 1875, the second fire destroyed a hastily rebuilt and heavily mortgaged version of McCourt and Cameron, as well as Lizzie's favorite building, the Harding Opera House. In 1875, the people of Oshkosh

again rebuilt, this time nearly five hundred brick and fireproof homes and commercial buildings. This reconstruction included a third McCourt and Cameron, a
solid brick and stone building owned almost entirely by the bank. Because
Lizzie's father was so deeply in debt, he essentially drew a salary as a clerk and
tailor rather than being an entrepreneur and owner as before.

Now in her early twenties, Lizzie watched her family descend the social
scale, herself with it. Her mother emphasized the need for "backbone" and her
father for spiritual courage, both principles that Lizzie later would draw on in
her own life. Clearly, the family's financial fortunes were not about to
improve. Rather than living in a fine house, Lizzie could only admire through
unfinished windows the elegant homes that rose, like the fabled phoenix, from
the ashes of Oshkosh.

It was while peeping into windows, probably during the spring of 1876,
that Lizzie met William Harvey Doe, the son of a staunchly Protestant mother
and an entrepreneur father who owned interests in far-off Colorado gold
mines. Lizzie seized the initiative, asking her older brother James to bring
Harvey Doe to the McCourt home for a visit. She approved of Harvey's quiet
ways and, undoubtedly, of his family's wealth. Within days, she became enamored
of him, while her renowned beauty and lively Irish wit drew Harvey to her.
Although Lizzie did not explicitly say so, Harvey must have seemed the
proverbial knight on a white charger who would fulfill her fire-scarred
dreams. If so, Lizzie was only following the messages she had internalized all
her life. Along with Lizzie's dauntless spirit, her looks would save her from
the wreckage of the McCourt family's hopes and ambitions.

Even though Harvey's mother disapproved, Lizzie saw a lot of Harvey.
During the winter of 1876–1877, Harvey mentioned to Lizzie that his church
was to hold a charity figure-skating event with prizes for the best skaters. He
added that he hoped to take first prize. In response, Lizzie demonstrated her
boldness and poor judgment, characteristics that would get her into trouble
many times during her life. Certain that no girls would enter the contest,
Lizzie signed up using the name "L. McCourt." People undoubtedly thought
the entrant was one of Lizzie's many brothers. Alone and hidden, Lizzie practiced on the frozen lake. When she confided in her mother, the woman remod-
eled an outfit for Lizzie, even lending her daughter her own mink stole and
muff to match. On the appointed Saturday afternoon, hearing her name
called, Lizzie hit the ice with a flourish. Before an audience of nearly all of
Oshkosh's residents, including the already judgmental Mrs. Doe, Lizzie
became a skating actress. As she cut the various figures, she brazenly showed

Elizabeth McCourt's (aka Baby Doe Tabor) first husband, William Harvey Doe, who she divorced in Colorado in 1880. (Courtesy of the Western History Department, Denver Public Library, #X-19602.)

flashes of leg. Her performance elicited smiles from the all-male judges, as well as warm approval from her mother. When the prizes were announced, Lizzie, rather than Harvey, won first place.

Lizzie's memories of the aftermath of this event were mixed. She recalled that she and her mother were proud of Lizzie's daring feat but that some town women snubbed Lizzie on the streets, even as female peers labeled her "common" and "fast." Although one might expect envy or anger from Harvey, Lizzie claimed that he came courting. He assured Lizzie that his father was about to send him west as manager of one of the McCourt gold mines. With the promise of riches in the air, Lizzie supposedly agreed to a secret engagement, which lasted only a few months—until the spring of 1877. When the couple announced their intentions, the Does reacted negatively to the idea of Lizzie becoming one of them.

In response, Lizzie demonstrated an amazing ability to live in a world of fantasy of her own creating. While her mother sewed for her an expensive trousseau, Lizzie reassured her skeptical father that she would pay him back after she and Harvey struck it rich in Colorado. At the same time, she used her lively Irish imagination to regale her brothers and sisters with tales of gold nuggets lying about ready for the picking. Lizzie undoubtedly believed her own fabrications. She had not been brought up to understand the realities of making a living, of marriage, and of raising children. Neither did she show any signs of accepting her father's new and lowly status as an Irish tailor. Although she may have been worried privately for the future, publicly she continued on with her gay social life. She appeared to hang on to her and her mother's early hopes and to draw on the brave spirit she had seen modeled in Oshkosh by people who attained wealth, lost it, and tried anew. If others who had fallen could rise again, why couldn't she?

At once selfish and wildly optimistic, Lizzie exhibited a persona that was the embodiment of frontier pluck and persistence. Of course, as a woman, Lizzie's paths of action were limited. Unsurprisingly, she turned to her most obvious resource, her looks. Living in a culture of beauty had convinced her that she had the necessary assets to advance herself beyond the status of her family. Because she no longer had a prosperous father who might underwrite her attempt to become an actress, Harvey Doe would be her stepping-stone.

Harvey and Lizzie's wedding took place on June 27, 1877, in St. Peter's Catholic Church. The occasion must have wounded Harvey's mother deeply, yet she pushed aside her own feelings for the good of her son. Although Lizzie feared that Mrs. Doe might refuse to attend, she was not only on hand, but greeted guests in a gracious, if reserved, fashion. Harvey's father appeared a bit more jovial. Lizzie remembered that her own parents also reacted in their own ways; her mother ecstatic and her father subdued, perhaps because he already knew that his many debts would soon result in a sheriff's sale. Lizzie added that Harvey seemed bewitched, unable to believe his fortune in winning such an attractive wife. For her part, Lizzie had already turned her thoughts and hopes westward to what she believed would be a land of gold.

As the couple, accompanied by Harvey's father, journeyed toward Colorado, Lizzie found everything to her liking. Harvey seemed a hero and, indeed, her one true love. When the party reached Denver, with its population of thirty thousand people, the city enchanted her. After Harvey's father went on to Central City, the couple honeymooned for two weeks at the swank American House. The hotel and its elite guest list convinced Lizzie that her chimerical goals were more possible than even she had dared to believe. As she and Harvey rode the narrow-gauge railway to Black Hawk to meet his father, Lizzie pledged lifelong allegiance to the stunning Rocky Mountains, which elated her and seemed to offer great promise. She also embellished her dreams. She would not only be rich, but would become a social leader in Denver, draped in fabulous clothing and jewels and admired by all.

Upon arrival in Black Hawk, an ebullient Lizzie and weary Harvey caught a stage to travel the mile to Central City, where Harvey's father was to meet them. In Central City, Lizzie saw favorable omens in the solid brick buildings, which, much like those in Oshkosh, had been rebuilt after rampaging fires in 1873 and 1874. Her heart soared even more when she saw the wooden framework of a new opera house silhouetted against Central City's spectacular sky. After the pair reunited with Harvey's father and visited the Fourth of July Mine, in which he owned half-interest, Lizzie thought the situation extremely promising. Harvey's father explained that his son had only to develop the mine, then buy out its other owner. As she stood listening to the din of pumps, steam hoists, and stamp mills, Lizzie believed that she and Harvey were on their way.

Sadly for Lizzie, nothing but disenchantment followed. She soon discovered that Harvey's shyness and reserve were only weakness disguised. From filing the necessary papers to sinking deeper shafts, Harvey lacked the will to follow up on his father's plans. Rather than pouting, Lizzie showed her mettle; she was willing to work for what she wanted. She left untended the rented cottage on Central's Spring Street and took the uncommon action of donning miner's clothes and helping Harvey in the mine. Lizzie's behavior fit the spirit of the times, filled as it was with women pushing into paid jobs and professions, and with women's rights campaigns. Such suffrage leaders as Susan B. Anthony, Elizabeth Cady Stanton, and Lucy B. Stone crisscrossed the West, including Denver and Central City, delivering pro-suffrage speeches. Although the frontier setting also allowed women a certain amount of latitude, there is no evidence that Lizzie was trying to exercise any "right" except that to find her fortune. As a result of Lizzie accompanying Harvey to the mine, the "better" women and men of Central City looked down upon her. Some even snubbed her in the streets, an insult Lizzie had first encountered in Oshkosh after winning the skating contest.

Even though Lizzie's conduct must have embarrassed him, Harvey either would not or could not restrain his wife. For the next six months, despite their lack of knowledge or experience, each of them commanded a crew on separate shafts. Their efforts brought up some gold ore, but, despite their sinking deeper shafts, the mine soon played out. When a poorly constructed shaft collapsed, Harvey made the sensible suggestion that he get a job as a common miner so he could learn the craft of mining properly. He told Lizzie she would have to don feminine clothing and stay at home. She did not take this setback graciously. Demoted overnight from a grand lady, at least in her own mind, to the wife of a poorly paid, lowly miner, she found herself forced to move to cheaper quarters in noisy and dirty Black Hawk, the smelting and milling hub.

As Harvey trudged off toward his mucker's job at the Bobtail Mine, where he shoveled out mud and slag, Lizzie despaired. She soon took to the streets of Black Hawk, walking up and down the hills, making circles, and repeating her route again. From her walks came three important consequences. First, rough miners called out to Lizzie, addressing her as Baby, a nickname she said had also been used by her family. When she stamped her foot and replied that she was a married woman, miners elongated the name to Baby Doe. The tale of Lizzie's beauty passed from man to man, thus making Baby Doe, at age twenty-three, something of a local legend.

Second, Lizzie persisted in her lifelong habit of failing to seek out women friends. Finding the other miners' wives dowdy and homely, she made only one female acquaintance, a Mrs. Richards, who loved to garden and was often outside when Lizzie passed. The woman called Lizzie to her, giving her flowers to match what she called Lizzie's astounding beauty. Telling Lizzie she looked like an angel, Richards stood in for Lizzie's mother, as well as adding her voice to the miners in chorusing Baby Doe's attractiveness.

Last, Lizzie went into shops where she daydreamed over fine fabrics, ornaments, and other goods she could not afford to purchase. Instead of taking in washing, sewing, or finding another way to produce some cash income, Lizzie held on to her illusions. She had no domestic skills she could translate into money. Besides, she was too beautiful to work. Everyone she met on the streets of Black Hawk told her so. Much as she used to dally in her father's clothing shop, Lizzie dawdled away time in the nearby shop of Sandelowsky, Pelton, & Company. Here, Lizzie caught the eye of proprietor Jacob Sandelowsky, who was twenty-six, unmarried, and devilishly good-looking. He too admired Lizzie, as well as proving a sympathetic listener to her stories of woe.

At home, the relationship between Lizzie and Harvey deteriorated. She spent long hours cutting and pasting articles in a scrapbook, a common hobby of leisure ladies of the day. But Lizzie was not a leisure lady, and she concentrated on clippings regarding social doings of the elite, as well as illustrations of their attire and jewels. Harvey retreated into composing lengthy letters to his mother. In all likelihood, Harvey, who many called a mama's boy, could not stand the pressure exerted by his father and especially by his wife. Only his mother would understand his plight.

Little wonder that resentment and distance developed between the newlyweds, especially when Lizzie prevailed upon Harvey to invest what money they had, most of it a Christmas gift from Harvey's parents, into mining claims she believed would pay off. When Harvey lost his job, Lizzie assumed that his employers had found him as unstable and unproductive as she had. Lizzie turned more and more to Jake Sandelowsky, with his golden tongue and welcome gifts. As Harvey drifted from job to job and from saloon to saloon, Lizzie spent her time with the adoring Jake.

Then Lizzie discovered she was pregnant and that Harvey was in debt. To escape creditors, the couple moved from one cheap boarding place to another. The senior Does decided to move to Colorado, in part because lumbering had passed its peak in Oshkosh and in part to be near their coming grandchild. Harvey's father assured Lizzie that he would straighten out Harvey and his financial affairs. When Harvey suggested that Lizzie's baby was not his but Jake's, she supposedly threw a specimen of Fourth of July Mine ore at Harvey, and he vanished out the door.

During Harvey's absence, Lizzie unwisely accompanied Jake to the Shoo-Fly, a variety establishment that housed a dance hall, stage, gaming rooms, and bedrooms. The Shoo-Fly attracted single men and sporting women, many of whom Lizzie found friendly and likable. Clearly, the Shoo-Fly was no place for a married woman; one can only wonder at Jake's decision to take Lizzie there. It was at the Shoo-Fly that people suggested that Lizzie divorce Harvey. They also entertained her with stories about the rise of the Silver King, Horace Tabor.

On July 13, 1879, Lizzie gave birth to a stillborn baby boy. Harvey was nowhere in sight, but Jake was on hand, making arrangements and paying bills. Lizzie wrote in her scrapbook, "My baby boy born July 13 1879, had dark hair very curly large blue eyes he was lovely, Baby Doe." Shortly thereafter, the senior Does established themselves in Central City and took in the wandering Harvey. After Harvey's father engineered a reconciliation between Lizzie and Harvey, he and Harvey's mother relocated in Idaho Springs. The younger Does returned to Denver. Since there was no grandchild to bridge the gap between the younger and older Does, their parting appeared easy enough.

In Denver, Lizzie and Harvey's life together remained so chaotic that Lizzie finally considered divorce. Although divorce would be a serious blow to Lizzie's Catholic family, it was fairly common in the West, which had a higher divorce rate than any other region of the country. At the end of the 1870s, the states or territories with the highest rates of divorce in the United States were Colorado, Utah, Nevada, Wyoming, and Montana. During the late 1870s and early 1880s, Colorado jurisdictions granted divorces on such grounds as adultery, bigamy, cruelty and desertion, habitual drunkenness, impotency, and neglect to provide. Given her frontier spirit, Lizzie probably thought she deserved another chance at marriage—perhaps with Jake Sandelowsky, who paid her fare for a trip to Leadville, where he had established a new store, to see if she would like it there.

The situation between Lizzie and Harvey boiled over early in 1880. According to her, a frightful row sent Harvey scurrying to a parlor house. She followed him and, in the company of a police officer, saw him enter Lizzie Preston's establishment on Denver's Market Street. On March 29, Harvey wrote to his parents that he had been on the trail of a man who might buy his mine, and "who should be across the street but Babe and [she] saw me going in there." It is doubtful that Lizzie would hang around Denver's red-light district waiting for Harvey to wander into a brothel; more likely Harvey was set up. At any rate, Lizzie had evidence for the charge of adultery, which appeared in the court summons. She got a quick divorce, granted March 19, 1880, but had to return the mining stock Harvey had put in her name. Because the divorce was not officially recorded until April 24, 1886, Lizzie, who had no knowledge of this slipup in court procedures, was technically not free to remarry.

Of course, marriage was Lizzie's only way to advance herself. Her other enterprises yielded little. While pregnant, she had mined the Troy claims that Harvey had signed over to her, but had no gold to show for her efforts. When she moved to Leadville after her divorce, Lizzie may have worked for a brief period for Jake, selling women's clothing, presumably at a less than munificent wage. Lizzie was unable to support herself, at least in the grand style that she coveted.

Evidence suggests that Jake Sands, as Sandelowsky now called himself, wanted to marry Lizzie. Although she referred to their relationship as a friendship, others described it as an affair. At least one of Jake's letters addressed Lizzie as "My Darling Love," but Lizzie found marriage to a clothing merchant much like her father unattractive. She also claimed that Jake gambled too much. Thus, Baby Doe was on her own. Once again, she drew upon her primary asset—her beauty—to parlay misfortune and hard years into good luck and high times. She would not again make the mistake of choosing an unproven individual like William Harvey Doe. As difficult as that relationship had been, however, it did get Baby Doe to gold rush Colorado.

The Tabors' Trek Westward

Well before Elizabeth Baby Doe McCourt was born, the other half of what would eventually become a scandalous intrigue was in the process of developing. In 1849, an unremarkable farm lad of nineteen left his home in Vermont to

Leadville mining magnate Horace A.W. Tabor in 1885. (Courtesy of the Western History Department, Denver Public Library, #X-22028.)

learn the stonecutter's trade from his brother John. Hopeful of finding a better way of life than had his English and Scottish parents, young Horace Tabor knew he must leave Vermont behind. At the time, the whole country seemed in a turmoil. Newspapers reported daily on the slavery issue, the outcome of the Mexican War, and the discovery of gold in California. Although Horace wanted to go west, he had neither the know-how nor the funds. For the moment, he seemed content to practice stonecutting in Massachusetts and Maine.

Tabor's course changed in 1853 when a stone contractor from Maine named William B. Pierce hired him and John to work in Augusta on the new state insane asylum. It was here that Horace met Augusta Louise, the Pierces' third daughter. Although Augusta was sickly, Horace found her charming and determined. Three years younger than Horace, Augusta not only came from a family of strong women who believed in rights for women, but she also agreed with Horace that the real opportunities lay in the West. Horace decided that Augusta was the perfect helpmate for a man like him; Augusta eventually concurred.

In 1855, Horace left Maine for Lawrence, Kansas, where his brother John had already settled. If prospects proved good, he would return to Maine for Augusta. Thus, Horace found himself once again a farmer. Because John and Horace migrated to Kansas under the auspices of the New England Emigrant Aid Society, dedicated to keeping the Kansas-Nebraska territory free rather than slave, the brothers also found themselves embroiled in local politics. After fighting in several skirmishes against pro-slavery forces and supporting the fiery abolitionist John Brown, John Tabor landed in jail and Horace Tabor in politics. In 1856, when Lizzie McCourt was only two years old, Horace's neighbors in Zeandale elected him their spokesman to the First Kansas Free State Legislature in Topeka.

After two years in the Kansas territory, Horace returned to Maine. During one of the most ferocious snowstorms on record, Horace and Augusta took their wedding vows in the same room in the Pierce home where they had first met. The date was January 31, 1857, and the promise of the rich and mighty West seemed to lie before them. A few days later, the newlyweds watched as Horace's brother John married his distant cousin Hannah. The two couples, plus Horace's sister Emily, set off to Kansas by railroad and steamboat, their hopes and their heads high.

During the Tabors' two years in Kansas, Augusta proved herself an archetypal frontier woman. She later said that her first sight of the crude log cabin that became her first home reduced her to tears. Like so many other women in similar situations, she "sat down on the trunk and cried." She explained, "I was homesick and could not conceal it from those about me." When she finished crying, the twenty-three-year-old bride took hold. Although she, like Lizzie McCourt, had been cosseted at home, she learned how to cook, even feeding family friends Samuel B. Kellogg and Nathaniel Maxey to earn a little extra cash. On October 9, 1857, probably while Horace was at Fort Riley cutting stone, Augusta gave birth to a boy. Although the child was named Nathaniel Maxey Tabor after their good friend, he was known as Maxey.

The Tabors failed to prosper in Kansas. Two bad winters and two summers of poor return on crops convinced the couple that it was time to move westward. As he had when he was a young man, Horace decided that farming was no way to achieve a comfortable living. The economic Panic of 1859 further exacerbated hardships for western farmers. Along with Augusta, Horace drank in tales of gold strikes in the Pikes Peak area of western Kansas territory. As a result, in 1859 the Tabors mortgaged their farm and set off in a covered wagon pulled by oxen, at last on their way to the promised land. Of course, baby Maxey was with them, as were Sam Kellogg and Nathaniel Maxey. Although the rigors of the journey along the Republican River route wore on Augusta, her first sight of the Rockies made everything seem worthwhile. As Elizabeth McCourt would so many years later, Augusta Tabor saw a bright future for her and Horace among the snow-crested peaks. While the rest of the nation suffered through the shattering Civil War and its aftermath, the Tabors sought their personal Eldorado.

Yet Augusta's fulfillment came even more slowly than Lizzie's would. Augusta followed Horace from gold camp to gold camp, such as Buckskin Joe and Oro City, chasing the wisp of fortune but always failing to find the strike that would relieve her wearying workload. Early in their many relocations, the Tabors settled at Payne's Bar, where Augusta was the first white woman. While Horace, Sam, and Nate panned for gold, Augusta discovered that she could earn cash by taking in boarders and by selling butter, eggs, baked goods, and other supplies. She also doctored local folks and eventually added postmistress to her list of titles. Horace had been correct in his assessment of Augusta; she was the perfect frontier helpmate.

Even though this pattern continued for some twenty years, Augusta seemed to grow stronger rather than weaker. In 1878, the Tabors were comfortably settled in Slabtown, known as "The Cloud City," but soon to be named Leadville. They appeared to have accepted the fact that gold had eluded them. Besides, the local gold rush was over, replaced by the deposits of silver in the heavy black sand and mud that miners, including Augusta, had complained about. The black muck turned out to be carbonate of lead contained approximately forty ounces of silver in each ton. Rather than joining the silver rush, the Tabors shared shopkeeping duties. In addition, the forty-four-year-old Augusta ran a boardinghouse in their comfortable clapboard home on Harrison Avenue, and the forty-seven-year-old Horace served first as postmaster and then as mayor.

In April 1878, two prospectors who approached Horace for a grubstake changed the Tabors' lives forever. Although Augusta objected, Horace was known as an easy mark. He barely blinked as he agreed to stake August Rische and George Hook to about seventeen dollars' worth of goods. A few days later, Horace supplied the men with a hand winch, drills, and blasting power. For the men's promise that Tabor would have one-third of whatever they found, Horace laid out perhaps sixty dollars of supplies. To Augusta's amazement and Horace's delight, Rische and Hook hit a rich lode of carbonates, bearing sizable amounts of silver. Because the two miners had promised Horace one-third of whatever they found, Tabor was well on his way to becoming the Silver King, and Augusta the Silver "Widow."

Horace lost no time establishing himself as a man of wealth and power. During the fall of 1878, Tabor successfully sought election as lieutenant governor of Colorado, which had become a state two years earlier. He bought the Henry C. Brown (of Brown Palace fame) home on Seventeenth Street and Broadway in Denver, and he and Augusta moved in. That November, Tabor, who had bought out Rische and Hook, founded the Little Pittsburg Consolidated Company. Within a year, the company was worth twenty million dollars. Tabor bought many other mines, including the celebrated Chrysolite and Matchless mines; the Matchless was said to average one thousand ounces of silver per ton of carbonates. One financial journalist predicted that within ten years Horace Tabor would be the richest man in America. He added that Tabor "does not look like a man whose head would be easily turned if the course of events should lift him to the highest pinnacles of fame in the councils of the nation or make him the greatest moneyed king of his day."

The writer was wrong. Horace's head was turned by his newfound wealth. He became what two Leadville writers later described as "money drunk." He liked to party and to spend money. Granted, Tabor put large amounts of his money into civic improvements, notably Leadville's Tabor Opera House, which opened in 1879. Tabor also formed the Tabor Light Cavalry, ostensibly to protect his mines, but in actuality used in 1880 to suppress a miners' strike and end picketing at Tabor's Chrysolite Mine. At the same time, Tabor bought a new house as well as jewelry for Augusta, who, the Leadville Chronicle reported in August 1879, "is admired by strangers as well as friends... [and] is known as 'The First Lady of Leadville.'"

When the ever-sensible and levelheaded Augusta objected to Horace's activities, Horace found "friends" who would accompany him in his increasing revelry. Although Horace and Augusta had argued many times in the past over such issues as money, work, and morality, their disputes increased in frequency and ferocity. In 1879, even though Augusta had always kept the Tabors' financial records, Horace ended her tenure as family bookkeeper, shifting the task instead to a professional bookkeeper. Nor could Horace deny himself the pleasures for which he had waited a lifetime. This should not have surprised Augusta; Horace was known as a fun-loving man who liked to fish, play poker, drink whiskey, and smoke cigars. Clearly, Augusta, with her staunch Maine background and reformist upbringing, could not accompany Horace in his meteoric rise to legendhood.

If either of them made a conscious decision to hold firm to his or her own viewpoint, it was probably Augusta. She knew how much she had invested in her marriage to Horace, yet evidently she was willing to risk that investment. Augusta, a debutante back in Maine, was not a homely woman; with her masses of dark hair, graceful figure, and gentle smile she could have made a convincing consort to the Silver King. Instead, Augusta found herself repulsed by Horace's carousing. In 1880, the same year that the newly divorced Baby Doe moved to Leadville, Augusta spent much of her time at the mansion at Seventeenth and Broadway in Denver. She thus left Horace to frequent Leadville, often in the company of such well-known prostitutes as Alice Morgan and Willie Deville.

As Horace gained a reputation as a big spender and a rake, Augusta achieved near sainthood. She participated in women's organizations and gave freely to charitable causes. In April 1881, a Gunnison banker named Sam Gill and his wife named one of their children Augusta Tabor Gill. The editor of the *Gunnison Review Press* remarked that "this is a token of the highest esteem and love to name a child after an acquaintance when so many relatives hope for that honor." Whether Augusta realized it, as she shook her righteous head in disapproval of Horace's actions, she was tacitly assenting to his acting like an available man. Thus the stage was set for a meeting of great consequence.

The Tabor Triangle

Because the Tabors and the Does had lived in the Denver and Leadville areas during the same years, Baby Doe was undoubtedly well aware of Horace Tabor and his incredible good fortune. She later said that she had even had some dealings with Tabor's right-hand man, William H. "Bill" Bush, in Central City. It is quite likely that Baby Doe met Bush when he was proprietor of the magnificent Teller House, which first opened in 1872. Because Tabor spent much time with miners and in saloons, he probably also knew of Baby Doe. He must have heard some of the rumors, including the one that Baby Doe was actually the model for the "face on the barroom floor" in the Teller House. In addition, at least one chronicler maintains that in Leadville, Baby Doe lived in the block across from the Tabor residence.

When Baby Doe set out for the Saddle Rock Cafe one fateful night when Jake Sands was gambling at a local hall, she may have been seizing a long-awaited opportunity. Or, as some suggest, Baby Doe may have already known Tabor and set up a public meeting with him. At any rate, shortly after Baby Doe was seated for a solitary dinner of oysters, Tabor and Bush strolled in. Later, Baby Doe explained that the tall, outgoing Tabor caught her eye immediately. According to Colorado historian Caroline Bancroft, Baby Doe fell in love with Tabor at first sight. Tabor noticed her as well; shortly a note from Bill Bush was delivered to her table. The message read: "Won't you join us at our table?" Once ensconced at the Tabor table, Baby Doe talked with the two men about mutual acquaintances in Central City. After the evening's performance was over at the Opera House, Bill Bush, its manager, excused himself. Baby Doe managed to dazzle Tabor with her description of her recent life and her feeling of gratitude to Jake Sands. The great man ended the evening with a gift of five thousand dollars to Baby Doe, partly so that she could pay back Jake for the help he had given her and partly to establish herself in Leadville. She remembered him saying, "Something's bound to turn up."

In the meantime, Jake found himself waiting at the Clarendon Hotel for Baby Doe, who had promised to join him for a late supper. The next morning he received a thousand dollars from Baby Doe along with a letter saying she had decided not to marry him. Jake immediately returned the money. After Tabor moved Baby Doe to the hotel where he stayed, the Clarendon, the situation was awkward; among the shops in the lower front of the Tabor Opera House next door was the new shop of Sands, Pelton, & Company, owned by Jake Sands and his partner. Despite their proximity, Baby Doe recalled that she saw Jake only a few times in passing on the streets of Leadville. He later moved to Aspen, where he opened a new store, married, and built a solid Victorian home, complete with a circular porch and a turret. Apparently Baby Doe spent little, if any, time regretting her decision to leave Jake behind.

Denver's Windsor Hotel, where Horace Tabor set up Baby Doe in a luxurious suite in 1880. (Courtesy of the Western History Department, Denver Public Library, photograph by Rose and Hopkins, #H-557.)

Instead, Baby Doe gloried in the relationship that blossomed between her and Tabor. Tabor found the covered catwalk that spanned the open space between the Opera House and the Clarendon very convenient. Although it was meant for the use of actors, actresses, and other theater personnel, Horace utilized the passageway to make frequent and discreet visits from his and Bill Bush's office suite in the Opera House to Baby Doe's rooms in the Clarendon. Later in 1880, Tabor moved Baby Doe to a luxurious suite in his newly leased Windsor Hotel in Denver, where he now had his headquarters. In 1879, a London firm had built the five-story, turreted hotel to look like England's Windsor Castle. On its opening day—June 13, 1880—the Windsor startled viewers with its opulence, including a seventeen-foot-wide entrance and diamond-dust mirrors. Tabor's suite at the Windsor boasted a marble fireplace and a gold-leaf bathtub. Its guests ranged from presidents and millionaires to renowned writers and actors.

The Windsor must have convinced Baby Doe that she made the right choice in Horace Tabor. Baby Doe's beauty had bought her the opportunity to beguile Tabor with her charming and earnest personality. Although most people dismissed her as a licentious woman taking advantage of a wealthy man, she protested that she loved Tabor—and that he came to love her. She turned out to be far more than the rumormongers predicted. Certainly neither Baby Doe nor Horace ever breached the trust between them by seeing another man or woman.

Naturally, none of this was a secret to Augusta. Like so many others, she assumed that Horace would eventually tire of Baby Doe. But rather than leaving Baby Doe, early in 1881 Horace moved out of the Tabors' Seventeenth and Broadway home and asked Augusta for a divorce, but she refused. Tabor publicly retaliated against Augusta by neglecting to invite her to the September 5 opening of the Tabor Grand Theatre. Even though Augusta wrote Horace a note pleading for reconciliation and their appearance together at the opening, he ignored her.

On opening night, Tabor's box stood empty. Horace sat near the stage, while a heavily veiled Baby Doe took a seat in the rear of the house to watch the proceedings. Representatives of Denver's citizens presented Tabor with a massive gold watch fob depicting his climb to fame. They also thanked him for his gift of the theater, a magnificent concoction of cherry wood from Japan and mahogany from Honduras, set off by a blazing crystal chandelier. On the stage an opulent curtain bore a quote that would eventually prove only too true for Horace and Baby Doe: "So fleet the works of men, back to the earth again, Ancient and holy things fade like a dream."

Augusta Tabor, first wife of Horace Tabor, in 1880, the year her husband first met Baby Doe. (Courtesy of the Western History Department, Denver Public Library, photograph by Alfred E. Rinehart, #X-21992.)

After the opening of the Tabor Grand, the struggle between Augusta and Horace intensified. When he refused to give her any more money, she sued him. After the suit failed in court, Horace demanded a divorce. Augusta again refused. Baby Doe claimed that she broke the stalemate by suggesting that Horace get a divorce in another jurisdiction without Augusta's knowledge. Horace duly obtained a divorce in Durango during the summer of 1882, presumably from a judge who owed him favors. On September 30, he and Baby Doe secretly wed in St. Louis. At the time, both Horace and Baby Doe were bigamists; he because the Durango divorce was questionable, and she because her divorce had not yet been officially recorded. Baby Doe was not as happy as she expected because she believed she had to have a church-sanctioned wedding. Certainly, this was the only way that Baby Doe's father would forgive her for divorcing Harvey.

A turning point came in January 1883 when a distressed Augusta finally sued for divorce on the grounds of desertion. In settlement, Augusta accepted the Seventeenth and Broadway house, the LaVeta apartment block in Denver, and mining stock. The same judge who divorced Baby Doe and William Harvey Doe now divorced Augusta and Horace Tabor. When Augusta ran from the courtroom crying out, "O, God, not willingly, not willingly," she became a renowned victim. Whether this last act was retribution

An 1885 graphic of Baby Doe Tabor. (Courtesy of the Western History Department, Denver Public Library, photography by Fred Mazzulla, #X-22030.)

against Horace is unknown, but it did cause irreparable damage to Tabor's political aspirations. When President Chester A. Arthur appointed Senator Henry M. Teller to his cabinet, Tabor was elected to finish out Teller's thirty-day term as senator from Colorado rather than the six-year term he had coveted.

Baby Doe Tabor

Even though Tabor was active during his short term as U.S. senator, he was often distracted. Augusta wrote to him saying that "the divorce is null and void" and that he should return to her after his thirty days were up. Obviously, Augusta had no knowledge of Tabor's plans for a lavish wedding to Baby Doe that would take place in Washington, D.C., near the end of his term. In the meantime, Baby Doe returned to Oshkosh to organize her family and explain to her father that a Catholic priest would preside over the ceremony. A gift of a new house and $150,000 from Horace Tabor to the senior McCourt made Baby Doe's news more palatable. Eight family members joined Baby Doe at Washington's Willard Hotel, where she personally addressed wedding invitations to President Arthur and other officials. The wife of Colorado senator Nathaniel P. Hill tore her invitation in half and bid Baby Doe's coachman to return it.

Still, Baby Doe remained exuberant. On March 1, she donned lace lingerie and a white satin dress, which cost seven thousand dollars. When

Tabor's gift, a diamond necklace said to be worth as much as ninety thousand dollars, failed to arrive in time, Baby Doe omitted jewelry. The ceremony was followed by a dinner accompanied by so many flowers and champagne that Baby Doe's mother sighed that it was "like heaven." If Baby Doe noticed that President Arthur and other important men attended without their wives, she did not allow the women's slights to spoil her wedding. She was now Baby Doe Tabor and proud of her new status.

The aftermath proved less happy. Within days, the priest — Reverend Placide Chapelle of St. Matthew's Cathedral — returned the two hundred dollars Horace had given him, publicly stating that he had not known that he was marrying a divorced Catholic woman. Because Horace was a Protestant, his divorce was not in question. Father Chapelle blamed the McCourt family for duping him regarding Baby Doe's divorce, however. He refused to enter the marriage into church records. He also prophesied that, "No good can ever come from such black deceit."

At the same time, headlines revealed the news of Horace's Durango divorce and his wedding in St. Louis to Baby Doe. Again, Baby Doe sought reassurance in her beauty. Although she was twenty-eight, she gave her age as twenty-two and in many ways acted it. On Horace's last day as senator she attended the session garishly attired in a brown silk dress and extravagant jewelry. In her journal, Senator Hill's wife sarcastically noted: "Tabors there; in front seat in full force." Afterward, Baby Doe concentrated only on newspaper reports that spoke of her style and grace. Although inwardly hurt by her husband's stalled political career, Baby Doe, who some called the Silver Queen, turned for solace to fantasies regarding the future.

Once again, Baby Doe's fondest dreams came to little. Less than two months after the wedding her father died, some said of remorse over deceiving a priest. In addition, despite exorbitant contributions to the Republican Party, Horace was passed over for the gubernatorial nomination he so wanted. He also publicly quarreled with Bill Bush, eventually replacing him with Baby Doe's favorite brother, Peter McCourt Jr. Because Horace's son, Maxey, sided with Augusta in most matters, his father disavowed him sometime during the 1880s, saying "he is no son of mine."

At the same time, Baby Doe received not one call from Denver's elite women. Even after the couple moved to one of the most ostentatious houses on Thirteenth Avenue and bought three carriages with six horses, Baby Doe was slighted by Denver's best. She did not enter high society, nor did she take part in the charitable and other activities of Denver's club women. The same

21

Alice Hale Hill who had torn the Tabors' wedding invitation in two and had once lived near Lizzie and Harvey in Black Hawk enjoyed a rich social life, but Baby Doe did not.

Baby Doe found ways to compensate for her exclusion, often by spending exorbitant funds on clothing, jewels, and parties. She added curls and frizzes to her hairdo. She even color-matched her coachmen's livery and her horses' trappings to her outfit of the day. Yet Baby Doe also became known for her bounteous charitable donations. Excluded by the women of Denver from their clubs and associations, Baby Doe gave generously on her own. Also, in 1893, she set aside two offices, rent-free, in the Tabor Block at Sixteenth and Larimer for the use of Colorado's woman suffrage leaders.

When Baby Doe bore a daughter, Elizabeth Bonduel Lily Tabor, on July 13, 1884, she seemed to grow up. Although Baby Doe dressed baby Lily in an ostentatious christening outfit that cost fifteen thousand dollars, she stepped into motherhood as if she had been born for it. Even when Horace traveled far from home to oversee his burgeoning financial empire that extended into Honduras and the state of Chihuahua in Mexico, Baby Doe usually refused to leave Lily with a nanny and stayed home herself.

Baby Doe showed her inner fortitude in other ways as well. When on October 17, 1888, she delivered a son who lived only a few hours, she grieved but did not break down. On December 17, 1889, she bore another girl: Rose Mary Echo Silver Dollar Tabor. Unlike the light-haired Lily, this child was a brunette, more like Horace than Baby Doe. Like Lily, however, she had Baby Doe's pouting lips and sensuous eyes. Although Baby Doe nicknamed the child Honeymaid, most people called her Silver. Publicly, she used Silver to display her disdain for Denver's elite. Not only did the baby's diaper pins have diamond tips, but Baby Doe defiantly nursed Silver as she rode through the streets of Denver in one of her carriages. Privately, however, Baby Doe sacrificed the pleasure of traveling with Horace to remain home with her children. Devoted and serene, Baby Doe promoted her children's love and respect for their father through copious letters. On one occasion Horace thanked Baby Doe: "The children through your teaching love me too much for me to be away."

When some of Horace's investments proved bad and he mortgaged such properties as the Opera House and the Tabor Block, Baby Doe continued to stand by her husband. Although Horace was a creative man who established everything from banks and life insurance companies to charity organizations, he depended more on the continuation of his good luck than on paying attention to market forces and the national economy. A contemporary of Tabor's

Elizabeth Bonduel Lily, the first daughter of Baby Doe and Horace, in 1890. (Courtesy of the Western History Department, Denver Public Library, photograph by Rose & Co., #X-22014.)

explained that Horace was a man of the frontier West, a man with a "reckless, pioneer spirit." Also, Tabor was far from alone. The boom psychology of the 1880s convinced many investors to believe that prosperity would last forever. When the U.S. government adopted the Sherman Silver Purchase Act in 1890, Tabor and others believed the erratic nature of the silver market was at an end. Yet extraction costs were spiraling, laborers were asking for better wages, mines had to be dug deeper, and ore was of poorer quality, all factors that affected the output of silver. Tabor compounded these problems through a series of bad investments and involvement in frequent lawsuits, some of which resulted from questionable or careless business practices.

Behind the scenes, Baby Doe shared with Horace the stress of lawsuits, debts, mortgages in her name, and recurring cycles of hope and despair. Yet she did not run at the first sign of trouble, as so many busybodies had predicted. Even Augusta had prophesied that Baby Doe only wanted "his money and will hang to him as long as he has got a nickel." In truth, however, Baby Doe not only stuck with Horace, but did what she could to keep his Denver interests going and to fend off creditors while he was away. As he had with Augusta, Horace seemed to harness Baby Doe's energy and inner strength. By frequent absences and putting responsibility into the hands of his wives, Horace helped create partners rather than dependents. Unlike Augusta, however, Baby Doe maintained her sense of humor. For example, when she learned that a neighbor objected to the classical nude statuary in her yard, she ordered her costumer to create outfits for each of them.

Even when the repeal of the Sherman Act in 1893 created a panic among silver producers and helped create the ensuing depression that wiped out much of Tabor's fortune, Baby Doe remained at his side. During the harrowing years of 1893 and 1894, Horace gave Baby Doe power of attorney to act for him when absent. He wrote, "I have no idea about our affairs there [Denver] except by your telegrams." In 1894, she despairingly jotted a memo to herself: "After doing all I could I find I have done nothing." Baby Doe offered her jewels to Tabor to pawn or sell. It was also Baby Doe who railed at the workers who came to turn off the mansion's electricity and who made a game of living by candlelight. And it was Baby Doe who went to her younger brother, Peter McCourt, with a plea to save the Opera House for Tabor. Brother and sister had had a series of earlier disagreements, and when McCourt rejected her plea, Baby Doe broke with her favorite brother forever.

After the mansion and its contents were repossessed or sold, Baby Doe followed Horace through a series of cheap rooms, where she did all the domestic chores herself. She spared no effort to make Lily presentable for school. She wept inwardly when the sixty-five-year-old Horace went off to hard labor in a mine, taking as her great consolation her youngest daughter, Silver.

It was during this period—in 1895—that Augusta died a millionaire in Pasadena, California, where she had gone seeking improved health. Augusta's body was brought back to Denver for burial in Riverside Cemetery. She was widely eulogized as a clubwoman, a benefactress, an astute financier, and a pioneer woman. A few years later, Augusta was memorialized in Tabor Valley near Zeandale, Kansas, where the Tabors had farmed between 1857 and 1859. An upright black granite stone lauded Augusta as "a pioneer mother," only mentioning Horace in passing and their breakup not at all.

During five long years of indignities and poverty between 1893 and 1898, a few friends tried to help the Tabors. It is said that gold magnate Winfield Scott Stratton gave Horace fifteen thousand dollars, or perhaps more, to develop the Eclipse Mine. Although Tabor worked at the mine site with a small crew, the venture came to nothing. In January 1898, possibly at the suggestion of Stratton, Senator Edward O. Wolcott got Tabor appointed postmaster of Denver. The family moved to a plain suite in Denver's Windsor Hotel, where Horace had once housed Baby Doe in opulence. Now they learned to manage on Horace's salary of thirty-seven hundred dollars a year. It was clear, however, that Horace's health was broken. Age, rich living, manual labor, and worry had taken its toll. He held his job only fifteen months before he developed acute appendicitis. Although Baby Doe nursed him for seven days, Horace died on April 10, 1899. On April 11, the *Rocky Mountain News* called Tabor "one of Colorado's chiefest benefactors." In the following days, sympathy letters and telegrams poured in, many from dignitaries and former friends.

Horace, who had converted to Catholicism a few days before he died, was to be buried in Calvary, a Catholic cemetery. The funeral procession began at the Windsor Hotel, where Horace's body had been embalmed before being taken to lie in the governor's reception room at the state capitol. During the well-attended service—some say ten thousand people—Father William O'Ryan of St. Leo's paid Horace a touching tribute: "May the turf lie lightly on his breast that pulsed with such a big heart. God, like man, loves the great heart. Surely, He loves Tabor." Afterward, a distraught Baby Doe reportedly threw herself upon the casket and had to be torn away.

Baby Doe later explained that she sustained herself through these difficult times only by remembering Horace's deathbed entreaty to "hold on to the Matchless mine...it will make millions again when silver comes back." Although Baby Doe believed this story until she died, it was probably apocryphal. The Tabors did not even own the Matchless at the time of Horace's death; it had been first mortgaged and then sold to pay his debts. Yet Baby Doe had always sublimated her problems through illusion and the Matchless myth would succor her for the rest of her life.

Baby Doe Tabor, only thirty-eight and still beautiful, declined the many offers she received from would-be lovers and even potential husbands. Instead, Baby Doe took her girls and went to Denver, where she pled with bankers for funds to reopen the Matchless Mine. Legend has it that Baby Doe, once the pampered daughter and coddled wife, did housework and other odd jobs to support herself and her daughters. One story alleges that in 1901, Baby Doe's sister Claudia McCourt redeemed the Matchless, but documentation is scattered and unclear. About the same time, Baby Doe moved the girls to Leadville, where brother Peter McCourt reportedly intervened on their behalf. Peter told a Leadville grocer that he would pay Baby Doe's bills but that his help must be kept secret from his sister. Within a short time, Lily, disgusted with her mother's seeming obsession with the Matchless, ran away to her Uncle Peter in Chicago. Some say that Lily never saw her mother again; others maintain that Lily saw Baby Doe once more in her lifetime. Certainly, Lily often disavowed being the daughter of Baby Doe and Horace Tabor.

Rose Mary Echo Silver Dollar, the second daughter of Baby Doe and Horace Tabor, in 1905. (Courtesy of the Western History Department, Denver Public Library, #X-21997.)

During those hard years, three things bolstered Baby Doe: her daughter Silver, a renewed interest in religion, and, of course, her hopes for the Matchless. After Baby Doe had pawned almost everything with the notable exception of the gold watch fob the citizens of Denver had presented to Horace in 1881, she and Silver moved to the Matchless cabin to save on rent. Although Baby Doe believed she had recouped the mine, it was more likely the kindness of friends that made it possible for her to live there. In 1914, Silver left Baby Doe as well, going first to Denver and then to Chicago, where she supposedly became an alcoholic and dope addict. Although Baby Doe always claimed her favorite daughter was in a convent, Silver died under suspicious circumstances in a sordid rooming house in 1925.

Baby Doe had very little left. Psychologically, she created a twilight world for herself. "Scrapbooking" was one habit she clung to during this dismal time, even though her notations were now frequently in code. In her scrapbooks, Baby Doe recorded her spiritual awakenings and the presence of otherworldly beings, especially the devil. Also, because her daughters were gone, she relied only on God, speaking to him through a knotted shoelace she wore around her neck as a rosary. Rather than looking back at her wealthy days with happiness, she saw them as pure vanity. Thus, she imposed small penances on herself, including twisting gunny sacking around her legs and tying it with twine against the stinging cold of Colorado winters. Physically, she barely existed. When hungry, Baby Doe ate stale loaves of bread that she bought twelve at a time, along with plate boil, a suetlike brisket of beef. When ill, she treated herself with vinegar and turpentine. She accepted charity only from those she judged sincere in their wish to help.

Baby Doe lived this way for thirty-some years. In 1935, a calamitous winter brought her tortured life to an end. Early in March, Baby Doe went into town for groceries. Upon her return, she wrote in her scrapbook:

"The snow so terrible, I had to go down on my hands and knees and creep from my cabin door to 7th Street. Mr. Zaitz driver drove me to our get off place and he helped pull me to the cabin. I kept falling deep down through the snow every minute. God bless him."

On March 7, Baby Doe's only friend—oddly enough a woman, given all the years Baby Doe had avoided the friendship of women—noticed that no smoke rose from the chimney of the old woman's cabin. When Sue Bonnie and a friend reached the Matchless cabin, all was silence. After they forced an entry, they came upon Baby Doe's body stretched out on the floor in the shape of a cross. Baby Doe was frozen to death, or perhaps had frozen after a heart attack. The one remnant of Baby Doe's beauty was her hair, which contained almost no gray.

Besides her legend, the once wealthy Baby Doe left little behind. The curiosity seekers and vandals who tore Baby Doe's cabin apart looking for hidden cash found nothing. It was from seventeen trunks stored in a Denver warehouse and additional trunks and burlap bags in the basement of St. Vincent's Hospital in Leadville that emerged the physical remains of Baby Doe's life. Among seventeen scrapbooks and voluminous notes regarding her forays into the spiritual realm were material treasures: a china tea set, bolts of expensive silk cloth, a box of Horace's cigars, and, of course, Horace's gold watch fob. Fortunately, enough unsolicited cash donations, probably the largest from Peter McCourt, came in to bury Baby Doe in Denver's Mt. Olivet Cemetery next to Horace, whose remains had been moved there from the abandoned Calvary Cemetery.

In assessing Baby Doe's life it is tempting to ask "what if?" What if young Lizzie's dreams for her and Harvey Doe had materialized? Would she have cracked Denver society and become a publicly acclaimed benefactress? What if she and Horace Tabor had been contemporaries who met and married early in life? Would she have loved him and worked next to him, as did Augusta? Or would Baby Doe have rejected the enterprising but young Horace as a bad bet? What if her parents and her contemporaries had not worshiped Baby Doe's

27

beauty to the point of elevating it above her other positive qualities? Would the determined Baby Doe have worked her way to the top some other way?

Perhaps the tragedy of Baby Doe was that although the culture of beauty encouraged her to use physical comeliness to advance herself, it also led to disgrace. From winning the skating match and Harvey Doe through charming Horace away from Augusta, Baby Doe capitalized on her most obvious asset, yet was spurned for her actions. Not only was she the subject of gossip and scorn, she forfeited the comradeship of other women. Even when she proved herself as a wife and mother, her family and her church rebuffed her. By believing in the culture of beauty, Baby Doe enjoyed the love of her husband, Horace Tabor, and a life of ease for nearly ten years. For some five more years, she had Horace and her girls. Overall, however, in the high-stakes game of beauty, wealth, and love, Baby Doe spent far more years losing than winning. Although she ultimately became far more famous than the elite Denver women she so wanted to join, Baby Doe spent most of her life in disgrace.

2

Emily D. West (Morgan)

The Yellow Rose of Texas

CARMEN GOLDTHWAITE

THE YELLOW ROSE OF TEXAS
There's a yellow rose in Texas
That I am going to see
No other darky knows her
No one only me
She cried so when I left her
It like to broke my heart
And if I ever more find her
We nevermore will part.

In common with many women during the 1830s in Texas, where women were scarce, Emily D. West Morgan was described as beautiful. A mulatto from Connecticut, Emily contracted—bonded herself—to go to Texas for a year to work for James Morgan, who was promoting real estate development.

Morgan was a slave trader from North Carolina, with a penchant for choosing mulattos. Morgan attached his last name to that of Emily D. West, a custom he observed with his slaves, although Emily was a free woman. He may have done so not only to distinguish her as his bonded servant, but also to differentiate between her and another Emily D. West, who sailed to Texas with her. This other Emily was the wife of Lorenzo de Zavala, a man who later became vice president of the Republic of Texas.

Morgan's Emily West would go on to inspire story and song in Texas. She is remembered as the Yellow Rose of Texas, and many believe the famous song of that name was written in her honor. The Texas war for independence from Mexico embellished her fame and fable. Many Texans and folklorists swear to the legend that Emily saved Texas with a timely love tryst with Mexican President Santa Anna

29

during the Battle of San Jacinto—though most historians see this as a Texas tall tale, many of which spun out of the war. Legends about her intertwine with key historical figures of the era: de Zavala, Santa Anna, David Burnet, Sam Houston.

Described as tall, lithe, and beautiful, with long black hair, and "looking Spanish," Emily Morgan also may have been a practitioner of the female wiles, enticing and satisfying the lusts of a woman-starved population. If she was indeed a beautiful seductress, it becomes even easier to comprehend her eventual prominence in Texas lore. Most heroines of Texas myth and legend are seen as tall, lithe, dark-haired, and beautiful. Undoubtedly some were, with the heavy doses of Indian and Mexican blood in their veins—and some of this beauty may have been imagined. But Emily's good looks and bravery, real or imagined, have captured the hearts of generations. In story and song, men have stepped off to battle with her in every United States war. She lives on in the words and music of "The Yellow Rose of Texas."

It may be impossible to fully separate fact from fiction in the story of the Yellow Rose of Texas. However, we can learn something about this woman who has remained celebrated yet mysterious by looking at her life in the context of the lives of well-known figures and the events of that time.

The Lure of Texas

History's lamp is dark on the matter of Emily West Morgan's beginnings, her family, and her ties to New England—and on why she eventually left home. We do know that when she was in her mid-thirties, she left New Haven, Connecticut, for New York City. At a portside coffeehouse on October 25, 1835, she signed up to sail for Texas, then a Mexican possession, with James Morgan, a merchant and shipper.

Morgan was point man for the New Washington Association, a band of western expansionist land developers brought together by Lorenzo de Zavala. Unknown to Morgan, or to Emily, Texans were then meeting in consultation over the question of continuing their allegiance to Mexico. So, not knowing she was sailing into a bloody war for independence, Emily bound herself for a year.

Her contract stated she would go to Texas and work for Morgan "at any kind of house work she...is qualified to do." She agreed "not to quit or leave said Morgan's employ after she commences work for him, at any time whatever, without said Morgan's consent, until the end of twelve months."

Morgan's part of the deal was to send her to Texas on board his ship, "free of expense," and to pay her one hundred dollars for a year's work, the wages to be paid every three months. He would also pay for her return trip to New York.

Emily joined a group of one hundred people described as artisans—
skilled house and field workers, craftsmen, and seamstresses—for the voyage
to the foreign land. These Highland Scots and freed Negroes, like Emily, were
bonded servants. She sailed on one of Morgan's schooners, the *Flash*, which
had as its home port Anahuac on the Trinity River in the Mexican province of
Coahuila-Texas, near the proposed town site of New Washington.

The *Flash* called at Baltimore, Maryland, where the ship picked up the
other Emily D. West—Señora de Zavala and her children, two boys and a girl
under five years of age. Her husband, Lorenzo, had sailed from France to
New Orleans months before. Formerly ambassador from Mexico to Paris, he
had resigned in protest of Santa Anna's increasingly dictatorial government.
After time spent in Washington and New York drumming up land sales, de
Zavala gave Morgan a letter authorizing him to escort de Zavala's wife and
children back to Texas. A simple "board and batten over log" house awaited
them near Harrisburg, close to New Washington and upstream from San Jacinto
on the San Jacinto River.

Historians can offer only conjecture on Emily's motives for going to
Texas. Perhaps the principal enticement was money, the assurance of one
hundred dollars a year. The eastern United States was wrapped in a depression, brought on by the financial burden of western expansion and flawed
banking policies, which would lead to the Panic of 1837.

Conceivably Emily also embarked on this journey for the adventure of
seeing a new land—a place prominently known both for its equality toward
Negroes and for an economy that looked the other way when slave smugglers
dropped off their chattels on the coast. When Emily sailed for Texas, the
Mexican flag flew over the province, and like the Spaniards before them,
Mexicans acknowledged no difference among emigrants, white or black.
Three freed black families were among members of the first Texas colony
established by Stephen F. Austin, receiving land for settling there. Other
blacks came out to Texas as freed craftsmen, laundresses, and housekeepers.
Some arrived escaping slavery.

Yet with the burgeoning of cotton plantations in the South, planters
required field hands, and there was a good bit of traffic in slaves from Florida
and New Orleans to Galveston, Texas. The distant Mexico City government
could not keep tabs on the planters and smugglers.

Never knowing slavery, Emily could not have known what to expect from
the slave-oriented society she was entering as Morgan's bonded servant. Morgan
had a number of young and attractive mulatto slaves to keep him company while

away from his wife on business for Texas, his "adopted country." However, chances are good that Emily Morgan came to Texas to do housework, as stipulated in her contract, and not to become another Morgan concubine.

James Morgan was working to help create New Washington, the town that was to rise amid oak and magnolia groves on the banks of the mouth of the San Jacinto River, below its convergence with Buffalo Bayou, above Galveston Bay. Five years earlier, Morgan had brought in some thirty slaves—duly vouched for by Mexican officials as ones he had owned long before emigrating to Texas. The slaves for his house—according to the official scripts authorizing their importation into Texas—were skilled in the "art and mystery" of washing, ironing, cooking, and cleaning. The field Negroes he brought were practiced in the "art and mystery" of tilling the fields and harvesting the crops.

Morgan bought Cloppers' Point, a peninsula of land jutting into San Jacinto Bay, and established his own plantation, Orange Grove, on several thousand acres, growing cotton and citrus. He renamed the peninsula Morgan's Point, and this is where New Washington would sprout. Morgan and his backers were selling lots and acreage at New Washington despite Mexico's ban on both emigrants and slaves from the United States. Emily and her fellow "artisans" were brought in to help in the building of the new town.

Samuel Swartout of New York, a principal backer of the New Washington Association, and his colleagues were enticed by cheap lands in Texas and by the anticipated wealth to be gained by supplying the goods needed by the new arrivals in Texas. The land was cheap because many people in Texas were selling their freely granted land to developers for fifteen to twenty-five cents an acre, like de Zavala. This was especially true of cash-strapped Tejanos—the native Mexicans who had settled in the province known to Mexico as Tejas. (The province acquired its name from a native Caddo greeting, *tayshas*, meaning *friend*, or *welcome*. Early Spanish explorers pronounced it Tejas—TAY-hahss—which stuck until emigrants Americanized it to Texas.)

To receive shipments of goods into the new town and to store cotton, sugarcane, and corn for export, warehouses would have to be built. Blacksmiths, carpenters, and shoemakers were needed. Most of the early Texas settlers were farmers and ranchers who whittled, sawed, spun, sewed, and hammered to craft their cabins, sheds, clothes, furniture, and tools. But New Washington backers saw the need for more, and better-skilled, craftsmen, such as those bonded artisans arriving on the *Flash*. And in a land of few women, more were needed to cook, clean, weave, and sew, the role for which Emily was contracted.

In the Midst of Rebellion

While James Morgan, and Emily, were sailing for Texas in late 1835, Texians (as the Americans who had emigrated to the Mexican province were known) and Tejanos alike hoisted the colors of rebellion. De Zavala represented the area of New Washington, called Washington-on-the-Bay by locals. He moved in with the "Father of Texas," Stephen F. Austin, to draft the document that would dispute Santa Anna's regime and frame a new government. The first "consultation" of these colonists' representatives began in San Felipe on October 15, yet they did not reach a quorum until November 3, because of the slowness of courier mail and the far-flung reaches of the colonies from the Red River to the Rio Bravo (also known as the Rio Grande).

Earlier, Morgan had been elected representative for the New Washington area, having proven himself "good for argument" in the first protests over taxes at Anahuac, site of his general store. Behind that disagreement was the Santa Anna government's requirement that ships bypass the ports of Velasquez (Freeport) and Galveston and sail upriver to Anahuac, a small port on the Trinity River, where customs officials would collect taxes. For years Mexican officials had exempted taxes on colonists' imports of goods, and people had become accustomed to living in a tax-free province. But this exemption had run out. Now the colonists resented the imposition of the taxes, not only for the cost, but for the time and inconvenience of sailing upriver to pay levies on cargo before returning to coastal ports to unload. Morgan had worked out an agreement with the government for ships to pay taxes at Velasquez and Galveston.

Across the channel from the townsite of New Washington, in the older community of San Jacinto, settlers kept pace with news of Texas, Mexico, and the United States through notices pinned to the side of the one-room log building that housed May & Bowman's general store. Here they learned about the upcoming "consultation" of colonists, and they elected de Zavala their representative, in Morgan's absence.

Meanwhile in Mexico City, alarmed by these billowing winds of discontent from the faraway province of Tejas, Mexican President Antonio López de Santa Anna ordered General Martin Perfecto de Cos and his army to quell the rebellion. Soon, Santa Anna himself would take the field.

By the time Morgan arrived at New Washington with Emily and other artisans, the de Zavala family, and supplies on board the *Flash* and another schooner, Texians were shouting huzzahs for independence. On the long voyage, Emily had occupied her time by helping Señora de Zavala care for her young children in the cramped and crowded vessel.

A week after arriving, Emily Morgan was set to begin her duties, as defined by Morgan. Yet he was embroiled in the political discord, heavily on the side of independence from Mexico, and he had a lot to do: raise money from the United States to stand an army; acquire more ships; obtain goods. He took the fledgling Texas government's note for a million dollars to begin acquisitions, a note most lenders expected to be repaid with land, not dollars.

Morgan's alliance with Samuel Swartout of New York was felt in the colony. Swartout and his associates strongly backed the Texans, advocating separation from Mexico and eventual annexation to the United States. The topsy-turvy, power-shifting regimes and wars of Mexican federalists and centrists had made the New York monied men nervous. They wanted a stable political scene in Texas. And because they profited from smugglers who beached slaves in camps, called *barracoons,* on Galveston Island while awaiting sale and transport to Louisiana, Mississippi, and Texas plantations, these New Yorkers had no qualms about Texas entering the United States as a slave state. Others did.

Mexican officials fretted over the increasing number of newcomers to Texas and the rising population of slaves. In 1823, Mexico outlawed the sale or purchase of slaves by colonists. Mexico never countenanced slavery. Here, Negroes were free to own land, be craftsmen, and intermarry without causing any Mexican brow to arch in disdain. Many Anglo settlers felt differently.

Mexican Texans, like de Zavala—the Tejanos—felt the pinch between New Washington's backers, like Swartout, and their own homeland's values. Sailing from New Orleans to Galveston, de Zavala cringed at seeing the slave barracoon on the beach. Although he winced at this scene, he continued to advance the interests of the New Yorkers while he drafted resolutions for Texas independence. Simultaneously, Emily Morgan assisted de Zavala's wife in settling into the de Zavala home across from Morgan's Point.

At New Washington, Emily was assigned to become a "hotel keeper," a term that in those times was somewhat nebulous. Texans were traveling now, via roadways and waterways, so taverns and hotels near the new town's wharf were in demand. Emily, educated to "read, write, and cipher," could ably serve the commerce of the region. In this land where the Mexican government made no distinction between black people and white, a literate mulatto woman from the East could serve the traveling public. With her education, she possessed abilities that only a few on this frontier knew. And since there were many mixed marriages—Negro, Mexican, Indian, and white—Emily would have had no problem in being accepted as the hotel clerk, or more.

Emily began her work at the small, one-story hotel with a tavern, recently built and opened by the New Washington Association. Morgan, however, turned around and was soon on his way to New Orleans to begin outfitting the Texas government, though it would be three more months before the Declaration of Independence was declared, on March 2, 1836, at Washington-on-the Brazos.

A Texas army had been formed after the first consultation, with Sam Houston named to head it. David Burnet was elected president of the Republic of Texas, with de Zavala as vice president. Stephen Austin, with two others, was sent by the consultation on a mission to the United States to drum up political support and entice adventurous young men from the states to come fight for Texas, and receive a bounty of land.

The Battle of San Jacinto

The Mexican Army crossed the Rio Grande, and President Santa Anna soon took the field, heading north from Mexico City to the border with more than six thousand troops, and the mantle of a conquering dictator. The upstart rebels would be quashed. His warnings spread before him. No one would be spared. Residents were frightened, but were convinced they could whip Santa Anna. The threats and tension made for a grim introduction to Texas for Emily, who also had to deal with winter weather that was colder and wetter than usual. Travelers bunched up in the hotel and tavern, seeking shelter for a dollar a night, and whiskey for twenty-five cents a shot.

As Santa Anna marched toward San Antonio, citizens fled before him. In mid-January, when Emily had been there a little over a month, the first of a stream of women and children, slaves, and the elderly streamed through New Washington, to wait for the ferry at Lynchburg to carry them across the Sabine River toward safety, in Louisiana.

News of the massacres at the Alamo and Goliad spread through the young Republic of Texas like a prairie wildfire. Word reached the Texians that the Alamo had fallen on March 6, every man slain, and that Santa Anna vowed to kill all rebel Anglos. The crowds of fleeing settlers jammed up when they reached bridges and ferries, and with the uncommonly wet winter, every river was over its banks.

At one point, more than five thousand people crowded the shoreline that included Harrisburg, Lynch's Ferry (also known as Lynchburg), New Washington, and San Jacinto, waiting to cross the swollen Sabine and escape to Louisiana, where American troops were marshaled to protect them. For those fleeing, the delay to take this last river crossing before they reached the protection of American soil lasted several days. Alligators snagged and drowned those who, growing impatient and frightened, decided to swim their mounts across.

This exodus is known in Texas history as the Runaway Scrape. Escaping families walked or rode as they hauled belongings through prairies churned into bogs by rain, oxen, horses, and wagons. Forced to lighten their wagons, they abandoned pianos, furniture, and treasured heirlooms, littering the bogs they crossed. Toddlers became easy marks for disease in the wet and constant cold, and tiny unmarked graves pocked the trail.

For some reason, Emily did not join this fleeing horde. Whether she sensed she was safe, with her mulatto coloring, whether she enjoyed the lively trade of customers, or whether she was determined to earn her money and paid passage back to New York is not known. It is only known that she stayed.

From her vantage point as hotelkeeper, Emily witnessed Texas's primitive, mobile government. The notables of the Texas revolution took rooms there, some lingering, some fleeing, and some shipping out to promote the cause of Texas. Among the hotel's guests only days ahead of Santa Anna's troops were David Burnet, the Republic of Texas president, and Lorenzo de Zavala, the vice president. They had left Washington-on-the-Brazos shortly after declaring independence and moved to Harrisburg, until Mexican bugles ignited their flight to nearby New Washington, which became another temporary capital. Emily waited. James Morgan, now a colonel in the Texas army, commanded Camp Travis at Galveston Island, so in the crush and confusion, she easily could have slipped away.

One day a teenage courier thundered into New Washington to warn President Burnet that Santa Anna was close. Burnet boarded a small sloop bound for Galveston, taking de Zavala's wife and family with him. Emily helped the family load their belongings. The courier escaped when a Mexican officer showed up. As the sloop sailed off, the officer held his fire because the de Zavala family was on board. Emily Morgan would not be so fortunate.

At Harrisburg, Santa Anna's troops looted two or three houses, "well supplied with wearing apparel, mainly for women's use, an excellent piano, jars of preserves, chocolate, fruit, etc., all of which was appropriated for the use of His Excellency and his attendants," according to Col. Pedro Delgado. Fortified with wine they had plundered, the troops torched Harrisburg and then headed for New Washington, Santa Anna leading the early April advance.

Having split his forces, Santa Anna arrived with nearly a thousand troops chasing the Texas government, only to find New Washington vacated. His men took prisoners, capturing Emily Morgan while she loaded goods onto the vessel carrying the fleeing Texas officials, the fledgling government.

Frustrated by the elusive Burnet, Santa Anna spent three days in New Washington. A small body of dragoons rounded up more than a hundred head of beef for the troops to feast on, along with corn they had confiscated. Also captured were the military stores from Morgan's shipments upriver, warehoused in a new building on the wharf. The Mexican Army snagged a bountiful supply of flour, soap, and tobacco. After three days of looting, well fed and resupplied, the Mexican Army burned the warehouse and all the town's houses.

Emily became part of the plunder, possibly for the dictator's satisfaction, along with the chocolates and whiskey. These spoils of victory augmented Santa Anna's caravan bringing champagne, silken clothes, and an elaborate tent. Certainly, El Presidente's brown-and-white-striped silk tent, with its comfortable bed and silken sheets, was far more sumptuous than the rustic settlement's accommodations.

Santa Anna was known to enjoy the favors of women, calling them the "gravy of society." Thus his magnificent coach followed him with some special passengers. "Decency and public morals," writes his secretary, Delgado, "do not permit further mention of the matter." Santa Anna surrendered none of his appetites for food, wine, sex, and opium to the inconveniences of army life.

When word came of Sam Houston's advancing Texas army, Santa Anna's forces entered the surrounding dense woods, traveling along a narrow lane on the route to the sea to capture the Texas coast. The trail allowed passage for pack mules in single file only, and to mounted men in double file. Delgado later wrote about Santa Anna's actions as his troops moved through the woods, saying the president made a "headlong plunge down the lane knocking aside soldiers and pack animals and shouting, 'The enemy are coming! The enemy are coming!'" It's presumed that Santa Anna's carriage, with its cargo of women, brought up the rear, along with camp followers, laundresses, and prisoners.

Moving toward the savannah at San Jacinto, Santa Anna's men spotted Houston's sentries. Meanwhile, Santa Anna's silken marquis tent, stocked with silver teapots, cream pitchers, monogrammed china, glass tumblers, and decanters with gold stoppers, was pitched under the shade of mighty oaks laced with Spanish moss. Here he entertained himself and his mistresses, and prodded his generals to plan for victory, confident his troops would overwhelm the scraggly army of the rebels led by General Houston.

The notion that the Texians would be anything but a pushover for Santa Anna's troops was preposterous. A small skirmish that day in the woods bordering the plain of San Jacinto was proof. When evening came, the Mexicans settled down and built a breastwork of packsaddles, leaving a break only for the cannons. More troops were due. They would dispatch the rebels tomorrow.

Houston's army, composed of Texians eager for a fight and on fire to revenge the massacres of the Alamo and Goliad, ate boiled beef, cleaned their rifles, and slept restlessly. They arose at 4:00 A.M.—a habit of recent weeks while their course carried them over the cold ashes of the Mexican Army's campfires and the burned-out homes and villages of Texians. These sights inflamed fears for the safety of their families, fleeing in the Runaway Scrape. The Texas soldiers agitated for battle. They needed no motivation, only permission to charge. Forced to tarry, to curb tension that mounted while they waited for Houston to arise from his first solid night's sleep in weeks, the Republic of Texas soldiers drilled, paraded, and monitored the arrival of reinforcements for Santa Anna's army.

In his tent, aware that his newly arriving soldiers needed rest before attack, Santa Anna ordered muskets stacked for the afternoon siesta, which he, too, would enjoy. In his tent was a bed on which he could lounge in his silken underwear, take his opium, drink champagne, and enjoy trysts with the conquered and the invited.

While Santa Anna and his forces enjoyed the afternoon siesta, Houston aligned his men, a column of determined Texians slipping through knee-high prairie grass toward the rise that would bring them into the Mexican camp. Not until they were thirty yards out did they open fire at the command, "Every man get yours," shouting "Remember the Alamo! Remember Goliad!" on their charge.

Eighteen minutes later, the battle was won. The Texians savaged every Mexican in sight, with some 630 killed and 730 taken prisoner. The Texians lost nine, and thirty were injured. Santa Anna escaped. After screaming at his officers again—"the enemy they come, they come"—Mexico's president, clad in silk shorts and a shirt, grabbed a horse and fled.

A couple of the women in the battle area were killed, but most survived, including Emily Morgan. After the battle, and throughout the night, the flash and roar of guns peppered the quiet on this April 21, 1836. Two files of Mexican corpses lined the battlefield. More Mexican soldiers met death on the banks of a deep, marsh lake, the bodies stacked so thick that they served as a bridge across the water.

Troops scoured the countryside by day, rounding up escaping Mexicans. Santa Anna was captured on the morning of April 22, wet, bedraggled, and wearing a peasant's blue cotton jacket and red worsted slippers and his own silk shirt, its diamond studs worth seventeen hundred dollars. Brought into custody, he pleaded for opium and his life. Santa Anna wrote to his generals elsewhere in the region to surrender. The Battle of San Jacinto won for Texas her severance from Mexico. Texas was a free and independent republic.

An auction of Santa Anna's opulent collection of comforts, an estimated twelve thousand dollars' worth, yielded the seven hundred Texas victors about $9.50 each, a bonus since the new republic had no treasury. Colonel Morgan acquired the Mexican dictator's famous tent for presentation to his financier, Swartout. Members of the Texas government steamed upstream to see the battlefield, proud of their army.

After the battle, Santa Anna and his fellow prisoners were shipped to Galveston Island, where Colonel Morgan, now General Morgan, was assigned the twin tasks of preventing their flight and protecting their lives. Several days later, Morgan's wife and daughters returned from the Runaway Scrape to a burned-out plantation. Immediately, work crews began rebuilding. The orange groves, undamaged, yielded their first crop in the fall.

Emily Morgan in Life and in Legend

Legend has it that Emily Morgan was seducing Santa Anna in his tent during the afternoon siesta, distracting him as Houston's men prepared to attack. However, given that Santa Anna's generals were happy to elaborate on their leader's failings but did not mention this incident, it's doubtful that it occurred. More than likely, Emily was kept with Santa Anna's laundresses at the rear of the battlefield, a common practice with prisoners.

Not surprisingly after her experience as a captive, Emily West was more than anxious to leave Texas. Her bond would be up in the fall, and her trip back to New York would be paid for. But a frantic search of the bloodied and trampled battleground failed to turn up her freedwoman papers and her passport. They were lost.

Morgan was informed, but he was incapacitated by bouts of yellow fever and preoccupied with containing the prisoners, provisioning and maintaining morale of his troops, and defending his reputation. Houston had accused him of reselling government horses and provisions for his own profit. So in July, Morgan dispatched his aide, Captain Isaac Moreland, to intervene for Emily. Moreland vouched, in a letter to the secretary of state, that Emily was a freedwoman and that her papers no doubt were lost on the battlefield, where she was held captive during the Battle of San Jacinto, in which he served as an artillery officer. The Republic of Texas issued a passport to Emily so that she could leave Texas.

This paper, documenting Emily D. West's status as a freedwoman, paved the way for the Secretary of State of the Republic of Texas to issue her a passport, allowing her to return to New York. (Courtesy of the Texas State Library & Archives Commission, Austin.)

Nearly a year after the Battle of San Jacinto, both Emily D. Wests left Texas the same way they had arrived, on board the schooner *Flash*. Emily D. West de Zavala, widowed when Lorenzo caught pneumonia after capsizing in a small boat on Buffalo Bayou, provided an escort for the lone, freed mulatto, Emily D. West (Morgan). In turn, Morgan's Emily once again helped with the small children on the several-week passage to New York.

The life of the Yellow Rose of Texas was again lost to history after her return to New York. The last public record of Emily West is her name recorded in the New York census of 1840.

Although the mulatto Emily West had left the new Republic of Texas, her role in Texas was really just beginning, a role that would live on in story and song.

Within a couple of years, a mail courier brought Sam Houston, now president of the republic, a tightly written verse inked on the light blue, heavy paper of the time. The rubric—an inked, symbolic drawing—stamped on the envelope resembled the "squashed" hat worn by Texans. Houston wore one like it, and used it to wave his troops into battle. The words were the lyrics of a song—"The Yellow Rose of Texas"—at times also known as "Emily, the Maid of Morgan's Point." The song, reputed to be about Emily Morgan, had grown to life among the slave quarters on Texas plantations, and it was believed to have been written by a slave, about the yellow-skinned mulatto, Emily Morgan.

Misspellings in the lyrics sent to Sam Houston have fueled historians' feuds. At that time, spelling by Texans—even among the better educated— was creative at best. The handwriting is far too legible to be General Morgan's, so he cannot be the actual writer. However, since this land specula- tor was an inveterate self-promoter, it is conceivable that he had the verses copied, claimed they were about his Emily, and sent them to Sam Houston.

In the tumult and bickering after the Texans won at San Jacinto, General Houston had questioned Morgan's integrity, so Morgan could have sent the lyrics to ingratiate himself with the new president. Who wrote, or sent, the let- ter is inconclusive, but most tales about Emily—fact or fiction—appear to emanate from Morgan, her proud "owner." He was noted for self-enhancing acts, such as sending an orange to another Texas official, Mirabeau Lamar, claiming it to be "the first produce" of the republic—yet Morgan was claiming the accomplishment that was the harvest of another settler.

Morgan's claims were not the only ones that began a Texas tradition of tall tales and bragging. In no time, the Battle of San Jacinto assumed mythical proportions. Texans celebrated the first anniversary by parading through the battleground even though it was private ranchland. By the second anniver- sary, invitations to a ball sallied forth around the republic. It was held in Houston, a town named for General Sam. Tales of bravery, legends of love, and other stories of uncertain origin swathed the battlefield like the thick clouds of black powder during the fight in 1836. Time buried the carnage, and the pasture returned to its native wildflower beauty. People walked the prairie, spinning yarns and remembrances. In ballrooms and taverns, citizens, veterans, and politicians reveled in reliving the glory.

With each retelling of the victorious battle scene, stories were embel- lished, or perhaps invented. One of the most famous stories from San Jacinto is that of the battle-winning seduction by Emily Morgan.

This Yellow Rose saved Texas, so the story goes. In the privacy of Santa Anna's luxurious tent, she seduced him, further clouding his alertness already dulled by opium and champagne, while the Texans stepped forward. Noted as an egomaniac, Mexico's leader shunned caution and would have denounced anyone who disturbed his siesta, so what he did—sleep or take one of his women to bed—is left to imagination. And legend.

An English traveler, William Bollaert, who visited San Jacinto several years later, drinking and enjoying James Morgan's hospitality, reported the following account by an officer who was at the battle, in his book *William Bollaert's Texas*.

41

The Battle of San Jacinto was probably lost to the Mexicans, owing to the influence of a Mulatta girl belonging to Col. Morgan who was closeted in the tent with General Santana at the time the cry was made, 'The enemy! They Come! They come!' & detained Santanna so long that order could not be restored readily again.

Much has been written both promulgating this story and refuting the legend. Those advancing the idea of Emily as heroine of San Jacinto believe they know what went on inside Santa Anna's tent because of his propensities for women. Twentieth-century writers picked up the tale and told and retold it through the years until it became a "Texas truth." The most notable of these was Frank X. Tolbert of the *Dallas Morning News*, who defended Emily's heroine role and went on to write a book about the battle, *The Day of San Jacinto*, in 1959. Where he left off, Martha Anne Turner picked up. A folklorist and English professor at Sam Houston State University, she championed the Tolbert version of the story and discounted critics when she authored *The Yellow Rose of Texas: Her Saga and Her Song*, in 1976. Both authors, fans of Sam Houston, sought to defend the tale against historians' demythologizing of Texas legends.

Those who refute the legend defend their position with some sage assumptions. They note that Santa Anna's officers omitted this supposed incident when they published accounts of the war—accounts designed to place blame on Santa Anna for the defeat and loss of territory. The Mexican generals and colonels blamed Santa Anna for sleeping, for showing fear, and for abdication of leadership, but mentioned nothing about a sexual liaison. Margaret Swett Henson, in the *New Handbook of Texas*, volume VI, is among the historians who challenge the legend, citing it as an illogical conclusion from the circumstances. More recently disputing the legend is James Lutzweiler in a paper presented at the one hundredth anniversary of the Texas State Historical Association, in 1997: "Emily D. West and the Yellow Prose of Texas: A Primer on Some Primary Documents and their Doctoring."

Lutzweiler traces Emily's famous tale to Sam Houston and to a note that Houston wrote to the traveler and writer Bollaert. Lutzweiler contends that the note found in Bollaert's collection recounts the original story and bears Houston's signature. Houston, a hard-drinking, carousing romantic, developed an affinity for fanciful tales of symbolism from his years of living with the Cherokee Indians. Most historians today, including those at the San Jacinto Museum, chalk up the legend of Emily West to barroom palaver. Tales abounded along the coast, in hotels and barrooms, and exaggerated battlefield accounts were common in the months and years following the Battle of San Jacinto.

Muddying the landscape of Emily's story are Mexican historians who have described her as Santa Anna's "quadroon mistress during the Texas campaign." Their account adds description, but also confusion, since she had not been in his camp for more than two or three days after the ransacking of New Washington. They also called her a slave, which she was not.

Yet today, she is known and loved by many people as the Yellow Rose of Texas, heroine of San Jacinto. Despite attempts to downplay her legend and doubts that she was the focus of the song, Texans have not yielded. In fact or imagination, Emily is the savior of San Jacinto and is the subject of the love song. Her memory continues to fire the spirit of Texans who love to embrace larger-than-life characters.

Although the bickering over the Yellow Rose continues, so does the song. Lyrics of the folk song, first sung in evening shadows around coastal plantation slave shacks after Emily left Texas, were sent to Sam Houston in 1838. Twenty years later, a composer known only by the initials J. K. first set down the melody in print. A lively tune in three-quarter time, it became part of a vaudeville routine in Nashville. Then "The Yellow Rose of Texas" became a marching song for the boys in gray during the Civil War, substituting the word "soldier" for "darky."

These are the original lyrics of "The Yellow Rose of Texas," written and posted to Sam Houston after he became President of the Texas Republic. Some words have changed over the years, but the love song of Texas's Revolutionary War has become one of Texas's best-loved ballads. (Courtesy of A. Henry Moss Papers, 1820–1897, Center for American History, University of Texas–Austin.)

The lyrics of "The Yellow Rose of Texas" changed slightly over time, embracing an ever-wider audience, but the sentiment remained the same: a fellow leaves a pretty girl, to his regret, and he dearly hopes to find her again. Perhaps it was because of this sentiment as well as the bouncy, upbeat tune that American soldiers have sung this song in every war, from the Civil War on. A story from World War II tells of a group of black U.S. sailors who were guarding Japanese prisoners on the island of Saipan. The sailors—a good number of them from Texas—formed a glee club, and their favorite song came as no surprise. At one point, even some English-speaking prisoners joined in singing "The Yellow Rose of Texas."

> *She's the sweetest rose of color*
> *This darky ever knew*
> *Her eyes are bright as diamonds*
> *They sparkle like the dew*
> *You may talk about dearest May*
> *And sing of Rosa Lee*
> *But the yellow rose of Texas*
> *Beats the belles of Tennessee.*
>
> *Where the Rio Grande is flowing*
> *And the starry skies are bright*
> *She walks along the river*
> *In the quiet summer night*
> *She thinks if I remember*
> *When we parted long ago*
> *I promised to come back again*
> *And not to leave her so.*
>
> *Oh now I am agoing to find her*
> *For my heart is full of woe*
> *And we will sing the song together*
> *We sung so long ago*
> *We will play the banjo gaily*
> *And will sing the song of yore*
> *And the yellow rose of Texas*
> *Shall be mine forevermore.*

~ 3 ~

Polly Bemis

Lurid Life or Literary Legend?

PRISCILLA WEGARS

With a poker hand that showed three queens and two threes, Charlie Bemis bested his Chinese opponent's three jacks and won Polly, the "sloe-eyed slave girl with the skin like whipping cream, the velvet hair and the smooth warm thighs." That's the way Ladd Hamilton tells the story in "How Mr. Bemis Won the Chinese Slave Girl," his 1954 article in the magazine *Saga: True Adventures for Men.* Hamilton said this tale from the 1870s was "handed down by old men who knew how the cards fell; old men who had long memories and who were there." Following the card game, Bemis and the young woman "set up housekeeping" in his Warren, Idaho, tent.

This and many other romanticized versions of the life of Polly Bemis have perpetuated myths about her that are now difficult to dispel. Such fantasies provide few glimpses of Polly's true character and personality and leave readers unable to distinguish the real Polly Bemis from the fictional one. In contrast, Polly's actual history is genuinely fascinating. As a refreshing antidote to the popular images of her, the real story illuminates how greatly the fictions have distorted our perceptions of a woman who is arguably the Pacific Northwest's most famous Chinese woman pioneer.

People often ask, "What makes Polly Bemis so famous?" Formerly, it was the romantic aura that surrounded her as a Chinese "slave girl" who supposedly led a risqué and lurid life, perhaps as a prostitute, and who was believed to have been the prize in a high-stakes poker game. As the Chinese wife of a Caucasian man, Polly Bemis was stereotypically "exotic." Being Asian and a foreigner made her a novelty and therefore intriguing. The legends about Polly that circulated even during her lifetime fed peoples' curiosity.

Since her death in 1933, pulp fiction writers have nourished the popular appetite for scandal by overshadowing and distorting her real life. Unfortunately, many people now perceive Polly as a "wild" woman, one whose character was not above reproach. The following interpretation of her life, based upon fact rather than fiction, should stimulate the disappearance of such demeaning literary legends.

Instead, Polly's fame can finally derive from her real life, which was both unconventional and dramatic. As a woman who was sold by her parents in China, smuggled into the United States, and brought to Warren, Idaho, to be the concubine of a Chinese businessman she had never met, Polly adapted to difficult circumstances. After the businessman's death, she made additional adjustments, first by keeping house for Charlie Bemis, a Caucasian saloon owner, and then by nursing him back to health after a disgruntled gambler shot him. Following her marriage to Charlie, Polly cheerfully complied with the arduous demands of residence in the Idaho wilderness. Widowed anew, and homeless, Polly settled into a two-year exile in Warren prior to returning to her new Salmon River home.

Ironically, marrying Charlie and living in this isolated location contributed to Polly's later celebrity status. In her role as a "featured attraction" for passengers who stopped at her home during trips on the Salmon River, Polly met wealthy and prominent people from all over the United States. Indeed, some of them may already have known about her through an article by Countess Eleanor Gizycka in *Field and Stream.* Her self-imposed seclusion captivated visitors and enthralled residents of the Idaho towns of Grangeville and Boise on her eventual visits to those communities.

A Chinese Woman in America

Polly Bemis came to the United States as part of a vast movement of Chinese people, mostly men, who began coming to the western United States during the mid-nineteenth century. The earliest arrivals came in response to employment opportunities made possible by the California gold discoveries in 1848. At first, they worked as laborers for Caucasian miners or provided support services, such as laundries and other businesses, to Chinese and non-Chinese alike. Later, others became workers for the transcontinental railroad, completed in 1869.

Polly's arrival in Idaho in 1872 was part of a dispersion of Chinese people within the United States. Beginning in the mid-1850s, new gold rushes encouraged Chinese miners and businessmen to relocate to other areas of the West. After settling in remote mining regions, such as Idaho Territory, some brought women into their new communities.

Chinese immigrant women were uncommon. They, including Polly, amounted to fewer than 4,000 in 1890, when the total population of Chinese in the United States was more than 107,000. Although some women accompanied

1880 census entry for Charlie Bemis and Polly. (Courtesy of Asian American Comparative Collection, University of Idaho, Moscow, #PB89.)

husbands, were family servants, or became concubines for wealthy Chinese men, most arrived unwillingly and unlawfully, as prostitutes. Whereas respectable Chinese women were usually secluded from public view, Chinese prostitutes were not. As a result, Polly and other visible Chinese women were stereotyped by mistaken assumptions. For Polly, the myth is further exaggerated by the prevalent belief that she was "won in a poker game."

Although the lack of available information regarding Polly Bemis's youth in China and her early years in Idaho has given rise to fictionalized accounts, some facts about her life are not disputed. After her parents in China sold her, an old woman smuggled her into Portland, Oregon. There, a Chinese man purchased her. He brought her to Warren (also Warrens), Idaho, in 1872 when she was not quite nineteen years old. By 1880 she and Charlie Bemis were living in the same household. They married in 1894 and soon settled on the remote Salmon River. Charlie died in 1922 and Polly died in 1933, shortly after her eightieth birthday.

In tracing Polly's life in Idaho, documentary records are important, but they are incomplete. For most people, such records would commence with a birth certificate. However, Polly's "paper trail" does not begin until the 1880 census, a document that is crucial for understanding certain facts about her, particularly her relationship with Charlie Bemis. There, his name appears as "Chas. Bemis." He is a white male, aged thirty-two, who runs a saloon. The next line in the same column reads simply "Polly," with no last name. She is a Chinese female, aged twenty-seven. Her occupational entry states that she was housekeeping—probably just keeping house for Charlie and not yet running a boarding house, as she later did. Charlie's place of birth was Connecticut, whereas Polly was born in, or near, "Pekin," a prior name for the northern Chinese city of Peking, now Beijing.

Little evidence exists for Polly's early family life. Interviews with her in 1921, 1923, and 1924 provide a few details, but are conflicting. Famed news-paperwoman Eleanor (Cissy) Patterson, on a trip down the Salmon River in 1921, interviewed Polly Bemis, then nearly sixty-eight years old. Two years later, writing under the name Countess Eleanor Gizycka, a legacy from her failed marriage to Count Josef Gizycki, the journalist quoted Polly as saying, "My folluks in Hong-Kong had no grub. Dey sellee me…. Slave girl."

Although Polly's folks sold her as a slave girl because they had no food, she did not explain why they were in Hong Kong instead of in the north, her birthplace. Besides the 1880 census, confirmation of her northern birth appeared in a November 1933 newspaper article, just before her death. Polly reportedly "was born September 11, 1853, on the Chinese frontier near one of the upper rivers of China…."

Even though Polly's parents sold her, they may not always have been poor. In a 1923 newspaper interview with her, the reporter observed that Polly wore "boys shoes on her tiny feet, bound in childhood in accordance with the ancient Chinese custom…." In China, women of the Han majority population and some other groups often had bound feet, indicating their social position. Since bound feet rendered a girl useless for physical labor, only the wealthier or upwardly aspiring families could afford the luxury of decoratively crippled women. If a family later became poor, a woman's feet could be unbound, allowing her to work. A fact seldom mentioned, but one of the main reasons that the custom lasted so long, was that the bound feet, called "golden lotuses" or "golden lilies," were sexually attractive to men. Fondling the tiny feet was an integral part of making love and is often depicted in Chinese erotic art.

Polly's plight was compounded by Chinese custom. Chinese women were considered to be the property of men and could be bought and sold like any other commodity. Since women of all races, especially Chinese women, were scarce on the western frontier, a Chinese man who wanted a woman, for whatever reason, had to pay a great deal of money for her; a price of several thousand dollars was not uncommon. In America as in China, women with bound feet were more expensive than those with normal feet. Polly's formerly bound feet may have contributed to her high selling price, an amount documented in Countess Gizycka's interview, published in 1923.

Although slavery was illegal in the United States, a Chinese man in America could buy a woman as a servant, a prostitute, a wife, or a concubine. Although Polly might have been purchased as a servant, her price—$2,500— is too high to justify that assumption. Chinese customs can help in determining which role Polly was bought to fulfill. Prostitution is also unlikely. A Chinese merchant or any other Chinese man of status found it distasteful to share a woman with other men, particularly ones of low rank. Such purchases by Chinese underworld groups were far more common.

*Polly Bemis in her wedding dress, 1894.
(Courtesy of John and Pearl Carrey and
Asian American Comparative Collection,
University of Idaho, Moscow, #PB111.)*

Other Chinese customs confirm Polly's purchase as a concubine rather than as a wife. For example, a man could choose his own concubine, but his parents chose his wife. To ensure there would be sons to carry on the family name, wealthy Chinese men often had more than one wife, as well as one or more concubines, all in the same household. In China, a concubine was not the same as a mistress. There, she had a legally recognized status and her children were legitimate. Although a concubine was not a wife, she was "like a wife."

Keeping the marriage and concubinage customs in mind, the 1880 census helps corroborate Polly's status as a concubine. One column, headed "civil condition," contained three narrow spaces for tallying marital status: single, married, or widowed. If Polly and Charlie had been married at that time, they would each have had a mark in the middle column. Instead, a diagonal mark in the first column shows that Charlie Bemis was single, whereas a similar mark in the third column indicates that Polly was a widow. Therefore, based on Polly's calling herself a widow in the 1880 census, her owner probably purchased her as his concubine. If he then died, she would have considered herself a widow.

Both the price paid for Polly and her mode of transportation to Warren indicate that her new owner was a wealthy Chinese businessman. Polly told the countess, "Old Chinee-man he took me along to Warrens in a pack train."

Polly's new owner may not have been able to leave his business for very long or may have wished to avoid the discomfort of traveling. Instead, he hired a Chinese pack train operator to buy a woman for him. A newspaper article based on an interview with Polly, in 1923, stated that she arrived in Warren "by saddle horse from Portland on July 8, 1872. As she alighted from her horse, she was greeted by a stranger who said, 'Here's Polly,' as he helped her from the saddle and ever after Polly [w]as…her name."

In later years, Polly gave contradictory accounts of her journey to Warren. A 1924 article, also based on an interview with her, stated that "she and two other young Chinese girls were enticed from their hamlet home in 1869 to Hong Kong and to America by an American woman, who told them she wanted them to work in the gold camps of America, where they could pick gold coins from the streets. They were taken almost directly to Florence, Idaho…." Perhaps the two other girls remained there, since no record exists of their coming to Warren with Polly. Those details differ from ones in a 1933 account stating that a bandit leader gave Polly's parents seed grain for her. The brigand supposedly took Polly to a Chinese seaport city, then to San Francisco, Idaho City, and finally to Warren, "where he either died or deserted Polly…."

In the beginning, Polly would have had a language problem. Since she was from northern China, she spoke Mandarin or a northern dialect rather than the Cantonese or southern dialect spoken by the other Chinese in Warren. Although the written Chinese characters are the same, or nearly so, their pronunciation is completely different. Because Polly lacked writing skills, her communication with Warren's Cantonese speakers would have been rudimentary at best. Despite being a concubine, which most likely saved her from becoming a prostitute, Polly may still have had to work in her owner's business, perhaps as a hostess or dance hall girl. That would have given her the opportunity to begin learning both English and Cantonese.

Life with Charlie

By 1880, Polly had somehow managed to extricate herself from her owner. In the absence of information about how that happened, many people believe the romantic legend of Charlie Bemis winning Polly in a poker game. However, there is no evidence for that event, and Polly denied it just before her death. If her owner died, as is implied in the census of 1880 and in a *Sunday Oregonian* article published in 1933, Polly would have considered herself a widow. As a widow, she would have needed both an income and protection from predatory Chinese and non-Chinese men. Charlie Bemis may have offered her a home in exchange for her housekeeping services. With both English and Cantonese being foreign languages to her, Polly could well have decided that an alliance with someone from the English-speaking majority would give her more hope for her future life in America.

Whether Polly just kept house for Charlie, or did more, is not known. Nevertheless, the Warren community soon considered them a couple. Even though Charlie and Polly were not yet married, a newspaper story in 1881 reported that "Mrs. Chas. Bemis" was one of only four women in the entire town.

In May 1887, the Bemis house in Warren burned down. *The Idaho County Free Press* reported, "The fire caught in the roof in some unknown manner, and had gained such headway that next to nothing could be got out of the house. The loss is considerable; $500 in greenbacks were consumed and several costly gold watches belonging to various parties, and other jewelry worth about $2000." The cash, watches, and jewelry suggest that Charlie acted as a pawn-broker in Warren, loaning money to people and holding their valuables as security for the loans. By early September, Charlie had rebuilt their home. A later tax assessment roll valued it at $275.

Another event that year in Warren also affected Polly. The 1880 census for Warren had listed just one additional Chinese woman; she was a prostitute. While we do not know the extent of their relationship, the two women surely knew one another. In the fall of 1887, the *Idaho County Free Press* reported that the only other Chinese female in Warren "died verry [sic] suddenly here sometime ago—cause natural, or otherwise, not known." Polly, Warren's last Chinese woman, did not see another Chinese woman for more than thirty-five years—not until she visited members of Boise's Chinese "colony" in August 1924.

On September 16, 1890, Charlie Bemis was the victim of a "shooting affray." His assailant, Johnny Cox, "a well-known hard case," believed Bemis owed him money, and Bemis refused to pay. Cox intended to shoot out an eye, but the ball shattered Charlie's cheekbone instead. A doctor removed part of the bullet, but feared the remainder would cause fatal blood poisoning.

By then, Polly was a fixture in the Caucasian community. Even if Charlie had perished, sympathetic neighbors would doubtless have assisted the resource-ful Polly by creating a demand for her washing, ironing, child care, and cooking skills. Charlie lived, however. A 1923 article about Polly stated that "she came to his rescue, and after weeks of faithful care, nursed him back to health."

Following the shooting, there was again no news of Polly until the fall of 1893. In September, a newspaper article reported that Warren's population numbered some one hundred Caucasians, seventy-five Chinese men, and one

Chinese woman, who, of course, was Polly. The account continued, "Chas. Bemis, who formerly ran the hotel, has now a private boarding house and also a stable. There is not a gambling house or saloon in the camp...."

Perhaps Polly ran the boarding house for Charlie. In a 1924 interview, Polly mentioned a man named Jay Czizek as one of her boarders thirty-two years before, about the time that Charlie had the boarding house. In the same interview, she also told how she silenced miners who complained about her coffee. An article based on the interview said Polly would appear "with a butcher knife and the question, 'Who no like my coffee?'" The article said that when Polly began running the boarding house, "she knew nothing of cooking ...and as no one was willing to teach her, she simply watched two American women who did cook, and then started in."

In 1894, Polly and Charlie formalized their relationship; they married on August 13 at Charlie's residence in Warren. The Bemises' marriage certificate gives the bride's name as Polly Nathoy, or possibly Hathoy. Justice of the Peace A. D. Smead performed the ceremony, witnessed by W. J. Kelly and George L. Patterson.

Although Idaho and other states had racist anti-miscegenation laws designed to prevent mixing of the races, the groups named in the Idaho regulation changed from time to time. When the Bemises married, Chinese were not mentioned in the Idaho law. Earlier, between 1864 and 1887, it was a misdemeanor for any Caucasian person to marry or cohabit with any African American, Native American, or Chinese person. From 1887 to 1921 the law prohibited only marriages between Caucasians and African Americans, so Polly and Charlie had a legal marriage. In 1921 the statute added "Mongolians" as another prohibited group. The Bemises, by then having lived on the remote Salmon River for nearly thirty years, were well out of reach of anyone inclined to prosecute them under the revised law, not repealed until 1959.

People who knew the couple sometimes wondered why Polly married Charlie, particularly since she was very industrious and he was known for being lazy. In later years, Polly's friend Pete Klinkhammer commented that "it was more a marriage of convenience on the part of both. They had known each other well for many years in Warren, where both were connected with the gaming houses. Polly was ever faced with the threat of being sent back to China."

Even though Polly Bemis was married to an American citizen, United States law did not allow her or any other Asian immigrants to become naturalized citizens. This racist law was only repealed in 1943, ten years after Polly's death, and then just for the Chinese. After 1892, under terms of the renewed

Chinese Exclusion Act, Polly had to apply for a Certificate of Residence showing that she was legally entitled to reside in the United States. Because a harsh winter prevented an official from visiting Warren to register the Chinese there, Polly and the other Warren Chinese missed the deadline for registering, thus risking deportation.

Polly's failure to register became a district court case in Moscow, Idaho, during May 1896. As was then customary during deportation hearings, a Caucasian person had to vouch for the accused; Polly did not attend the court proceedings. The court determined that impassable roads and inaccessibility had indeed kept her from registering, and a Certificate of Residence was issued to her a few months later.

The Shepp Diaries

Soon after their marriage in August 1894, Polly and Charlie left Warren. They took up a mining claim on the south side of the Salmon River, about a seventeen-mile trip on foot or horseback from Warren. For the next few years, almost nothing is known about their lives. Beginning in late 1902, however, the Bemises appear in what are known as the Shepp diaries.

Charles Shepp had a mining claim several miles away, on the north side of the Salmon River and up in the mountains. He often came down to the river to purchase produce from the Smith and Williams ranch across the river from the Bemises, at the mouth of Crooked Creek. To retain his mining claim, Shepp had to prove that he worked it regularly. He kept track of his mining operations by writing daily entries in small pocket diaries. Besides mining particulars, his notes furnish a detailed account of pioneer life on the Salmon River. Most importantly, Shepp's diary entries provide revealing glimpses of Polly and Charlie Bemis.

Shepp's first mention of either of the Bemises is on November 8, 1902, when he states, "Bemis…over this am." From then until Polly's death in 1933, his diary entries tell a great deal about Polly and Charlie's personal possessions, their garden, their everyday activities, and their ranch buildings. Like neighbors anywhere, Shepp and the Bemises helped each other out and entertained one another. For example, on November 20, 1902, Shepp wrote: "Went over river after dinner [the noon meal]. Got parsnips & onions…Envited [sic] to Thanks[giving] dinner the 27th."

It is typical of Shepp's diaries that very succinct statements can evoke vivid images or carry a wealth of meaning. For example, in mid-January 1903 Shepp visited Polly and Charlie again. In reporting that he "Got jar tomatoes,"

Shepp implies that the Bemises purchased or saved tomato seeds; planted them; weeded and watered the growing plants; picked the fruit; owned canning jars, lids, and a canning kettle; put up their produce; and shared it with their neighbors. During other seasons, Shepp obtained pie, sauerkraut, strawberries and other kinds of berries, and a wide variety of vegetables including onions, peas, and string beans. Occasionally Shepp paid Polly for food items. She also earned money from selling fruit, vegetables, and eggs to passersby, or by sending produce to Warren, Dixie, or Concord to be sold for her.

Shepp occasionally mentioned the Bemises' animals. One fall, someone coming down to the river from Warren brought Polly a dog. In February 1910, Shepp noted that he "took picture of Polly & Nellie & Julie." Nellie and Julie were horses, one named after Shepp's sister Nellie. The following year, Shepp's mining partner, Peter Klinkhammer, brought Polly a cat. Shepp often got eggs from Polly and occasionally chickens.

At times Shepp referred to events of national interest and importance, news that he surely shared with Polly and Charlie. On April 21, 1906, he wrote that an acquaintance "brought word that San Francisco was destroyed by earthquake." In April 1912, a letter from his sister Nellie reported "the loss of the *Titanic* by hitting an iceberg."

Shepp was handy, probably more so than Charlie Bemis. He made a meat safe for Polly and fixed both her clock and her sewing machine. Shepp also installed a battery-operated telephone between his ranch and the Bemis place. Later, he ran the line on his side up over the mountain to town and repaired the telephones as needed.

During Polly's leisure time she enjoyed sewing, crocheting, and other kinds of needlework. Some evenings, the Bemises, Charlie Shepp, and Pete Klinkhammer listened to a radio that Shepp had built. Pete recalled that the radio "delighted Polly, but completely mystified her." Pete remembered that Polly especially liked Shepp's wind-up phonograph, marveling at "how the voice could come out of that big horn amplifier." Her favorite record was Cal Stewart's comic monologue "Uncle Josh in a Chinese Laundry." According to Pete, "Uncle Josh's troubles invariably made Polly chuckle."

Polly's fishing exploits were almost legendary. Shepp once wrote, "Polly & Bemis over to dinner. Polly caught 27 fish." In later years, Pete Klinkhammer commented, "Polly loved to fish and was good at it. We'd see her [gardening] & she'd bend to the earth real quick, then shove something into the big pocket of her long dress. Come three o'clock every day Polly had her gardening done and her fish bait, ready and waiting in her pocket. We used to know what time it was by watching her."

From right, Polly Bemis, Captain Harry Guleke, and members of the R. E. Shepherd boating party, July 19, 1922. (Courtesy of Philinda Parry Robinson and Asian American Comparative Collection, University of Idaho, Moscow, #PB232.)

In 1910 Shepp purchased the Smith and Williams ranch at the mouth of Crooked Creek and began living there. Pete Klinkhammer soon joined him, and they and the Bemises often visited back and forth. Shepp was much more fastidious than the previous owners, Smith and Williams. A story about them related that they had five dogs. One was named Water, and the men's dishes "were as clean as Water could make them."

If Shepp had a sense of humor, it rarely peeked forth in his diaries. When it did, it was probably unintended. One sequence, involving a rooster, began, "Put George in chicken house." The following day, Shepp "killed George, he weighed 4# [pounds]." Later Shepp wrote, "Bemis & Polly over to dinner. Cooked George with noodles."

Every fall, Shepp helped Polly order the Bemises' winter food supply. When it arrived in town, up the mountain on Shepp's side of the river, he and Klinkhammer took care of getting it down to the river and across to the couple. Shepp also wrote up Polly's orders to Montgomery Ward and other businesses. He got shoes and eyeglasses for her and once measured her for a dress.

The stretch of river between the two ranches was a popular Salmon River crossing point for people going between Warren, south of the river, and Dixie or Concord, north of the river. Other travelers hazarded a downriver journey on "The River of No Return." Any visitors were a welcome diversion from the daily routine. In early September 1919, Shepp wrote, "Boat down with 9 men.

They stopped here tonight." The intrepid Captain Harry Guleke, a Salmon River legend, piloted the boat. In an *Idaho County Free Press* article dated September 25, passenger Will Shoup said, "Another interesting character...was Charles Bemis, who has lived with a Chinese wife on a little 4-acre patch of land on Polly [C]reek...for the past twenty-five years. He is getting too old to work and Polly, the wife, does it all."

Two years later Shepp chronicled a similar visit, one that ultimately brought Polly Bemis to the attention of a much wider audience. In July 1921, he wrote, "Boat down this eve." On that trip, again captained by Harry Guleke, passenger Eleanor (Cissy) Patterson spoke with Polly. In 1923, an account of her visit with Polly Bemis appeared in the magazine *Field and Stream* under the byline of Countess Eleanor Gizycka. It is the first known interview with Polly.

The countess wrote that Polly "stands not much over four feet, neat as a pin, wrinkled as a walnut, and at sixty-seven she is full of dash and charm." Polly told the countess, "I cost $2,500. Don't looka it now, hmm?" and chuckled. The countess asked Polly where Charlie Bemis was, and she replied, "Abed. He bin abed most two year now." When Polly indicated that Charlie was pretty cross and implied that she had to wait on him a lot, the countess suggested that maybe Polly should get another husband. Polly laughed and said, "Yas, I tink so, too."

With Charlie Bemis bedridden, Shepp and Klinkhammer increasingly took over many of the Bemises' chores. During 1921, for example, Shepp recorded that they crossed the river many times to cut wood for the Bemises, put out a stovepipe fire, plow and plant their garden, burn brush, cut hay, and do the watering.

Captain Guleke continued to stop so that his passengers could meet Polly and take photographs. In July 1922 the R. E. Shepherd party from Twin Falls, Idaho, visited with Polly; she was then sixty-eight years old. One of the men on that trip kept a diary, and his entry for that day notes, "About 5 pm we stopped at Polly Bemis's place. Bemis is an old timer here, probably 75 years old and confined to his bed. His wife, Polly, is a Chinese woman. She looks after him and tends to the garden, orchard, and farming operations. Polly has been in the Salmon River country for more than 40 years and has never been off the ranch for 28 years."

Then, less than a month later, catastrophe visited the Bemises. In mid-August, the Bemis house caught fire and burned to the ground. Pete was away taking produce to Dixie, so only Shepp could help. That evening he wrote, "The Bemis house burned at 12 [noon]. Had a hell of a time. Got the old man out by the skin of my teeth. Lost Teddy [Polly's dog]. He got burned. Polly & I got the old man over [the river] about 4. Had hard time. Didn't save a single thing. The whole place was on fire when I got over."

Charlie Shepp's diary entry for August 16, 1922, when the Bemis house burned. (Courtesy of Asian American Comparative Collection, University of Idaho, Moscow, #PB147.)

Although he was not badly burned in the fire, Charlie Bemis never recovered. Stress and smoke inhalation doubtless worsened his already weakened condition; on October 29, 1922, Charlie Bemis died. Shepp wrote, in the margin of that day's entry, "Bemis Dead," underlining the words for emphasis. The entry read: "Bemis passed in at 3 am. Up to camp. Left at 5 am. Gus & Holmes down. We buried the old man right after dinner. Fine day."

Charlie Bemis's grave is still at the Shepp Ranch, confounding romanticists who want to reunite the couple in death. Since Polly surely helped choose his final resting place, it is not surprising that it is in a nearly perfect setting with respect to the Chinese principles of *feng shui*. In that belief system, the ideal location for a grave is in the center of a south-facing slope overlooking a body of water, preferably a meandering stream or river. A curving hillside embraces Charlie Bemis's grave, which would still view the river if modern buildings did not intervene.

A Look at the Outside World

Protective of the new widow's reputation, Shepp and Klinkhammer realized she could not remain with them. On October 31, Shepp wrote, "Polly going to Warren." He took four horses across the river, plus her belongings and some food—onions, squash, and one hundred pounds of potatoes. Pete took her up the next day and found her a cabin in Warren. Polly lived there for nearly two years. During that time, Shepp wrote to her occasionally. Although Polly could not read or write, she had many friends in Warren who surely read the letters to her and who probably wrote the replies that she dictated.

In July 1923, Charlie Shepp's sister Nellie and brother Harvey came for a long visit. When they left, in August, they returned through Warren. From there a car took them, and Polly, to Grangeville. In Grangeville, the *Idaho County Free Press* interviewed Polly. Described as a "little, old, gray-haired woman, weighing less than a hundred pounds," Polly wore "boys shoes on her tiny feet, bound in childhood…and…a plain cotton dress." She stayed at the home of Mrs. Anson Holmes, where many people visited her. She also found time to be fitted with glasses and to have dental work done.

Polly had never seen a train, so friends took her to the Grangeville station. There she marveled at the evening train's arrival. *The Free Press* article said, "When the trainmen were advised that she had never before seen a locomotive or cars, they lifted her into the engine cab, opened the firebox, and allowed her to peer at the seething, roaring furnace," which frightened her.

Polly gave the interviewer details about her life in Warren before the turn of the twentieth century, observing, "When school come to Warren, I can't go to school. I got to make money. God gave me that much," and here she pointed to her head. "I learn right along."

The reporter commented at length on Polly's remarkable memory for children's names and birthdays and dates and details of events. Called a "modern Rip Van Winkle," Polly professed astonishment at the magnitude of Grangeville, then a community of sixteen hundred people: "She stands aghast. She chuckles for joy. She walks…grasping the arm of her companion, for fear she may become lost—that she may be engulfed in the maelstrom of the mad throng." In reaching and touring Grangeville, Polly took her first automobile ride and saw her first train. Those were memorable experiences, but Polly's first motion picture fascinated her the most.

Although Polly thoroughly appreciated visiting Grangeville, she missed Warren. After a week of the city's hustle and bustle, she had had enough and wanted to go home. Polly returned to Warren on the Salmon River stage. One interviewer noted that Polly exclaimed, "I have best time in fifty year! …Maybe I come back next year." Thanks to gifts of new clothes from her many friends, Polly was "bedecked in a new dress, a gay hat and white shoes." She appeared to be "as happy as a child after the annual visit of Santa Claus," and was "particularly proud" of her "new gold-rimmed spectacles."

Shepp and Klinkhammer agreed to build Polly a new house and look after her; in exchange, they would get the ranch on her death. Between October 1923 and the following May, Shepp often wrote about sawing and putting up house logs, cutting shakes for the roof, installing a new telephone, laying flooring, and constructing windows.

In the meantime, Polly kept busy in Warren. She was always extremely fond of children, and Johnny Carrey was a very special young friend. Johnny, his parents, and his two sisters lived on the South Fork of the Salmon River. To attend school, the Carrey children had to live in Warren, away from home. Johnny stayed at a hotel, but when his younger sister Gay started school, she lived with Polly that term. In turn, the children's parents sent Polly money and garden produce and Johnny helped Polly with chores, such as bringing in wood.

A trip to Boise in August 1924 was another high point in Polly's life. She went with Jay Czizek and his wife and they stayed at the Idanha Hotel. Polly told a reporter who interviewed her there, "Czizek eat in my boarding house 32 years ago. I know him long time." In Boise, Polly saw "her first street car, her first high building, her second movie show, and rode in her first elevator, all in one day." The reporter seemed to find in Polly a most enchanting person, describing her as "a tiny woman with iron gray hair, the brightest of eyes, dressed in a blue cotton dress, her whole appearance scrupulously neat. Her speech is excellent, with just enough of the 'pidgin English' to make it fascinating. Her memory is remarkable, particularly for dates, and her eyes twinkle as she tells jokes on herself...."

Polly had a lot to tell the interviewer: "My husband say, 'We will never see railroad, I guess,' and he die, then I come out to get dentist to see my teeth and I see railroad at Grangeville last summer. Now I see Boise, big city, stores five, six stories high, street cars run middle of street. Lots of people, I like it, but it makes me tired to look so much." Although Polly did not care for bobbed hair, she approved of modern dress. When asked how she liked the movies, she said, "Some very nice—ships and big sea—and some very bad, shut eyes."

Meanwhile, Charlie Shepp accelerated construction of Polly's new Salmon River house. By September 1924, he worked on it nearly every day. In early October, Pete traveled to Warren. The next day he returned with Polly and took her over the river to the Shepp Ranch where she stayed for just over a week, until construction was finished. Polly finally moved into her new home in mid-October 1924. Charlie Shepp built a bed for Polly, as well as a table and chairs, and Pete cut firewood for her. As she became older, Shepp and Klinkhammer did more and more of the heavy work. Polly still kept very busy; in a single two-week period, she killed four porcupines, notorious for damaging tools and other gear around a ranch.

In later years, Pete Klinkhammer's comments about Polly further illuminate her lively personality. He observed that Polly "was a sharp gambler in a crib[bage] game & used to pit her wits against the best of 'em. Two fellows came & camped across Crooked Creek & did some placer mining over there. One of them liked to make a big show. He used to get vegetables and a few little things from Polly. She never charged for the stuff. But he kept flashing this one hundred dollar bill—to show off, I think. Well, Polly let it pass a few times. Then one day she got tired of this and she surprised him. Two things Polly could do good—count money and fifteen two [cribbage scoring]. She changed it for him. After that he didn't flash no more money."

Polly's final illness came upon her suddenly, but lingered. On Friday, August 4, 1933, Shepp went across the river in the morning and found Polly had collapsed outside. He wrote, "she is bug house [meaning, insane] and nearly helpless." Two days later Pete and a friend took her halfway out on horseback, where they met a car sent from Grangeville to get her. The following Friday, Shepp learned Polly was "getting along fine." She probably had had a stroke. Polly languished in the Grangeville hospital for three months. On November 5, 1933, reporter Lamont Johnson, writing for the *Sunday Oregonian*, published a lengthy article with sensational headlines: "Old China Woman of Idaho Famous. Polly Bemis Seriously Ill in Grangeville Hospital. Career Nearly Ended. Patient Denies That She Was Won in Poker Game by Man Who Later Married Her."

Johnson did not interview Polly himself. Instead, he obtained his information from Eva Weaver, Polly's nurse in the Grangeville hospital. During the three months she had cared for Polly, Weaver had learned a great deal about her patient. In his article, Johnson referred at length to a letter from Weaver, in which the nurse "related personal traits to show the old lady as a most likable character. She has been a friend to all unfortunates, and particularly fond of children, although she never had any of her own. Her wrinkled face lights up with a lovely smile when she hears the little folk, or of them. She had a keen interest in an expectant mother at the hospital and was anxious to see the baby when it was born. Polly has been an expert angler and loved to fish in Salmon River, but she was so frail and small – 'only as tall as a broom,' she said—about 4½ feet high, and was always afraid the fish would pull her into the river. She made pets of any kind of bird or animal she could find. Once she took a nest of baby robins and raised them, letting them come and go as they pleased. When they found fresh meat at a nearby market in Warrens they spent so much time there that a French clerk killed them. This made Polly very angry, Mrs. Weaver said."

On November 6, 1933, Polly Bemis died in the Grangeville hospital; she was just over eighty years old. Her death certificate lists cause of death as chronic myocarditis, defined elsewhere as "an inflammation of the muscular part [myocardium] of the heart wall." In his diary, Shepp wrote, "Polly passed away this afternoon." He underlined that sentence, emphasizing its importance. Two days later, Polly was buried in Grangeville. Neither Shepp nor Klinkhammer could attend. Over the next few weeks Shepp crossed the river to get things — sugar, flour, and even a bed, presumably the one he had made for Polly. He also fed her cat, Johnnie. By January he no longer saw Johnnie across the river and in February he wrote, "Over river PM. I guess Johnnie is gone."

Polly Bemis in Fact and Fiction

In the seven decades since Polly Bemis's death, historians, biographers, journalists, and fiction writers have profiled her with more imagination than fact. Numerous magazine articles, several book chapters, two books, and even a film have presented versions of Polly's life, building upon one another to the extent that the factual Polly has become submerged beneath the fantasized Polly. These works include supposed details about her being won in a poker game; discussions of her possible role as a prostitute; and the use of the undocumented Chinese names *Lalu* for Polly and *Hong King* for her Warren owner.

The best-known of these writings is Ruthanne Lum McCunn's biographical novel, *Thousand Pieces of Gold* (1981), together with a motion picture of the same name very loosely based on the book. A dramatic highlight of both the novel and the film occurs when Charlie Bemis and a Chinese man called Hong King play poker for very high stakes — ownership of Polly herself. The book and the movie make Polly's story both fascinating and believable.

The "won in a poker game" story is a common theme pervading much of the popular literature about Polly Bemis. One article describes how Charlie, playing against the "Oriental saloon-keep, Hong King," had a poker hand containing "4 bullets" — four aces — with which he won the "delicately lovely" Chinese girl whose "round, young body" was "seductively sheathed in red brocade satin." The same author inexplicably forgot having earlier written about Polly's "yellow oriental dress slit to the knees revealing a pair of shapely legs." In both renditions, a gentlemanly Charlie took her home to his cabin, gave her his bed, and "threw his bed-roll on the floor."

Polly Bemis's restored home on the Salmon River. (Courtesy of Asian American Comparative Collection, University of Idaho, Moscow, photograph by Priscilla Wegars, #PB35.)

Sister M. Alfreda Elsensohn's version of this episode was, predictably, the antithesis of titillating. In her biography *Idaho County's Most Romantic Character, Polly Bemis* (1978), Polly merely "appeared dressed in yellow." After Charlie won her, he moved Polly "to one of the twin cabins." Although Elsensohn did not mention the winning poker hand, other writers amply compensated for her omission. One writer noted that Charlie Bemis had four of a kind while his opponent, named Hong Kong, held only three aces. Another observed that "Johnny" Bemis's four kings and a queen beat Wing Toy's three aces, whereas a third author wrote that Charlie's full house overcame Hong King's straight.

The inconsistencies in the stories are intriguing. If Charlie Bemis really did win Polly in a poker game, logic dictates that the cards he held to win her would have become an integral part of the story, together with his name, his opponent's name, and the color of Polly's dress. Like the "telephone game," where a group of players whisper the same story to one another in succession, retelling has distorted the details.

The challenge of the "won in a poker game" story calls for more information. Is this assertion true and verifiable, or should it be relegated to the realm of legends, myths, and folklore? In reconstructing Polly's true history from the available contemporary documents, one major point stands out. None of them, particularly the Shepp diaries and the interviews with Polly herself, mention Polly being won in a poker game. Since Polly herself denied that the poker game incident happened, how did the story get started?

One explanation is contained in a tape-recorded interview with longtime Warren resident Otis Morris. Morris, who began living there in 1890, was the stepson of W. J. Kelly and the nephew of George Patterson, the two witnesses at the Bemises' wedding in 1894. Morris stated, "My stepdad died in 1911 and up to that time I had never heard a thing about it but sometime after that in the next five or six years they got the story out that she was won in the poker game." Therefore, Otis Morris first heard the story about 1916 or 1917. He also thought he knew where the story originated. He stated, "I'm satisfied in my own mind that Jay Czizek started that."

On the other hand, respected historian Sister M. Alfreda Elsensohn firmly believed that Charlie won Polly in a poker game. In her writings, she accepted that story, but argued that Polly "was not a poker bride." In other words, Bemis won her, but did not marry her until later. Elsensohn probably relied on the recollections of Warren pioneer Taylor Smith, who explained how Charlie won Polly in a gambling game. Smith named five men who reportedly saw the game and told him about it. Interestingly, one of the five was W. J. Kelly, Otis Morris's stepfather, but Morris never heard the story during his stepfather's lifetime. Clearly, unresolved contradictions remain.

If the poker game did occur, it happened between 1872, when Polly arrived, and 1880, when the census listed her with Charlie Bemis. During those years, tremendous anti-Chinese sentiment flourished. Such racist attitudes culminated in the United States' Chinese Exclusion Act, passed in 1882, prohibiting new Chinese laborers from arriving. The rallying cry "Chinese Go Home" united unemployed Caucasian workers, who blamed the Chinese for their plight. Since similar anti-Chinese attitudes also prevailed in early Idaho, common sense dictates the unlikelihood of a scenario in which a lone Chinese man sat across the table from a Caucasian man, in a roomful of other Caucasians, staking his entire fortune, and his Chinese concubine, on the turn of a card.

Anti-Chinese attitudes also impacted Chinese women, but to a lesser extent. Although none of the primary sources link Polly with prostitution, some later writers insist she engaged in that occupation. Warren's lack of Chinese prostitutes in 1870 may be the inspiration for that myth; later authors may have assumed Polly was brought to Warren for that purpose. Another source for "Polly as prostitute" may simply be the pervasive stereotype that "all" Chinese women engaged in that occupation. Before and during the

1870s, most Chinese women in the United States were indeed prostitutes. This fact caused people to mistakenly attribute that occupation to every Chinese woman, no matter what her status.

Purchasing Chinese girls from poor parents was one important manner by which prostitutes were obtained for the American market. Therefore, Polly's experience of being sold has contributed to the myth that she herself was a prostitute, despite the lack of evidence for this assumption.

If anti-Chinese prejudice ever impacted Polly specifically and directly, no record of it has been found. Interviews, newspaper accounts, and reminiscences from former friends and acquaintances are overwhelmingly favorable and speak of her kindness, friendliness, and neighborly qualities. When Robert G. Bailey wrote that Polly "has a yellow skin, but a white heart encased in a sheathing of gold," he intended it as a compliment, never suspecting that his patronizing remarks would survive to reek of racism in the twenty-first century.

Even contemporaries with anti-Chinese attitudes perceived Polly favorably. As an individual, her adoption of many Western traits and customs may have insulated her from anti-Chinese prejudice. In her daily life and behavior, whether deliberately or not, Polly effectively countered anti-Chinese stereotypes. For example, she spoke English, wore Western-style clothing, and cooked mostly American food. Polly had a Western-style marriage ceremony and was reported to be a Christian. She was clean and neat, she interacted successfully with members of the Caucasian community, and she did not smoke opium or send money back to China.

An unsolved puzzle about Polly Bemis remains. Her Chinese given name is often said to be Lalu, but where does that name originate? It is not in any of the newspaper accounts, in the interviews with Polly, or in the Shepp diaries.

Several possible explanations have been advanced. The transcript from Polly's 1896 court case includes what look like two Chinese characters. Although one hypothesis suggests that they stand for "Lalu" or "Lalu Nathoy," several people literate in Chinese stated emphatically that the characters do not read "Lalu" and are apparently meaningless. Recently, however, Emma Woo Louie, an authority on Chinese names, has suggested that the characters are very similar, although not identical, to ones that would be pronounced P'o and Lee, in Cantonese. Perhaps, since Polly could not read or write, she may have learned an approximation of these characters and used them to symbolize her signature.

The earliest occurrence of "Lalu" seems to be in *Pioneer Days in Idaho County* (1947), by Sister M. Alfreda Elsensohn. There she states, "As previously indicated, in the Certificate of Marriage, her Chinese name was Lalu

Nathoy." The certificate, however, reads as follows: "This is to certify that on this 13th day of August 1894 I have joined in the holy bonds of matrimony Chas. A. Bemis and Miss Polly Nathoy at the residence of C. A. Bemis."

Why Elsensohn ascribed the name "Lalu" to the marriage certificate, and thus to Polly, is unclear, but subsequent authors have perpetuated the name. Western writer Caroline Bancroft, who wrote about Polly as Lalu, obtained her information from a manuscript written by her father, George J. Bancroft, a mining engineer who knew the Bemises, but not until about 1917. However, George Bancroft's manuscript itself does not contain the name Lalu.

According to the Bemises' marriage certificate, Polly's Chinese family name was Nathoy (possibly Hathoy), but Chinese name authority Emma Woo Louie's search of the Chinese surnames dictionary did not find that word used as a Chinese last name. Instead, she suggests that "Nathoy could have been written down for the sound of Ah Toy [also Atoy], a common given name for women." Even if Nathoy really stood for Ah Toy, it remains unclear how Polly would have acquired that name. Ah Toy is "a southern Chinese name custom," but Polly Bemis was from northern China. Perhaps Warren's Cantonese-speaking residents gave her that name.

The name of the Chinese businessman in Warren who owned Polly is also a mystery. No original sources name him. Although Elsensohn called him Hong King, she herself questioned the name's existence. In a 1943 letter to a local "old timer," she asked, "Do you know whether there was a Chin[ese man] by that name at Warrens in the early days?" Subsequent writers continued using Hong King. They also stated the "fact" that he owned a saloon, but detailed research in primary sources failed to confirm either statement. No Chinese man with that name, or that exact occupation, appears in any documentary sources. Although early tax records indicate that two Warren Chinese dealt in "retail liquor" in 1870 and 1871, prior to Polly's arrival in 1872, they were named My Yick Chung and Ye Yick.

The search for the name Hong King in the Warren census of 1870 also sought wealthy Chinese men of any name. Only one man could have afforded to pay $2,500 for a woman. He was a thirty-year-old placer miner named Ah Yung, with wealth valued at $3,500. His nearest Chinese financial rival was Ah Hon, a thirty-five-year-old merchant with a building and possessions worth $1,900.

"Ah" was often used before Chinese names. Not a name itself, it simply means, "that person is called," so Ah Hon meant "that person is called Hon," with no indication of any last name. With "Hon" as his first name and no last name given, Ah Hon might be the Hong King referred to, but that coincidence is not sufficient to say that his name was Hong King or that anyone in Warren was so named.

The person who provided the money to buy Polly in 1872 may not even have been listed in the Warren census of 1870. For example, Charlie Bemis is not listed. Other records show that Bemis lived in Warren that year, but he may have been away, perhaps mining in a remote area. A deed dated 1876 for property in Warren may provide the closest connection to the so-called Hong King. A man named Ah King sold Ah Hong a house, lot, and house furnishings for $140. Perhaps Polly lived there, and her association with one or the other of the men may have fused the two names in public memory.

Legacy of an Indomitable Spirit

Polly Bemis died oblivious to the enigmas that still perplex researchers. On her death, Pete Klinkhammer became the owner of the Bemis Ranch. Previously, in 1929, he had applied to claim it as a homestead. Although Idaho law allowed Polly, as a widow, to inherit land from her husband, Bemis had only held the land as a mining claim and had never filed for a homestead patent. Despite her marriage to Charlie, Polly was an alien ineligible for citizenship, so she could not homestead the land they had improved together. Claiming it as Klinkhammer's homestead was the most expedient way for Shepp and Klinkhammer to protect Polly's interest in her home during her lifetime and to ensure that Pete obtained the land on her death.

Charlie Shepp died in 1936 and was buried next to Charlie Bemis on the Shepp Ranch. Over the years, Pete Klinkhammer gave many of Polly's personal possessions to The Historical Museum at St. Gertrude in Cottonwood, Idaho, in care of Sister Alfreda. Following Pete's death in 1970, his heirs purchased a gravestone for Polly Bemis in accordance with his wishes.

In June 1987, the Salmon River Resort Club, then-owner of the Polly Bemis Ranch, dedicated her restored log cabin as a museum. The seventy guests who attended the ceremony included Idaho Governor Cecil Andrus and other dignitaries. Prior to the event, Polly's remains were exhumed from Grangeville's Prairie View Cemetery and reburied adjacent to her restored home, so she is across the river from her husband, who is still buried at the Shepp Ranch. Her gravestone, which was also moved, reads, "Polly Bemis, Sept. 11, 1853 - Nov. 6, 1933." Because Caucasian people selected her grave site, it lacks the *feng shui* characteristics of her husband's burial place. Charlie's grave site is more typically Chinese than Polly's.

Polly Bemis's grave adjacent to her restored home. (Courtesy of Asian American Comparative Collection, University of Idaho, Moscow, photograph by Priscilla Wegars, #PB1995.2.)

Through her perseverance and her indomitable spirit, Polly Bemis symbolizes all the forgotten Chinese women who came to the United States during the late nineteenth century, women who arrived often unwillingly, without knowing English, and with no prospect of ever returning home. While here, these women usually faced racial prejudice from Caucasian people, as well as sexual discrimination from Chinese men. Polly Bemis lived in Idaho for over sixty years. During that time, her strength of character enabled her to rise above adversity, winning respect and admiration from everyone who knew her.

In doing so, Polly successfully surmounted a host of anti-Chinese stereotypes. Her Caucasian friends gave her gifts, took her on trips, welcomed her in their homes, and prided themselves on their friendship with her. More than fifty years after her death, Polly's friend Fred Shiefer remarked at the museum dedication, "I don't think there was a better person than Polly Bemis. There couldn't have been. Polly was one of the nicest people I ever met."

Shiefer's statement embodies Polly Bemis's unique legacy. Although her birth in China prevented Polly from ever becoming a naturalized American citizen during her lifetime, she has nonetheless amassed honors that most citizens never attain. Polly continues to be acclaimed and memorialized. The National Register of Historic Places lists her Salmon River home and the Idaho Hall of Fame counts her as a member.

Priscilla Wegars wishes to thank the Idaho Humanities Council and the John Calhoun Smith Memorial Fund of the University of Idaho for much-needed support to carry out her research on Polly and Charlie Bemis.

Part Two

∽Sellers of Sex∾

_₀ 4 ₒ_

Mattie, Katie, and Ida
Western Women at Risk

ANNE M. BUTLER

According to local lore, in 1877 two well-known Denverites faced off in a classic place outside the town saloon, on an abandoned main street, with its tightly closed bank, land office, and dry goods store sheltering the cowering "good" citizens of a little frontier community. "Respectable" folk—men in their top hats and women in their sunbonnets—did not scurry to havens of safety, leaving the "hero" to protect the sanctity of law and order. No virtuous U.S. marshal strode forth against a ruthless hired gun. After the shots rang out, no wretched villain lay dying on the dusty street, while the now-relieved, if cowardly, residents slowly emerged from their hideouts to gawk at the corpse and offer their embarrassed thanks to the town's savior for his steely courage and deadly aim.

Rather, this gunfight allegedly occurred between two well-known local madams, Mattie Silks and Katie Fulton. The women took up arms against each other in the midst of a lively collection of raucous onlookers gathered near the South Platte River, a short walk from Denver's Holladay Street dance hall and brothel district. A snappy band kept the crowd entertained, while revelers enjoyed generous amounts of food and alcohol. Armed with pistols, and by some accounts, topless, the two women confronted each other and opened fire in a jealous dispute over Cortez Thomson, who, by bad fortune or one woman's deliberate misdirection, was the only person wounded in the escapade.

The American West offered unusual opportunities of many kinds to women and permitted them to explore nontraditional ways of employment, to pursue unusual style and taste. Here, one woman roamed the countryside as a traveling butcher, there one tried her hand at taxidermy, whereas another managed a train station, a fourth administered a workers' hospital for a mining company, and a fifth herded cattle for a living. Yet, along with enhanced prospects for work came greater social, economic, and political risks, especially for those, such as prostitutes, who stepped beyond the safe confines of a private world into the glare of a public life.

$50 REWARD!

Reward of $50.00 will be paid by Zepheniah Smith for the recovery or information leading to the recovery of Mrs. Nannie Bell Smith; age 26 years, height about 5 feet 4 inches, weight 120 pounds, brown eyes, dark brown hair. Disappeared from her home near Trousdale, Okla., Oct., 20, 1905. Was traced to Oklahoma City, Okla. Will likely seek employment such as light house work, as health would not permit her to do hard work. Was in very poor health at time of disappearance. The above picture is good of her taken about a year ago.

ADDRESS ALL INFORMATION TO
ZEPHENIAH SMITH
Trousdale, Okla.
Box No. 3.

Once married, western women were not always happy with their choices and simply disappeared. In this "wanted" poster, an Oklahoma husband is seeking his runaway wife. (Courtesy of Glenda Riley.)

Although all women functioned under a weighty mantle of gender constraints in nineteenth-century America, those who violated widely held codes of womanly conduct could expect to face added burdens. Women who transgressed moral boundaries suffered severe consequences imposed by those who controlled the agencies of society. This proved especially true in the West, where the cast of characters appeared to be easy to identify, etched so starkly against the horizon of a western landscape. In nineteenth-century Denver, for prostitutes Mattie Silks and Kate Fulton, the bawdy scene along the South Platte River would have represented only one afternoon of public display and personal hazard in a professional life generally spent in harm's way.

Indeed, was this boisterous outing, with its picnic atmosphere, merely part of a publicity stunt by the two women—planned in advance, widely advertised, and staged for the moment? Were intoxicated customers and employees in the vice district invited to stagger out of their watering holes and bordellos to witness the gala event? Did the altercation, instead, explode spontaneously out of a festive but liquored party turned angry?

One question leads to another. Were the quarreling madams stripped to the waist? Did Cortez "Cort" Thomson sustain a glancing wound to the neck, or did he escape unscathed? Had Thomson once ridden with Quantrill's Raiders during the Civil War? Did a "brokenhearted" Kate Fulton leave Denver on the next morning's train? Did Kate Fulton, angry and sullen, remain in the Mile High City and continue to stalk her rival, Mattie Silks? Did this outlandish afternoon catapult Mattie Silks into unparalleled fame as the "West's most notorious madam," whatever that term might mean?

Ambiguity surrounds these questions, and even careful historical research does little to resolve them. Indeed, investigation of this event only provokes yet another set of questions. Did the duel take place in April or in August? Did a band actually provide music? What band was it, and how were its services secured? Was it a group of several musicians, or did a single fiddler strum a jaunty tune? Was Mattie Silks born in Kansas, Indiana, or New York? How did it happen the two women were conveniently armed with weapons? Did "Cort" or "Cortez" spell his name "Thomson" or "Thompson?" Was Thomson really the focus of the fight? Were the two madams warring entrepreneurs or conniving partners in Denver's highly competitive prostitution industry? The most important question, of course, remains buried beneath this avalanche of disputed trivia: did an encounter between Mattie Silks and Katie Fulton, even one remotely resembling the fanciful tale, ever take place in nineteenth-century Colorado, along the banks of the South Platte River?

For the purveyors of romantic and dashing tales of western history, correct answers to all these questions, especially the last one, remain irrelevant. For them, it is the ribald excitement of the story, rather than its authenticity,

Many western women made livings by offering solace, sex, and entertainment to men. Chicago Joe (Josephine Hensley) ran a saloon and supplied dancing girls, circa 1880, photograph by C. W. Carter, Salt Lake City. (Courtesy of the Montana Historical Society, Helena, #944-615.)

that captures the magic of the West. Clearly, some find flashy accounts of a grand Wild West a thrilling way to explain the essence of the so-called American personality. Their perception of western history centers on those nineteenth-century anecdotes that underscore improbable adventure, unfettered lawlessness, and dashing conquest. They inhale the frontier, they believe in its uniqueness, they celebrate its Anglocentric nationalism. They relish the gritty environment of the West and mutate its very real physical demands into abstract philosophical values connected to the rise of democracy.

They find their history and their democracy in a West filled with the exploits of gamblers, cowboys, soldiers, and miners. It is a flamboyant, if lopsided, narrative. Further, this view of the West tilts toward a highly masculine and far-fetched world, although one championed by many male and female fans of frontier history. It is one that has no significant analytical place for women and minorities, except as supporting players who keep the historical lens trained on the astonishing accomplishments of male westerners.

What highlights the extreme behaviors of daring men more than a sprinkling of outrageous women, whose actions shock and titillate? For those who love their history served with an attractive topping of imagined glory, the most important element in the story of Mattie Silks and Kate Fulton is its "proof" that "wild women of the West" added to the glamour of a masculine frontier world. These "denizens of the demimonde," these Matties, Katies, and Idas, provided the sexual tartness that keeps America convinced of the existence of a once wild West, where the antics of prostitutes and madams served to amuse frontier observers, past and present.

Even a quick glance confirms that these so-called notorious women of the West, their daily lives in conflict with accepted gender standards, flitted along the margins of society. Excluded and ridiculed, poverty-stricken and uneducated, most western prostitutes scrambled to survive in a region of economic extremes and social complexity. In all cities and towns, they lived in the shabbiest neighborhoods, paid the most exorbitant rents, worked in the most uncertain circumstances, and tangled with the most powerful adversaries. Their closest associates were other prostitutes who competed for their business, men who frequented their places of employment, or law enforcement officers who oversaw the conduct of the vice district. In their domestic arrangements, they often lived with their pimps, as husbands or consorts, and raised their children in the shadow of the red lights.

For these women, steady employment, with its few rewards and many liabilities, required a booming local prosperity, to which their irregular access depended on the largesse of notoriously tightfisted customers. Theirs was an ancillary profession, without an independent financial foundation, that thrived when close to the good fortune of others. Profits were accrued through a haphazard system of covert scams and overt dishonesty. Their personal stories shrouded in half-truths and historical tidbits, prostitutes, their employment resting on a shallow base, represented the most vulnerable workers in the unstable and burgeoning economy of the nineteenth-century West.

Public Disapproval

First, western prostitutes felt the constant press of moral and legal disapproval from those outside the vice community. Municipal authorities, religious leaders, business owners, women reformers, and male patrons all had an impact on the way a town responded to the presence of prostitutes. While these civic groups generally agreed on the corrupting influence of prostitution, they were less united on what civic strategies should be employed against it.

In this uncertain area of public policy, local newspapers led the way in shaping attitudes about prostitution. In a frontier world with its few forms of communication and limited service institutions, newspapers provided the main source from which citizens learned about local social, economic, and political happenings, including those regarding prostitutes. Prostitutes' behaviors, whereabouts, and arrest records were all regular components in the weekly news. Indeed, sensational news reports from the vice district added spice to the otherwise painfully banal accounts of small-town life or tedious listings of declining silver prices.

In addition, editors enjoyed considerable latitude in the manner in which they chose to report on women's activities. For example, some editors appeared to relish using humor or derision when writing about episodes involving prostitutes. The language choices of newspaper reporters seldom suggested concern for the personal privacy or civil rights of a prostitute. Rather, news about prostitutes seemed to be an opportunity for indulging in the worst journalistic taste, with excessive language, sly jokes, and bad puns.

The most dire life crises for a woman, such as an assault or a suicide attempt, evoked a supply of stock descriptions from journalists. News articles were quick to describe altercations as "brawls" between "beefy old tarts" and make light of injuries, whereby the "blood flowed freely," for the combatants, who "were none the worse for wear after the cat fight ended." Women of color were particular favorites for local news articles, which referred to them as "dusky daughters," "ebony Jezebels," "mulatto whores," or "Chinese harlots," adding yet another layer of linguistic censure for prostitutes from ethnic cultures.

A "dancing girl" in Virginia City, Nevada, no date. (Courtesy of the Montana Historical Society, Helena, #PAC74-23.)

When, however, the circumstances called for it, an editor shifted with ease and apparently little reader notice to a sympathetic or nostalgic tone concerning prostitutes. The deliberate and accidental shootings that occurred so frequently in saloons and brothels gave reporters plenty of fodder for sentimental prose. If a prostitute actually perished as a result of the violence so endemic to her life, newspapers slid effortlessly into a tone of formulaic regret for the "departed frail one," who it seemed "came from a wealthy family back east" and had been "led to a life of shame by a heartless older man." How reporters acquired so much private information about women who migrated from town to town, changed their names with regularity, and left only scant personal possessions remained unclear. Undaunted by such factual constraints, reporters further announced that the recently mourned always "sent regular support money" to "a beautiful, innocent daughter," who "knew nothing of her mother's slide into sin." Elaborate depictions of the wake and funeral overflowed with sorrow for the deceased, empathy for her co-worker friends, and warnings about the inevitable fate of all prostitutes.

Overall, a frontier newspaper used local political situations and a changing social ambiance in a community to gauge its response to prostitutes. During the burgeoning of a bonanza town, when city organizers wanted to draw new-comers and desired a resident prostitute population to attract the bachelor labor force, newspaper editors indirectly publicized the women's availability through numerous references to their many aliases, most recent addresses, and places of work. To blunt the criticism of eastern observers, who sniffed about "western rowdiness and immorality," reporters typically kept hometown stories brief. They reserved their most forceful anti-prostitution moralizing for editori-als about the unsavory conduct found in other communities. Yet, at the local level newspapers effectively supplied citizens and transients, such as miners and cowboys, with clear directions to nearby red-light districts, known by such quaint names as Hog Town, Barbary Coast, or The Bottoms.

Thus, flamboyant journalism became one weapon in the arsenal to support and to control local prostitution. Legislation regulating brothels and saloons, moral condemnation of the vice districts, and reform petitions gained momentum from the bully pulpit of the town press. For example, in most western communi-ties, laws outlining the fines against "houses of ill fame and gambling dens" were among the first passed by a city council concerned with organizing a new munici-pal government. The statutes embraced a range of persons and their offenses—landlords who rented property for use as a brothel, those inside the house, women and customers, as well as the off-site managers of bordellos.

Men, especially brothel customers, usually escaped arrest and prosecution. In practice, those most commonly inconvenienced by these statutes were the

Madam Laura Evans's "sporting houses" in Salida, Colorado, after she gave up her business in Denver, undated. (Courtesy of the Western History Department, Denver Public Library, #X-13361.)

prostitutes themselves, who were arrested on a regular—weekly or monthly—basis and taxed for their illegal profession. Madams and their employees might be scooped up in a brothel sweep, taken to court, fined, and released to secure the needed court costs.

A madam—Mattie Silks, for example—who knew how to manipulate the system usually negotiated a monthly fee paid to the appropriate official to elude the Saturday night dragnet—thus, leaving her house in operation, whereas other, less well-connected madams, perhaps of the Katie Fulton category, lost hours of employee work during the wholesale arrests. To further cement protection for herself, a well-placed madam might regularly bestow expensive gifts on important local officials; in one town, a well-known brothel owner sent the chief of police a diamond replica of his badge via the local chapter of a men's benevolent society. Such a circuitous route for graft deflected the obvious connections between law enforcement personnel and prostitutes.

Other statutes, related to illegal professions, touched the vice community in a general way. For example, police officers vigorously implemented prohibitions of public drunkenness, disorderly conduct, illegal gaming, personal assault, and lewd behavior against those who lingered in and around the saloon and brothel neighborhood. Obviously, such persons routinely included prostitutes who depended on staking out a public presence to advertise themselves. When the women disrupted dance halls or took loud behaviors into the street, they became targets for arrest, as they violated not only town law, but also flaunted their ongoing, even "arrogant," disregard for gender rules about correct conduct for a woman.

Thus, early in the process of community building, city officials, who had neither the desire nor the intent to eliminate vice, identified prostitutes and gamblers as populations to be regular contributors to local treasuries through the imposition of fines. It must have seemed to police officers that the vice community could not have cooperated in this process any more fully, as its very existence rested on breaking the law at all times. These laws gave officials a powerful hand in the management of brothels, saloons, and gambling halls, as well as the streets and sidewalks of a town. The statutes, which established a local mechanism for taxing "immorality," could be ignored, enforced, or used as a regulating agent, according to the current wishes of a town.

Other constituencies drawn from the "respectable" quarter often dictated how vigorously law enforcement personnel acted on their collection of "morality" laws. Elected officials and religious leaders found that, when needed, prostitution provided a handy cause to be publicized on behalf of law and order. Both groups, often pressured by business owners, tolerated brothel operations when it was evident that sexual commerce advanced local economic development. Yet, either politician or preacher, at a moment's notice, could raise the crusader's voice against the "evils of loose women" who threatened the lives and spiritual well-being of the "best" of the young men. These outcries tended to be sporadic and of short duration. In more than one frontier community, the insistence by civic leaders that prostitution either be driven from the town or tightly restrained enjoyed a short life.

Indeed, these sudden campaigns for "cleaning up" the community often seemed to catch other officials by surprise, and they did not necessarily rush to support their colleague's burst of moral fervor. In reality, while a town prospered with a cattle, mining, railroad, or lumber boom, civic organizers accommodated the presence of a vigorous vice industry. Given to town boosterism, politicians, business owners, and clergymen all wanted to encourage the promotion of civic success. When that success depended on cultivating the careless spending habits of a large group of working-class men, prominent leaders spoke solemnly about the uselessness of trying to eradicate the "oldest profession" and implemented little significant action. Once a community stabilized, lost its bonanza aura, and saw its economy slide into more conventional patterns, high-profile prostitution as a local service seemed less desirable. Prostitutes adjusted quickly to the changed atmosphere, assessing their depressed business opportunities and drifting off to more promising boom locations, while their less mobile colleagues were left to absorb the extra hindrances of life in a suddenly "moral" town.

In part, women—married and single—from the ranks of the middle class had an impact on these attitudes and events. "Respectable" women often found themselves with an intellectual conflict over the circumstances of prostitution. On the one hand, they objected when prostitution invaded their social space. In an intimate frontier urban setting, the daily routines of women's lives or those of their children might well require travel near or through a red-light district.

Prostitutes, with access to few community power initiatives, did not hesitate to hoot at respectable women, inviting them into their houses and enjoying the opportunity to shower discomfort on the "ladies." This lewd behavior and public bawdiness by prostitutes, who undoubtedly delighted in their moments of interaction with the town's "acceptable citizens," antagonized those women from more genteel homes. These women drew on their better status in the local society in an effort to curtail public displays they found offensive.

Wives and mothers from the "respectable element" used the newspaper—operated by editors and reporters with whom they circulated in social circum-

The large male population of mining camps like Leadville wanted female companionship and were willing to pay for it. Numerous brothels are among early Leadville's makeshift buildings, 1879. (Courtesy of the Western History Department, Denver Public Library, #X-498.)

stances—as a venue in which to articulate their distaste for the public loudness of prostitutes. They called on their domestic power with husbands, sons, and brothers, clergymen, and council members to demand greater regulation of visible "sin," if for no other reason than to validate their own status as "ladies" in a frontier world that appeared not to understand that term. Ironically, they then complained if new zoning rules—prompted by their input—designed to close brothels, pressured prostitutes to move out of the commercial vice area and into residential sectors of the community.

On the other hand, women everywhere in the nation felt the rising tempo of reform that gained momentum in the late nineteenth and twentieth centuries. These impulses prompted them to think deeply about gender issues. Increasingly, women reformers pointed to a common bond with prostitutes, whom they saw as examples of the worst of female oppression. Still, women's political rhetoric about gender equality often clashed with their personal familial expectations for their own neighborhoods. Despite their best intentions, it remained difficult for women to accept the spread of prostitutes' housing beyond the streets and alleys of the saloon district. They feared the influence of prostitution within their own residential areas and they objected to loosening local controls over vice regulation. Middle-class white women failed to reconcile these conflicting perceptions, especially those centered on class and race differences; thus, although they emerged from their homes as articulate and concerned reformers, middle-class women sometimes undercut their public impact because of ambivalent attitudes toward prostitutes who lived in close proximity to them.

With this formidable array of civic forces lined up against them, prostitutes tried to manipulate all aspects of the system to their best possible advantage. Although their direct contacts with civic leaders, members of the clergy, and middle-class women remained uneven and problematic, they often knew newspaper reporters and law enforcement personnel quite well. Their welcome at the centers of a community always uncertain, prostitutes exploited their closest civic associations in ways that permitted them to continue working and stay out of jail. Thus, they did not hesitate to use an intricate system of bribes, payoffs, and gifts to keep the law at bay or to win more kindly treatment in the press.

Brothel owners—typically in control of more property and money than their resident employees, back-alley crib occupants, military camp followers, or streetwalkers—were in the best position to jockey for place in local society.

The grand entrance to successful madam Mattie Silks's "parlor house" in Denver, Colorado, which operated during the early 1900s. (Courtesy of the Western History Department, Denver Public Library, #X-2052.)

As propertied taxpayers, they used connections with city leaders to protect their operations in a society that did not offer them much legal grounding. Madams, especially those who owned real estate, pursued any possible advantage for themselves within local government.

For example, Mattie Silks was able to secure a liquor license for her establishment, a mark of business legitimacy, at the very time other Denver brothels selling illegal spirits drew the scrutiny of police. Further, it has been suggested that in 1885, eight years after her supposed clash with Katie Fulton, Silks cooperated with the city in hosting a visiting executive who had stopped in Denver to explore railroad development. Whether the tale, including the allegation that the chamber of commerce cleared a five-thousand-dollar loan for Silks so she would embark on a monthlong California vacation with the supposedly smitten railroad magnate, encompassed any more truth than the infamous Silks/Fulton duel, it reflected the personal advantage a few prostitutes managed to carve out with influential public officials.

In fact, the apparently successful business and political connections of a Mattie Silks obscure the usual economic history for prostitutes and madams. Few, in the whole population of those working in western prostitution, ever accumulated sufficient capital to purchase multiple properties—brothels, saloons, rooming houses, and rows of cribs, where the poorest and least employable prostitutes paid exorbitant surcharges to work. That Mattie Silks, in 1909, had the resources to acquire, from the estate of a recently deceased madam, Denver's elegant House of Mirrors should not be misread as the typical business initiative of prostitutes in the West. Those women, including Mattie Silks and the former owner of the House of Mirrors, who made a financial mark could not have done so without bargaining and bartering inside local offices of government.

Lesser prostitutes, especially those of color, had fewer successes in manipulating a quasi-place within the infrastructure of Denver. In the late 1880s, Ida Jones, a black prostitute, found that her numerous arrests for public disturbance, destruction of property, and "running a lewd house" combined to place her in a precarious legal position. By 1890, when charged with a murder for which the actual perpetrator remained uncertain, Ida Jones was already burdened by her well-known criminal record, routinely publicized in the Denver newspapers.

Jones lacked support from her African American neighbors with whom she had frequently quarreled, she faced animosity from a powerful white family of saloon district entrepreneurs, and she brought a lengthy criminal history to her trial. Every avenue of support was lost to Ida Jones, as those in public

This 1890 mug shot of Ida Jones, once described as the "most dangerous and vicious woman in Denver," was taken when she entered the Colorado State Penitentiary on a charge of murder. (Courtesy of the Colorado State Penitentiary, Colorado State Archives, Denver.)

authority and the vice community—black and white—closed ranks against her. A woman of color, who was unable to read and write, Ida Jones, not yet thirty years of age, was convicted of murder by a jury of twelve white men and went to the Colorado State Penitentiary for fifteen years.

Unlike Mattie Silks, who knew how to ingratiate herself with high-ranking local officials, Ida Jones lived at the edges of Denver society. There, as Ida Jones could see of Mattie Silks, only a privileged few managed to negotiate relationships with influential public figures. When Jones's actions challenged public limits and when all allies, whether from the "respectable" or the "vice" citizenry, abandoned her, Ida Jones confronted a formidable barrier: the cumulative power of the local establishment—"legitimate" and "illegal"—to control criminal women.

Actually, Jones's case proved somewhat distinct in that forces from the vice and non-vice districts cooperated to work for her conviction. Denver officials within the justice system showed themselves quick to exploit the testimony of other known vice operatives, if that would secure the conviction of a prostitute known to be a regular nuisance. At the same time, those who lived in the saloon and brothel neighborhood united across racial divisions to punish a woman judged to have broken intragroup bonds of loyalty.

Personal Dangers

As seen in the Ida Jones case, a second risk for prostitutes came from the uncertainties within their own community. Although they might lie dormant for weeks and months, these hazards threatened to overtake a prostitute in any number of life situations. The form of this risk almost always involved some aspect of violence.

Even though it seems that prostitutes would form a sisterhood of comfort and support for one another, and many historians have so argued, such did not always materialize. Certainly, Ida Jones did not feel connected to everyone in the vice community, and some acted aggressively to bring about her conviction. At least eight of her black neighbors from the saloon district of Market and Blake Streets testified against Jones for keeping a house of prostitution. Although it is not certain all these citizens worked in vice occupations, they were associated with Ida Jones, and at least one woman had been involved in physical fights with Ida. Four other black women, who in some manner participated in the homicide, gave state's evidence against Jones, and, to their legal benefit, their court case was separated from hers.

In addition, it remains unclear why Ida Jones so offended the white saloon owners, the Ryan and Wallace kinfolk. Perhaps the murder victim, Stephen Zemmer, was their friend, employee, or relative, but the insertion of this family into the fray against Jones opened a window onto the hierarchy found within prostitution. Despite the fact that many prostitutes remained essentially powerless in the political sphere, others built practical relationships that shielded them from legal harassment, as well as provided enormous clout inside their vice circles. The Ryan and Wallace family, with its profitable saloons, brothels, and cribs, enjoyed a comfortable place in Denver. Indeed, when Annie Ryan, daughter of matriarch Jane Ryan Wallace, shot her lover in one of the family saloons, she escaped a sentence that might have sent any other prostitute to the Colorado penitentiary. Ida Jones did not find the authorities so understanding.

Yet, the internal dangers of the profession exempted no one. Even the influential Mattie Silks, whose life has taken on lavish and merry descriptions, fell prey to the potential for hazard inside prostitution. Not only was Silks theoretically physically threatened in the famous duel along the riverbank, but other episodes in her life also captured the disorder and insecurity of prostitution. The rumor that she always carried a pistol, concealed within her voluminous clothing, pointed to the way in which all prostitutes understood the ever-present shadow of violence. That violence typically emanated from persons closely associated with the routines of prostitution.

In the Mattie Silks and Kate Fulton account, the violence spewed from one woman to another. Such occurrences proved more ordinary than not. Across the West, newspapers, jail dockets, and cemetery records attested to the physical attacks prostitutes heaped on each other. In one town, a woman beat another severely and left her to die on her bordello bed. In another, two prostitutes repeatedly fought in the street outside a saloon. In yet another, an intoxicated prostitute shot and killed a co-worker because the woman would not stop singing an offensive ballad. Ida Jones, once described as "the most dangerous and vicious woman in Denver," was well acquainted with violence and had herself, on one occasion, destroyed the home and furnishings of another black woman.

Even though friendships certainly existed inside prostitution, they tended to rest on thin loyalties. Women did travel together, operate brothels, and pay jail fines for each other. On those occasions, and when one prostitute nursed a sick colleague or arranged for the funeral of a former co-worker, perhaps circumstances suspended the generally vexing ambiance of prostitution. Competition, drunkenness, fear, and anger, however, too easily disrupted this friendly veneer and led to explosive exchanges. In the best situations, the environment of prostitution remained charged with the suggestion of violence; in the worst, that suggestion burst forth in injury and death.

In addition, male clients in brothels and customers in dance halls furthered the occasions of personal danger. Cloying reports of Mattie Silks's business arrangements with the ever-so respectable chamber of commerce and a subsequent "vacation" with the railroad executive shroud the usual relationships between female prostitutes and male westerners. Most frequenters of brothels were not local judges and mayors, seated about a richly furnished parlor, lavishly accented with heavy velvet drapes; the clients did not sip fine liquor, smoke expensive cigars, and pursue elegant conversation with a tastefully dressed and well-educated madam and her "girls."

Rather, the men came from the same economic environs as the women. Together they added to the laborers transforming a vast region into a part of an immense nation. Intensity, hostility, fear, and greed marked much of that national endeavor. These forces did not necessarily instill in western laborers common notions about work or shared values about personal relationships. All hoped to extract the most wealth, as quickly as possible from a promising West; they only rarely cared if they trampled on each other in the process.

In reality, most, illiterate or close to it, scraped along, making the wages of the lower class. When a windfall came their way, men and women usually frittered it away in a short time, and the dreamed-of escape to luxury never materialized. Prostitutes "entertained" men of their own rank, and, accordingly, the emotionally turbulent ambiance inside a brothel mirrored the outside physically coarse environment of industry. In general, customers soliciting

Madam Mattie Silks had a personal life as well, which included her horse, 1880. (Courtesy of the Western History Department, Denver Public Library, #X-27055.)

western prostitutes were not particularly interested in helping the women advance to a higher economic realm, looking to establish long-term meaning-ful friendships, or seeking a sophisticated brothel world akin to a seventeenth-century European salon. The men wanted a sexual encounter, and they went to those western locations where they could buy it.

In fact, the nature of this sexual trading called for negotiations that were carried out in confusion, when one or both parties usually had consumed considerable alcohol. Women tried to get the highest possible sum of money; men tried to give the least possible. Each tried to distract the other during the bargaining. Women pushed for the cost agreed on and the cash delivered in advance of the physical act; men preferred to delay the money transaction, in the hope of not paying or cutting the price. In the alcohol-induced sleep of customers that often followed, women did not hesitate to increase their wages through thievery, carried out alone or with the help of other vice workers. Certainly, the regulations inside a brothel, where a madam set fees and col-lected them in advance, offset some of these problems. Overall, however, an atmosphere of exploitation and suspicion did not produce agreeable relation-ships between prostitutes and their customers.

Just as accounts of prostitutes attacking each other fill the ledgers of the West, so do those episodes when brothel and saloon customers accidentally or intentionally wounded and killed prostitutes. Madams, like Mattie Silks, carried their own weapons, not only for personal protection, but to suppress disputes between customers and employees that might bring the unwanted attention of law enforcement officers. In numerous locations, as fights erupted in brothels, a prostitute caught the bullet intended by one client for another. In more than one dance hall, a weapon was fired by mistake, and a young dancer died by misfortune.

Domestic violence of every sort was a regular feature inside the prostitutes' community. Jealous husbands, pimps, and customers did not hesitate to beat and shoot prostitute wives, companions, or workers. These attacks occurred in homes, rented rooms, saloons, cribs, tents, well-to-do and shabby brothels, on streets and in alleys. In every place where prostitutes lived and worked, they were subjected to sudden and potentially deadly attack. On occasion, the assaults were so frequent, so intense, and so public that a local newspaper complained about the perpetrator or a town sheriff intervened on the woman's behalf.

Predictably, prostitutes sometimes responded to repeated instances of domestic violence by lashing out at the attacker. Although such actions would appear to be obvious attempts at self-defense, prostitutes rarely found the legal system inclined to accept that explanation. For example, in Wyoming, a twenty-one-year-old prostitute shot and killed her companion of several months as he pummeled her about the head while shoving her toward an alley, complaining about her low earnings and yelling obscenities and death threats. Despite the many bystanders, including the marshal, who witnessed the scene and testified for the young woman, the jury rejected her plea of self-defense and sent her to the penitentiary for three years on a charge of manslaughter.

While prostitutes dodged an assortment of physical dangers inside brothels or on the street beyond, they also lived with the assault they inflicted on themselves. The demands of their lives were not conducive to good health. Other than those in an extremely well-regulated brothel, the women lived by an erratic schedule, ate poorly and sporadically, and seldom sought medical care. Their work exposed them to sexual disease and unwanted pregnancy. Home-done abortions were common, unsanitary, and often fatal.

Alcohol and drugs permeated the world of prostitution. If the newspapers can be believed, prostitutes were almost constantly inebriated or had the opportunity to be. Beer sold for five cents a bucketful, and a large quantity of an opiate could be obtained with ease for a quarter. Suicide and near-suicide accounts of prostitutes almost always noted the victim had consumed a deadly combination of both substances. Time and again, as a prostitute lay in an irreversible coma, her co-workers admitted to a helpless physician that the one near death had been locked in her room for a week, consuming vast quantities of beer, followed by a full bottle of laudanum. Alcoholism and drug addiction, not always recognized as such in the nineteenth century, played a prevalent role in the daily lives of prostitutes. Even the supposedly respected and distinguished Mattie Silks was described as publicly intoxicated (and half-dressed) during her fight with Katie Fulton.

In general, prostitutes entered the profession as very young women, perhaps thirteen to fifteen years of age. Many were women of color, from the ethnic cultures of the West, or were recent European immigrants. They possessed few skills, had little schooling, and frequently could not read or write. Their chances for leaving prostitution were limited, and only a few rose to the more prosperous role of madam. Most trudged on as common laborers in an intensely competitive and unstable business.

Prostitution was often one of several forms of employment for a woman, who might earn additional income as a seamstress or laundress. Some made small economic gains and supported themselves for a time, but many did not. Like most poor people, they found the cost of living was high in a frontier world that was generally pricey. The women knew life to be a continuous round of arrests, fines, court costs, and attorney fees. On occasion, prostitutes supplied the liquor for customers and lavish gifts for officials; property disputes, political graft, and lawsuits undercut profits of even the successful madam. The women spent their working lives paying off pimps, hack drivers, sheriffs, and gamblers; landlords charged them double, and so did undertakers.

Those who husbanded away economic resources lived in the same tumultuous world as their poorer sisters, a world whose unpredictable ways cared not for whether one was madam or streetwalker. A fancy brothel did not guarantee exemption from physical danger. Fights broke out, knives flashed, and pistols discharged in the locked rooms of a plush bordello as quickly as in an alley behind a crowded saloon. Prostitutes—whether with many dollars or without a penny—in every western location worked hard in the most arduous and uncertain circumstances. They died young, often under hideous conditions, by the hand of a customer, a colleague prostitute, or from their own self-inflicted battery. For prostitutes, generally, the dangers to their personal well-being and safety loomed over them with a greater shadow than the elusive monetary advances everyone in the West hoped the frontier world would bestow.

Romanticized History

Even with these many disadvantages a third risk embraced prostitutes. It has proven to be one they could never have anticipated and could least control. This peril, unlike their lives, not only had no end, but has inflated with the passage of time. It concerns the way in which modern America has treated the historical memory of prostitutes. Few prostitutes, eking out a living under the weight of social and economic hardship, could ever have imagined that future Americans would care so much about them, but would paint their experiences with such fictional hues.

In the nineteenth-century West, towns and cities, military garrisons, and roadhouses wanted prostitutes. In a largely bachelor world, the women were welcomed for their feminine presence and their assumed sexual availability. Few seemed to understand them as women, their loud public behaviors confusing observers about their attitudes and feelings. No matter—they provided sexual service, often in a seedy entertainment setting. Then, the West regarded them with a less kindly eye, as the environment stabilized and the signposts of Anglo middle-class society overtook the rugged frontier. So, cities, energized by middle-class men and women, implemented their laws with more vigor, closing down the bordellos, chasing prostitutes from the streets, and driving the "harlots" out of the rows of cribs that had once beckoned to the bachelor hordes of the West.

Yet, no sooner had this taken place than western communities, moving into the modern surroundings of the twentieth century, began to find a new way to exploit nineteenth-century prostitutes. Prostitutes, after a few decades in obscurity, reappeared as folksy examples of an earlier and more interesting way of life. Their lives were dusted off and sanitized, their personal histories made "colorful" and "frolicsome," and prostitutes, most of them conveniently long dead, were given new careers as glamorous accoutrements of the Old West.

Both the television and film industries of the 1940s and 1950s contributed to the new updated prostitute identity. Gone were the grimy details of the women's lives, the working-class realities, addictive drugs, physical brutality, the social and economic exigencies. In their place came a parade of stunningly beautiful thespians—healthy and vivacious, costumed, adorned, and perfumed. They lounged about in opulent houses, sang alluring torch songs by a saloon piano, twirled across a dance-hall stage, and walked into the sunset of a "respectable" life with a handsome cowboy of the John Wayne genre. They dropped their eyes in modesty during a marriage ceremony or died heroically in an act of attrition for their "sinful" ways. Most of all, they had no sexuality.

The day-to-day sexual commerce of their lives evaporated to be replaced by an all-American, wholesome, "heart-of-gold" beauty queen.

It became impossible to imagine that prostitutes, like working women everywhere, struggled with low wages, sexual harassment, and a devalued role, when portrayed by such glamorous actors as Gene Tierney, Marlene Dietrich, Patricia Wymore, Amanda Blake, and Doris Day. No child prostitutes here— girls of twelve soliciting for their own mothers—no women of color mocked in the public press, no grasping sheriff demanding an extra dollar, no ill-tempered husband assaulting a woman for working too little or too much, depending on the jealous mood of the moment, no brutal rape for women whose sexual employment made them unworthy of legal justice. For the American fan of film and television, prostitution, devoid of these unpleasantries, appeared to have been a sophisticated and lucrative way to enjoy the West.

This cinematic renovation of prostitution meshed nicely with the West's most recent boom industry—tourism. Particularly after World War II—as Americans entered into a new era of domestic travel, fueled by the rise of the airlines, the construction of superhighways, and the growth of the motel/hotel industry—the West became accessible as a vacation destination in ways that it had never been before. Yet, the fundamental reality of the West—cities and towns remained scattered far from one another—reintroduced the old nine-teenth-century problem of local communities competing fiercely for dollars spent by passing visitors. More than one locale turned to the commercial pos-sibilities in resurrecting the town's "frontier past," to attract tourists from around the nation and the world. Just as prostitutes had added some sparkle to early western newspaper accounts, now they would do so again—only this time their lives could be defined as fit for family amusement, as the film indus-try had already demonstrated.

In a splash of enthusiasm, various western cities, with tourist prospects, evoked their "history," promoting these so-called "wild women" as a way to sell a local version of the "true West." Tourists were lured to purchase a picture booklet, brothel token, fancy garter, or decorated mug, all publicizing the local prostitutes a town had elected as the "least inhibited," the "boldest," or the "most outrageous" in the West. Photographers stocked an array of costumes so that couples could pose as a "fancy lady and her gambler man," giving them a personalized touch of the nineteenth-century frontier to carry home. Old brothels were spruced up and transformed into museums, where one could tour the very rooms where the women brought their customers. There seemed to be no end to the gimmicks that sold notoriety as the souvenir of the prostitutes' West.

Denver looked into its past and found its own collection of madams to publicize, while ignoring its legions of young and nameless prostitutes from the heyday of frontier living. Mattie Silks won the title as "most notable," perhaps for her longevity, since she did not die until 1929, long after that storybook era of the "Wild West." Whatever the reason, Denver showed itself happy to advertise her fame, but always with tongue-in-cheek descriptions. The city delighted when it could send modern-day tourists for an upscale dinner in Silks's House of Mirrors brothel, restored as a fancy restaurant, complete with exhibits dedicated to prostitution. What could be more engaging than sitting at a bar, surrounded with sexual memorabilia, in the very building where the infamous Mattie Silks had once reigned as the queen of Denver vice?

But beneath this merriment lurk some troubling matters. Any number of popular publications recount the story of the famous "duel" by the river involving Mattie and Katie. At least an equal number of scholars try, in vain, to refute the historical inaccuracies in the tale—most especially asserting that it never occurred. Most recently, the West has gone to the Web, and brief biographies of Mattie Silks can be found at several Internet sites. The content

The circumspect, properly attired Mattie Silks shown in this photograph does not suggest a woman who would engage in a lewd drunken brawl with a prostitute. (Courtesy of the Colorado Historical Society, #F-32942.)

of these Denver tales contradict one another, although most claim Silks herself never worked as a prostitute, as if this solemn, albeit unverified, declaration of her "personal purity" elevates her beyond the moral condemnation "respectable" society has always accorded women employed in sexual commerce. Further, much is made of the unclear assertion that Silks "left the life" and spent her declining years outside the vice profession. How could Mattie Silks—in life or in death—have been excluded from the world of vice, when the rationale for her place in the western lexicon is predicated solely on anecdotes about her role as a madam? Without her identity as a worker in the western sex industry, Mattie Silks, in all probability, would have remained an ordinary and anonymous Denver resident.

Nowhere in these fun-spirited, poorly documented treatments of Mattie Silks's life does one find even a hint that perhaps all the jolly press she receives in modern society is far different from her own experience in nineteenth-century Denver. Although it is a boost for tourism, this lighthearted look at Mattie Silks ignores that the woman herself left no historical voice. Her words are not found in diaries and letters. Her joys, her sorrows remain a secret. Her life plan, her deepest fears, her inner hopes, her sense of self and kin—all are missing. What she found personally beneficial as a businesswoman in prostitution and what she detested about its place in Denver's world cannot be known.

The report that she paraded new employees through the streets of Denver each year may well underscore her skill at advertising her business. At the same time, it may point to her public objection to the mechanics of how she was required to manage both her personal and professional affairs. Given that possibility, one can only wonder what the woman herself would think of the current marketing of Denver prostitution as an example of "wild and carefree" frontier life.

It seems, whatever the case, ludicrous to overlook the essentially capricious professional conditions that had little respect for power or status inside the vice world. For a prostitute, the local climate could change in an instant. A political upset for the party in office, a new mayor, a change at the sheriff's headquarters, the building of a church, a shift among the brokers in the vice community, the death of a competitor—any of these and a dozen more could place a woman, prostitute or madam, in a precarious position. Those were some of the public hazards prostitutes faced. In their personal worlds, they confronted additional uncertainties, including eviction, family loss, transiency, poor health, divorce, erratic employment, and violence. The strain of working for years under such circumstances certainly exacted a toll for those in prostitution.

Yet it is hard to know about this, to document the patterns of the difficulties. Kate or Katie Fulton serves as a reminder of the elusive evidence that inhibits modern understanding of prostitutes' lives. In the 1877 account, Fulton has remained the shadowy figure, known only for her appearance along the bank of the South Platte River; her earlier life and her subsequent fate have no place in the narrative. Accordingly, she represents the thousands of western prostitutes about whom little or nothing is known, women who passed through western history but failed to come into full view. Their lives, captured only in a newspaper article or two, have been reduced to an arrest record or a public fight. Thus, Fulton, along with thousands of her colleagues, slipped past the historical record; the chance to re-create these lives in a full manner remains beyond reach. As women, participants in an immense regional transformation, they stand in the background, frustratingly removed from the centers of historical knowledge.

Perhaps, after troubled times, a woman moved a hundred miles, changed her name, and started once again to court a clientele, one suggested outcome for Katie Fulton, following her clash with Mattie Silks. Perhaps upon release from prison, sick and alone, a woman disappeared into the historical landscape: this seemed to be the case for Ida Jones.

These prostitutes at Bell Birdard's brothel lived only a few doors from Mattie Silks and Katie Fulton, sparring neighbors from the 500 block of Holladay Street in Denver. (Courtesy of the Mazzulla Collection, Colorado Historical Society.)

Jones, whose life in Denver can be followed for about ten years, left only shards of information. Her experiences fit into the context of the African American community in Denver, thus illuminating some notion of the dynamics that enveloped her. But one has only to look at the inmate photograph of Jones to wonder if she should really have been called "the most dangerous and vicious woman in Denver." Ida Jones and others of the demimonde, their lives so filled with little-known aspects of gender history, seem fated to be nearly invisible women in the narrative of the West.

Mattie, Katie, and Ida were, indeed, western women at risk. Their professional lives as prostitutes guaranteed certain kinds of public danger in their communities. They negotiated that rocky terrain with the best available means. Yet, they were left to juggle, usually by themselves, a second risk, the dangers of their personal lives. It is tempting to think that Mattie Silks did so better than Ida Jones and Katie Fulton, but that might be said if lives are measured only by a monetary standard.

Madam or prostitute—Anglo, Hispanic American, African American, Asian, or Native American—all women working in western prostitution did so while dealing with hazards that came to them from outside and inside the profession. Little did they suspect that a modern world would add to these two risks a third—a splashy and romanticized memory of western prostitution—one that treats prostitutes as background props in a masculine frontier world, crafted to memorialize regional glorification from an Anglo perspective.

Had they known such a historical destiny awaited them, Mattie, Katie, and Ida might have requested a less shallow remembrance and forcefully insisted on one that addressed the race, class, and gender complexities for themselves and other western prostitutes who lived inside the frontier world of saloons and brothels. Had that recognition not been forthcoming, Mattie Silks, Kate Fulton, and Ida Jones might have ignored the risks and demonstrated ways they could legitimately be called "wild women of the West."

Sadie Orchard

A Hard-Working Woman

GLENDA RILEY

A twenty-something woman named Sarah Jane Creech who grew up on a Kansas horse farm during the 1860s and 1870s seems an improbable candidate to become a western legend. Yet when this woman migrated to the Black Range Mountains of New Mexico during that area's silver and gold rushes of the 1880s and 1890s, her life became the stuff of which myths are made. During the mid-1880s, Sarah Creech joined the ranks of soiled doves on Kingston's Virtue Avenue. Known by such names as Big Sal, Frenchy, and Missouri Lil, these women included Anglos, African Americans, Asians, and Hispanas. Sarah was known simply as Sadie.

Of course, Sadie might have chosen to work as a cook for a camp full of miners, a washwoman of miners' grubby clothing, or a clerk standing long hours behind the cash register or counter of a mercantile, all for low wages. Because prostitution was more of an economic than a moral decision in the "Wild" West during the 1880s and 1890s, Sadie's choice made financial sense. She stood to gain from the lack of women among Kingston's population. Although Sadie's family back home might not have approved, she was living in a very different milieu from farm-dominated Kansas. As a "bad" woman, she had numerous colleagues and many customers, few of whom worried about the moral implications of prostitution in a raw mining town.

In addition, economics would have affected the way in which Sadie launched her career. Even though Sadie reportedly set up a brothel of her own on Virtue Avenue, there is little evidence that the newly arrived adventuress brought with her the necessary funds to rent and furnish a bawdy house. It is far more likely that Sadie Creech took employment with an established madam or perhaps found customers in Kingston's twenty-two saloons, at least until she created her own local reputation. Given her gregarious nature, Sadie appears to have made her mark on Kingston and its male population in less than a year.

Sadie Orchard during the 1890s, probably in front of the Ocean View Hotel in Hillsboro.
(Courtesy of the Geronimo Springs Museum Archives, Truth or Consequences, New Mexico.)

During that time, Sadie also learned a valuable lesson: the promise of the West did not come easily. Rather than falling into people's hands, the riches of the West usually went to the incredibly lucky, the dishonest, or those willing to commit themselves to years of toil. Luck was not Sadie's strong suit, and dishonesty was incompatible with her ingenuous personality. Consequently, Sadie became a hard-working woman, yet one who exhibited such charm and grace that western tall tales transformed her into a darling of the demimonde. Reportedly, she was an irrepressible, dauntless, and, at times, even glamorous woman.

The Road to Kingston

As with all such legends, the reality of Sadie's life was far more complex—and far more difficult to discover—than the colorful stories. For example, although some stories claim that Sadie hailed from the Limehouse district of London and came to New Mexico via New York City, she was, in truth, just another young American anxious to escape the confines of home and explore the opportunities offered by the West. Despite the fact that Sadie seemed to have given a variety of birth dates and birthplaces to different people, the 1870 Mills County, Iowa, census indicates she was born in the county in 1860. Although Sadie's death certificate lists her birth as August 20, 1862, in Kansas, it seems certain that Sadie was born near Tabor in Mills County in 1860, but the exact date is unknown.

Sadie came from a large family. She was the fifth child of Bennett L. Creech and Nancy Ann Davis, who had married in Arkansas on September 5, 1850. The wedding took place in Nancy's home county, Madison, where Bennett resided for a while. The couple remained in Arkansas, where Nancy bore their first two children, Delila and Mary, and probably their third, John Walker. During the mid-1850s, the Creeches relocated in Mills County, Iowa, where the remaining seven children were born. They included Martha in 1858 and Sarah (Sadie) in 1860. Two more were born during the Civil War, in which Bennett served. These were Isabella in 1862 and Tecumseh Sherman in 1864. An infant daughter who did not survive birth arrived in 1867. Phil Sheridan came the year after, and Mae in 1870, making a total of ten. On March 6, 1873, Nancy Creech died and was buried in Mills County.

Sometime after that, Sadie's father seems to have taken the children to Kinsley, Kansas, and perhaps sent a few of the children to live with relatives. Creech and some of his children eventually lived in Oklahoma and California. Creech's son, T. Sherman, joined the horse business. During the 1920s and early 1930s, he took horses to the Caliente Race Track in Tijuana before pari-mutuel racing was legal in California. Although two of Creech's daughters married horse trainers, Sadie apparently wanted to find her own way in the world.

When Sadie reached Kingston, probably in 1885 when she was in her mid-twenties, she saw before her an incredible panorama of high life and low life, of riches and poverty, and of goodness and depravity. Even her rich imagination had been unable to concoct such a scene from newspaper reports, travelers' accounts, and miners' tales. Savvy as the rest of the horse traders in her family — a line of horse people named Creech strung out over Iowa, Missouri, and Kansas — Sadie quickly assessed the situation. Like many young, unmarried, and tolerably good-looking women in western boom towns, she chose prostitution.

After all, Kingston proffered only so many possibilities to women. The mining camp was in its infancy, working its way through a chaotic phase that people often referred to as "rip-roaring" or "hell-bent." Kingston had sprung into existence in southwestern New Mexico in August 1882, after miner Jack Sheddon discovered the Solitaire Mine. Within weeks, surveyors laid out the townsite of Kingston, which took its name from another rich strike, the Iron King Mine.

Kingston's first winter brought record-breaking cold, as well as a smallpox epidemic that raged through the town's populace. Tents and crude buildings bore signs reading Small Pox and warnings for people not to enter or leave without special permits. During the winter months, sorrowful funeral corteges made their way to the newly established graveyard, where men used dynamite to blast open the frozen, rocky ground. Eventually spring came, and those people who survived remained enthusiastic about the area's prospects. Building lots on Main Street escalated in value to the hundreds and even thousands of dollars. Within the year, Kingston boasted a post office and a population of some eighteen hundred people.

Despite fearing attack by Warm Spring Apaches who had lost their homes and lands to the mining boom, Kingston's inhabitants saw their occupation as permanent. To prove their point, Kingston's people feverishly erected sturdy buildings. Legend has it that in one single day thirty thousand feet of oak and pine building lumber was freighted in from Lake Valley, twenty-six miles to the south. Within a few years of its founding, Kingston metamorphosed from a collection of battered tents, flimsy shacks, and twenty-two saloons to a community of substantial structures, including a double-gabled brick assay office and an impressive-looking stone bank whose state-of-the-art vault often held thousands of dollars worth of gold and silver.

Eventually there was also the Union Church, which some say Sadie and her "girls" funded by passing the hat among miners. Thankful that the Apaches gradually left Kingston alone, the builder of a new three-story hotel named it the Victorio in honor of the dauntless Apache chieftain who had once tried to live in harmony with settlers but had ended up embattled. Despite stories to the contrary, Victorio never attacked Kingston. He had met death earlier—in October 1880—at the hands of Mexican troops at Tres Castillos, Mexico.

In the meantime, a printing press retrieved from the bed of the Rio Grande near Mesilla not only cranked out sporadic newspapers like *The Clipper* and *The Shaft*, but printed handbills intended to swell Kingston's population. One widely distributed handbill describes the allure of the Black Range, including its health-giving climate:

HO! FOR THE GOLD AND SILVER MINES OF NEW MEXICO!
Fortune hunters, capitalists, poor men, Sickly folks, all whose hearts
are bowed down; And ye who would live long, be rich, healthy And
happy: Come to our sunny clime and see For Yourselves.

By 1885, seven thousand people had thronged to Kingston, Sadie among them. When she looked down Kingston's main street, she saw on her left a dressmaking shop, the two-story Occidental Hotel, and the small, one-story Opera House. The mud street was wide, to accommodate stagecoaches and freight wagons. A water ditch ran through the road, while trash littered its dirt surface. On the street's other side stood a printing office and a variety of shops, offering an assortment of "staple and fancy goods." In their dim interiors, lit only by hanging kerosene lamps, were shelves stocked with food items, household goods, clothing, hats and shoes, and mining supplies. Saloons, including the ubiquitous Long Branch, were liberally scattered among other businesses. The "tonier" places advertised the "best of wines, bourbon whiskies, and the choicest cigars." Some saloons even sold strawberry and lemon beer, a temperance beverage. Reaching upward from the business district were Hillsboro's hillsides, where two- or three-room clapboard houses with glass-pane windows and shingle roofs clung to the slopes. When Kingston's population, as well as visitors and curiosity seekers, thronged into town on Saturday nights, the crowd was so thick a person could progress only by inches.

A Working Girl in Hillsboro

Why Sadie chose to leave Kingston sometime around 1886 and move approximately nine miles east to the gold mining town of Hillsboro is unclear. It is unlikely that she foresaw the events that would drain the life from Kingston, including the Panic of 1893, the repeal of the Sherman Silver Purchase Act, the Gold Standard Act of 1900, and the eventual playing out of Kingston's silver mines during the late 1890s and early 1900s. It is more likely that Sadie was alarmed by an Apache foray in 1886 that left a family named Yates dead and several others wounded. Later, former Black Range miner James A. McKenna explained that soldiers stationed in the area could not "go against the Indians without order from Washington." In this case, according to McKenna, the soldiers' inaction caused "much hard feeling among the settlers in the Southwest."

This incident alone would have been enough to encourage Sadie to move. Also, she surely had visited Hillsboro via the Kingston-Hillsboro stage line. As a result, Sadie probably recognized that, even during Kingston's peak years, Hillsboro offered her more opportunities. For one thing, Hillsboro, more established than Kingston, had jumped to life during the spring of 1877 after two miners, Dan Dugan and Dave Stitzel, found gold along Percha Creek, supposedly named for hundreds of wild turkeys that perched in trees lining the stream. Dugan and Stitzel called their finds the Ready Pay and the Opportunity. In June, Dugan and another miner, Frank Pitcher, found the Rattlesnake Mine. After they and other miners established a raw camp near Percha Creek, they named it Hillsborough, perhaps because one miner wanted the new town named after his hometown in Ohio or because the men drew names out of a hat. Whatever the case, Hillsborough soon became spelled in a more manageable way as Hillsboro.

Hillsboro also was beyond the worst of its Indian problems. During the town's early years, residents experienced great anxiety regarding Warm Spring Apaches who were desperate to recover their homes and lands in the Black Range. Between 1874 and 1877, these and other Apaches had been assigned to the Ojo Caliente Reservation in New Mexico. In 1877, many were relocated in Arizona on the San Carlos Reservation. Because of dismal conditions and broken promises, hundreds of Apaches escaped, especially following the then very much alive and vital Victorio back to the Mimbres Valley. Once in New Mexico Territory, the Apaches fought for their ancestral homeland, where they believed the Creator had given them life, ceremonies, and all the resources they would ever need.

Hillsboro's citizens were unwilling to back down. Town officials sought protection from the United States government, especially from troops at Fort Bayard, whose infantry and cavalry soldiers pursued the Apache throughout southern New Mexico. During the late 1870s, however, Fort Bayard was woefully understaffed. In 1878, the post's commander even asked, and received permission, to assign horses and weapons to members of the regimental band. In 1880, Hillsboro was fortunate in having several companies of U.S. troops stationed in town. Miners also organized themselves into military-style companies. With Victorio's death in 1880, the situation promised to quiet down, but the aged Nana tried to take Victorio's place as chieftain of the Apaches. When Geronimo escaped from the San Carlos Reservation for a time during the mid-1880s, he posed a very real threat to the Anglos and others who had taken over the valley of gold and silver that had once belonged to his people. Still, the clear possibility of Indian attack did not stop large numbers of Anglos, along with lesser numbers of Hispanics, African Americans, and Asians, from entering the area.

When Sadie relocated in Hillsboro around 1886, she found a pleasant, established town with a post office, school, and church, as well as grocery stores, hotels, homes, and, of course, saloons and brothels. For the next ten years, Sadie reportedly worked as a "fair but frail" woman, perhaps even running her own house. Times were changing, however. Mining towns in the Black Range area were beginning to adopt codes meant to control such businesses. Growing numbers of citizens viewed these establishments as what one code called "offenses against good morals and decency." In nearby Silver City, an 1885 provision made illegal the operation of "any bawdy house or house of ill fame, house of assignation, or place for the practice of fornication, or common ill-governed or disorderly house."

Persons running bordellos could be brought before a justice of the peace and fined "a sum not exceeding one hundred dollars and not less than ten dollars." Usually, however, anti-prostitution laws were enforced loosely, if at all. It is highly likely that such restrictive provisions also existed in Hillsboro, but that the town's prostitutes and madams followed the widespread practice of paying fines in advance on a weekly or monthly basis. This procedure allowed brothels to operate without the risk of police raids and provided a regular source of revenue for a town's government.

During the late 1880s and early 1890s, Sadie faced other dangers as well. Into the 1890s, troops stationed at Fort Bayard continued to hound a small number of Indians who supposedly threatened miners, ranchers, and settlers. Under the command of such colorful figures as First Lieutenant John J. Pershing, later known as Black Jack for his leadership of the 10th Regiment U.S. Colored Troops, and Colonel Zenas Randall Bliss, who oversaw the longest command in the fort's history, infantry and cavalry harassed Indians that Anglos considered "renegades" because they had fled from deplorable reservations and returned to their homelands. Not until 1900 did the last troops leave Fort Bayard, which was converted into a hospital to serve navy and marine veterans.

In the meantime, miners and settlers created a fractious society among themselves. In such towns as Hillsboro, Silver City, and Chloride Flats, men and women, including Anglos, Hispanics, African Americans, and Asians, regularly assaulted one another. Reports of murder, along with such lesser crimes as stealing and rustling, frequently appeared in Hillsboro's *Sierra County Advocate.* Farther afield, to the south of Hillsboro, Silver City's *Enterprise,* and to the north, Chloride's *Black Range,* regaled their readers with stories related to knife slashings and shootings. People shot other people in saloons, brothels, homes, and on the streets. At Fort Bayard in 1889, two African American soldiers, reportedly fighting over a woman, shot each other. In the same year, a Pinos Altos woman shot at her lover after a quarrel. Although the woman claimed she only meant to frighten the man, her bullet killed him.

Additional kinds of violent incidents reminded people of their own mortality. In Española in 1889, a bear killed and ate most of an aged Hispanic woman, leaving only some torn clothing, bones, and hair. In the mines, accidents were endemic; premature explosions of dynamite or other catastrophes claimed numerous lives. Some people's desire for revenge created further havoc. In Doña Ana County, a dying gunman confessed that he had been hired to kill the deputy sheriff for an unexplained offense. In more than one instance, people with revenge on their minds used widely accessible "giant powder"—

dynamite—to blow up someone's home or office. Others simply resorted to setting easily ignited wood buildings on fire.

Even the supposedly healthful climate made life tenuous. In 1889, the snow in the Mimbres Valley was reported as "hip deep," and in the foothills drifts of snow reached to a horse's back. On one occasion, three cowboys perished in a blizzard; their lifeless bodies were found lying in the snow, frozen. That spring, when the snow melted, flood waters rolled out of the mountains, cutting a fourteen-foot-wide path of destruction and claiming several more lives.

During the late 1880s and early 1890s, Sadie lived in this perilous environment and practiced one of the most dangerous professions in the West. Madams and prostitutes sustained frequent injuries and sometimes death, often at the hands of their associates. For example, in 1888, prostitute Bessie Harper was out of jail on bond awaiting the action of a grand jury because she had attacked another prostitute, Millie Forest. With a stone tied up in a towel, Bessie had allegedly beaten Millie senseless and left her with multiple lacerations of the face and scalp. In 1889, a Miss Cordelia languished in a Pinos Altos jail after she "shot up" and wounded denizens of a house run by a Miss Williams. The following year, a French woman who managed the house called Nettie's Place was found dead with a .41-caliber bullet through her forehead. The newspaper account left little to the imagination: "She had bled terribly as the bed clothes were saturated and there was a large pool of blood on the floor."

In addition, many of Sadie's customers were unstable and reckless. Some experimented with opium, available at a price from apothecaries, as well as from Chinese merchants and laundrymen. Many men routinely ingested far too much alcohol. One drunken cowboy shot a clean hole through his own ear. In other instances, firearms went off unintentionally. In one case, a shotgun exploded and blew off the side of a man's head, exposing his brains. Amidst all this mayhem, Sadie remained alive and unscarred. Clearly, she was a survivor.

Moreover, through these tumultuous years, Sadie seems to have kept her name out of the newspapers and away from police blotters. Apparently she did not walk the streets or work in a crib (a small, flimsy shack), both of which afforded a woman little regard and no protection. Instead, Sadie worked saloons and bawdy houses, which gave her more status and protection from rowdies and aggressive clients.

Despite her occupation, Sadie, who was literate and had some education, seems to have viewed herself as a modest Victorian woman. Like other Victorian women, Sadie collected and pasted in a scrapbook moral sayings, flowery poetry, didactic stories, and articles she had clipped from newspapers and magazines.

Sadie's manner of dress was also typically Victorian. She preferred high-buttoned shoes with dark stockings, ankle-length skirts with petticoats, and white shirtwaists, topped off with a fashionable hat. She wore her hair upswept and favored a modest amount of jewelry. In addition, she usually rode horses sidesaddle and carried a dignified horsehair quirt. Standing five feet tall and weighing about one hundred pounds, Sadie was small in stature but not in presence.

Even though Sadie avoided headlines, mention of her counterparts and their misdeeds appeared regularly in newspapers and in legal documents. In Black Range communities, members of what the Silver City *Enterprise* called the "Lost Sisterhood" sometimes made themselves into public nuisances in various ways. By day, such women sat on doorsteps or walked through the streets, often smoking cigarettes and dressed in revealing Mother Hubbard gowns intended for wear at home. These women insulted passersby with "vile and obscene language." Some women even sassed officers of the law. In Silver City in 1889, the marshal arrested one Claudie Lewis for being what the *Enterprise* described as "entirely too flip." About the same time, a "colored girl" went to jail for "corrupting the morals" of the people of Central City. Although such women usually paid a fine and perhaps spent a night in jail, the most obnoxious women were asked to leave the community.

A New Mexico territorial law banning women from saloons, which took effect in May 1889, exacerbated the situation. Women who pursued saloon-based occupations developed creative—and often bothersome—evasions. In a Lordsburg saloon, for example, the female piano player kept on performing by reaching the keys through an open window. Two female faro dealers continued to deal cards in an annex whose door led into a saloon. In many towns, women of disrepute had their drinks brought to them in the street, where they solicited business among male customers entering and leaving saloons. This practice created a noisy and unsavory disturbance is front of virtually every barroom and saloon.

Similar occurrences must have taken place in Hillsboro, but Sadie apparently stayed out of them. Meanwhile, she witnessed dramatic changes in Hillsboro that could deeply affect her own life. Farm and ranch families settled outside Hillsboro in an area known as Happy Flats. In 1884, the town became the seat of Sierra County. Then, in 1892, the silhouette of the imposing Sierra County Courthouse rose against Hillsboro's southwesterly skyline. Within a year, the windowless adobe cell adjoining the old courthouse downtown was no longer needed as a jail because a sturdy stone prison with numerous cells took its place right behind the courthouse. The new jail handled what one commentator called "a flood of drunks, thieves and highwaymen." A criminal could be tried by a judge and incarcerated by a jailer, all within a few yards of each other. Also in 1892, the brick Union Church went up near the courthouse. Two years later, a stolid black-stone Victorian cottage with whimsical gingerbread trim appeared near the church.

In other words, Hillsboro was no longer a rough mining camp with loose behavior tolerated and sometimes applauded. Nomadic miners who were ready to leap up and leave at the news of a strike elsewhere were now in the minority. Instead, families made up the bulk of Hillsboro's population. Middle- and upper-class families, mostly Anglo, lived in solid homes with servants and gardens. Concurrently, as happened in many other western settlements, some of Hillsboro's people, especially women who defined themselves as "good," wanted officials to enforce existing legislation against prostitutes. These women hoped to see local prostitutes restricted or run out of town. Many of these good women were clubwomen who wanted all kinds of reforms. They happily staged such charitable events as ice cream socials and church bazaars to fund their causes. They were determined to bring their version of civilization to the West. In other words, they envisioned a modified eastern culture in the West. Sadie and her ilk did not fit into these women's hopes and plans for Hillsboro.

Even if Sadie lived and worked in a segregated part of town usually called the red-light or tenderloin district, she had to realize that not everyone tolerated her presence in Hillsboro. If she wanted to become "respectable," she had a number of choices. Most notably, she could get married, or she could establish a legal business. Whether to achieve respectability or for other reasons of her own, Sadie eventually followed both of these routes.

A Married Woman

On July 17, 1895, Sadie Creech wed James W. Orchard. The ceremony was performed by Sierra County Justice of the Peace R. A. Nickle. How Sadie met James, as well as details of their wedding, are unknown. At last, Sadie was a respectable married woman. It was not unusual for a prostitute to marry. A significant number of prostitutes remained in the profession after they married. Even during the twentieth century this was true. During mid-century, for example, Silver City's renowned madam Mildred Clark married a local rancher, Wendell Cusey, who had no objection to her continuing her business activities. Apparently, however, Sadie left her career behind when she married James.

James had also led a harried life. Some years before he married Sadie, he had purchased the Lake Valley to Kingston stage line. Horse-drawn vehicles shuttled passengers, mail, and bank deposits to the railway depot in Lake

Sadie Orchard during the late 1890s with her husband James. The child may be the groom who Sadie called Boots. (Courtesy of the Geronimo Springs Museum Archives, Truth or Consequences, New Mexico.)

Valley, which, in 1878, became a mining town after blacksmith John Leavitt discovered the Bridal Chamber Silver Mine. The coach line was especially busy with deliveries when such companies as Sears and Roebuck and Montgomery Ward issued the heavy catalogs that served as dream-books for families in the relatively isolated Black Range area. Soon, coaches made daily runs, connecting Kingston, Lake Valley, and Hillsboro in an awkward loop that involved driving through creek beds and steep-walled canyons, where the stages were moving targets for Indians and robbers. In 1892, Orchard sold his line to William Matthewson. Orchard continued to manage the company and in January 1894 became Matthewson's partner. In that same year, Orchard ran for election as Sierra County assessor, but he does not appear to have been successful.

When James and Sadie married in 1895, she took an active interest in the company and participated in its affairs. The Orchard-Matthewson firm advertised itself as the United States Mail, Express, and Stage Line, which "always connected with the arrival of trains in Lake Valley." Using one of several buckboards, flat-bed wagons, and at least one coach, probably a Concord called the Mountain Pride, the company promised to change horses every ten miles, making it a "comfortable" five-hour run from Kingston to Lake Valley through "grand" scenery and "prosperous" towns. The Mountain Pride was the glory of the two men and of Sadie. Designed to carry nine passengers, six inside and three more on top in a seat mounted behind the driver, this vehicle could carry considerably more passengers — if they were willing to ride inside sitting on the floor, or with the driver on the top, or dangling from the vehicle's sides. The stage had one baggage boot at its rear and another under the driver's seat. A remuda of eighteen or twenty horses supplied teams of four. These teams were composed of two nervy, excitable leaders in front to provide a fast start, and two large, muscular horses, known as wheelers, to keep the team moving so the lurching coach did not roll into them.

Despite the stage line's grandiose assertions, it provided an undependable living for James Orchard and his bride. Because mail contracts were periodically put up for bids and went to the lowest bidder, the company could not always count on carrying the mail. In addition, necessary expenses included the employment of stock-tenders, a bookkeeper, ticket agents, and drivers. The horses required feed and heavy-duty harnesses and other special tack. For coach brakes, the company purchased sacks of men's old shoes for leather to daily reline brake housings. In addition, coaches often needed repair. If a coach was about to upset or had a runaway team, the driver could disengage the coach from the horses by a single kingpin holding the body to the front wheels and axle — but considerable damage could occur, demanding expensive mending.

The greatest difficulty was not bad roads, Indians, or highway robbers, but the hiring of drivers. Some say that Sadie herself regularly drove for the Orchard stage line, but others refute such stories. The truth probably lies somewhere in between, with Sadie driving occasionally when drivers were in short supply. Coming from a horse background, Sadie would have had neither fear of horses nor awkwardness in handling them. The agility of a driver's hands and his or her sensitive handling of the reins, or ribbons, were far more important than a driver's size and weight. A driver had to have the dexterity to start the lead pair slightly before the wheelers, or back pair, so that the leaders gave impetus to the wheelers, while the wheelers supplied power for the leaders. A driver also had to control leaders and wheelers when turning the coach to avoid a leader turning so sharply as to trip the slower wheeler behind it. Jolting along the rock-strewn bed of Percha Creek, with its greenish water and steep, rocky hillsides leaning inward, would have required a dexterous driver indeed.

Undoubtedly, Sadie would have been an effective driver. In fact, on January 18, 1899, the *Santa Fe New Mexican* complimented the Orchards, and seemingly Sadie, by saying that the Orchard stage line "is one of the finest

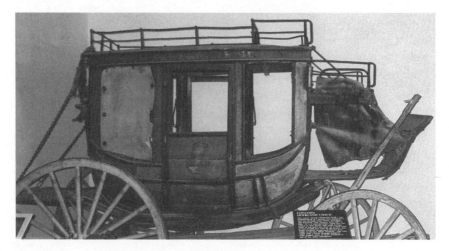

The Mountain Pride coach that Sadie said she drove during the late 1890s. A likeness of Chief Victorio is painted on both doors. (Courtesy of Glenda Riley.)

stage lines in the territory and sports the best vehicles, best horses and best looking driver in the Southwest." How the good-looking Sadie handled Indians and robbers would have been another matter. By the late 1890s, however, Indians were becoming scarce in the Black Range. Someone, maybe Sadie, had a portrait of Victorio painted on the doors of the Mountain Pride. The portrait could have been a tribute or some sort of good-luck charm. As far as robbers were concerned, Sadie carried firearms and knew how to use them. The most popular story regarding Sadie's foiling of thieves — that she hid $175,000 in the horses' collars — is probably untrue. Sadie herself is said to have given credit for this scheme to driver Bill Holt, who received a hundred-dollar reward from the Orchards for his quick thinking.

Yet stagecoach driving was not really "proper" for a lady. If Sadie did indeed seek respectability, driving her husband's coaches would not achieve that goal. Apparently she and James knew this.

The Ocean Grove Hotel

In 1896, James virtually gave Sadie a Main Street building lot in Kingston on which to build a legitimate hotel. She constructed a modest, one-story adobe building with a shingled roof and half a dozen rooms, most leading one into another. A water tank and a "necessary house" were located in the backyard. Sadie furnished the hotel in customary Victorian fashion, including some of the finer things that she so loved: horsehair furniture, a cut-glass fruit bowl, a china

Because Sadie Orchard liked quality,
she bought this massive, modern wood
stove for the Ocean View Hotel.
(Courtesy of Glenda Riley.)

teapot, and a bone-white condiment set. Sadie named the place the Ocean Grove Hotel. Since there was not an ocean in her past, in her present, or likely to appear in her future, the Ocean Grove was a fanciful name at best.

Sadie equipped the Ocean Grove's kitchen with a formidable black Banquet cast-iron stove; it had ovens below and above, with a commodious range top in between. Sadie hired a Chinese immigrant, Tom Ying, away from a Lake Valley eatery. On the huge wood-burning stove, the small man cooked for hotel guests, as well as for local people who stopped in for a meal. Typical menus included courses of soups, fish, roast meats, boiled meats, and such relishes as tomato catsup, Worcestershire sauce, pickles, and chow chow (chopped pickles in a spicy mustard sauce). Biscuits and gravy were ever-present. Pastries and dessert followed. Sometimes, cookies were offered, as well as Limburger and Swiss cheeses.

By supplying clean accommodations and tasty, filling food, Sadie's establishment soon built a clientele of visiting businessmen, farmers, and ranchers. When court was in session, the Ocean Grove also housed surveyors, lawyers, and politicians. Even though Sadie did not break into the upper strata of Hillsboro's female society, she had many paying guests, some of whom became influential friends as well.

Sadie played her new role well. She appeared quite happy immersing herself in the Ocean Grove Hotel. For work, she favored dark dresses or dark skirts and white shirtwaists, often covered by an apron. She was pleasant to everyone, whether young or old, male or female, Anglo or of color. Her business grew slowly but steadily until 1899, which was an extraordinary year for Sadie, Ying, and the hotel. On May 25, a court case began—the Territory of New Mexico vs. Oliver M. Lee and James Gililland—widely known as the Fountain case. Lee and Gililland were the alleged murderers in the 1896 killing of Albert Jennings Fountain and his young son. Fountain had gained notoriety as a newspaper editor who crusaded for law and order, as well as becoming, in 1879, the captain of the Mesilla Independent Cavalry, or Mesilla Scouts. Fountain led a vigorous campaign against Victorio and his warriors. Later, Fountain helped pursue white fugitives who had fled from Texas to southern New Mexico to join with robbers, rustlers, and murderers. In between, Fountain proved himself a brilliant trial lawyer, as well as an outspoken advocate of statehood for New Mexico.

Because Fountain had many enemies, foul play was immediately suspected. Witnesses and solid evidence of a crime proved elusive, however. Two years elapsed after the disappearance of Fountain and his son before Sheriff Patrick F. Garrett, known for shooting Billy the Kid in 1881, swore out warrants for the arrest of Lee and Gililland. After a long and difficult chase, Lee and Gililland

Women standing in front of Ocean Grove Hotel, Hillsboro, New Mexico. Mrs. Sadie Orchard is on the right. (Courtesy Museum of New Mexico, photograph by George T. Miller, neg. #76560.)

were taken into custody. Although the case should have been heard elsewhere, a change of venue assigned it to Hillsboro, whose citizens were generally delighted to have the traffic and business the sensational trial brought to their town.

Apparently, Sadie Orchard took advantage of the windfall. At least one historian states that Sadie drove one of the stagecoaches that brought swarms of prisoners, lawyers, witnesses, and onlookers from Lake Valley to Hillsboro. Sadie's hotel filled to capacity, as did the rest of Hillsboro's boardinghouses and hotels. Tom Ying set bounteous tables that not only fed hotel guests, but those staying in tents, wagons, and the open air. Sadie and Tom also fed the prisoners housed in Sierra County's relatively new jail. Defense lawyer Albert Bacon Fall, however, took his meals at the chuck wagon in the tent camp set up for witnesses.

The trial lasted eighteen days. When a jury declared Lee and Gililland innocent, Sadie was reportedly on hand to drive the stagecoach returning people to the Lake Valley railroad depot. Some say that the principals, especially the humiliated Pat Garrett and the prosecuting attorneys, were so anxious to leave Hillsboro that one stagecoach carried twenty-three people. Within a few days, Sadie's business had returned to as near-normal as it ever would. Meanwhile, Hillsboro and Sadie had gained widespread attention.

Unfortunately for Sadie and James, her new notoriety and prosperity seemed to upset whatever balance they had achieved in their marriage. Although rumor says that James liked to drink and was adept at hiding whiskey around the Orchard home, it is more likely that the energetic, successful Sadie overshadowed James. In 1900, Sadie's growing tension and distress became public and resulted in Sadie spending time at Hillsboro's courthouse. On June 8, the Sierra County *Advocate* reported that Sarah J. Orchard was charged with "unlawfully discharging a deadly weapon." During the summer of 1900, the apparently irascible Sadie claimed that Mrs. Guniocinda Rubio, better known as Enchilada, had assaulted her with a deadly weapon.

Next came a spat between Sadie and James. The *Advocate* announced that "Mr. and Mrs. J. W. Orchard" were "in trouble." After a disagreement over a carriage, Sadie had taken a potshot at James with her revolver. Although Sadie maintained that the weapon had gone off by accident in James's hands, the court set a two-hundred-dollar bond for Sadie. Near the end of September, she was back in court regarding a property dispute. She was blamed for "illegally appropriating from Mr. J. W. Orchard a buggy and a set of harness." In November, Sadie was again accused of "drawing, flourishing, and discharging a deadly weapon." The *Advocate* noted, however, that Sadie

Sadie Orchard, circa 1901. (Courtesy Museum of New Mexico, photograph by Jacob Pasevich, neg. #58824.)

ended the year with a positive step, making in mid-December "some desirable changes to the interior of the Ocean Grove Hotel."

In the meantime, James Orchard had his own troubles, not the least of which was Sadie shooting at him. On January 1, 1901, a legal notice showed James owing back taxes on a stable and corral in Hillsboro; a stable, office, and house in Lake Valley; a stable and brick office in Kingston; a toll road; a house at Jarralesa; and other personal property. In sum, Orchard owed precinct number three of Sierra County just over fifty dollars. Two months later, James's holdings were threatened by a fire in his express office, which adjoined his stable. Although the fire started sometime around 1:00 or 2:00 a.m., the alarm was promptly sounded, and men from "Shorty's place," a saloon, came to the rescue. They were able to subdue the flames, while Orchard's stock-tender cut loose the four horses in the stable.

According to the *Advocate*, the blaze at the Orchards' place was set by a "fire fiend" who "had carefully arranged plans of destruction." The culprit had disconnected the water pump and liberally doused the stable with coal oil. "The dastardly affair," the editor wrote, "caused no little indignation." Was James the miscreant, who perhaps hoped to collect insurance money? Or could the guilty party have been a vengeful Sadie, determined to burn her husband out of town? The *Advocate* refused to speculate, only saying, "Who committed the act is yet a mystery."

The end of the marriage came sometime in 1901 with a divorce. The following year, James failed to secure a mail contract; he sold the stage line to Fred Mister and relocated in Belen, also in New Mexico Territory. Almost immediately, rumors circulated regarding the Orchards. One reported that, in the dark of night, Sadie had run James off with a shotgun. One of the most fantastic was that Sadie and James made a trip to her supposed home in England, but only Sadie returned. Perhaps, to escape the onus of divorce, Sadie spread her own rumors. Yet many other divorces had occurred in the Sierra County Courthouse prior to the Orchard split. One of these was the controversial Hiler case, which resulted in the shooting death of the very popular Dr. Mason and the suicide of a key witness. Although the national divorce rate of the era hovered around one out of thirteen or fourteen marriages, Sadie was embarrassed by her status. Instead of a divorcée, she always referred to herself as a widow. However she chose to explain her situation, Sadie was again on her own without family.

Madame Sadie

After James's departure, Sadie remained in Hillsboro, where she retained control of the Ocean Grove Hotel and the Orchard Hotel. A newspaper advertisement of the time also mentioned the "Hillsboro Hotel, Mrs. J. W. Orchard, Proprietress." This place may have been a third hotel or another name for the Orchard Hotel. Or it may have been a brothel; one advertisement included a phrase open to interpretation: "Headquarters for Commercial Men." Back at the original hotel, the Ocean Grove, Tom Ying continued to cook and manage the business. It is said that Sadie essentially sold the property to Ying, even though no legal sale existed because Asians were not allowed to own property.

Sadie evidently put her time and energy into the Orchard Hotel, presumably constructed sometime before the divorce. In an oft-published photograph—usually dated 1884, well before Sadie met James, and more likely taken in the mid-1890s—Sadie is captured in the yard of the Orchard Hotel. Sadie is mounted sidesaddle on a fine horse, perhaps a bay or a black. The horse's bridle is worked in silver, and Sadie holds the reins in hands covered by soft-as-butter leather gloves. Her long skirt flows across the horse's side, her shirtwaist is crisp and very white, and jauntily cocked on her head is something resembling a man's silk, high-top hat. Also in the original photograph (although usually cropped off for publication) is Sadie's husband, James. He appears to be a mild-mannered man attired in dark trousers, a light-colored shirt, suspenders, and a broad-brimmed felt hat. His handlebar mustache and sad eyes block attempts to discover his personality or his feelings.

Next to Sadie's horse stands a small black lad, who some accounts identify as Boots, Sadie's groom. The child appears again in a photograph including a group of boys posing next to the Mountain Pride stagecoach. One local tale told of Sadie's befriending a child, perhaps this one. As far as is known, the Orchards never had children of their own. In her will made in 1937 (presuming she gave her correct age), Sadie stated, "I aver and declare that I have no living issue, my children having long since died." This may have been a legal formality, however, or perhaps she referred to the child she befriended. After all, during her marriage Sadie was in her mid-thirties, not an age then considered propitious or healthy for childbearing. Or perhaps the Orchards did not want children and Sadie had picked up enough knowledge to know how to prevent pregnancy.

During the early 1900s, Sadie converted the Orchard Hotel into a brothel, furnished with brass bedsteads, wicker furniture, and an oak curio cabinet in Sadie's parlor. The hotel's backyard—a commodious corral, with five- to six-foot walls of piled stones, seemingly intended for the Orchards' stagecoach horses—now accommodated a small number of guests' horses or automobiles. Madame Sadie, as she was now known, appears to have run a discreet house that attracted local men, as well as men visiting Hillsboro. Because some of Sadie's clients were men of importance, she had little trouble with the law. In addition, Sadie maintained an image at which few people could take offense. She dressed modestly, rather than in silks and satins. The jewelry she left behind is little more than costume pieces. If her fabled necklace made of five-dollar gold pieces ever existed, it disappeared somewhere along the way.

Even though the divorced Madame Sadie's dream of becoming "respectable" apparently suffered a setback, during these years she retained qualities of the Victorian lady she had once hoped to become. Most notably, Sadie had always been kind to people, especially children, but a growing spirit of philanthropy marked her later life. When in 1914, floodwaters roiled down Percha Creek and through Hillsboro's streets, they left behind a mass of destruction, as well as hurt and homeless people. Following the calamitous flood came an influenza epidemic. It is claimed that Sadie not only nursed the sick, but also cut up her gowns to provide linings for children's wooden coffins. Given Sadie's generous personality, she doubtless rendered such services.

During the next years, Sadie continued her benevolence. For example, after the United States entered World War I, Sadie resumed her aid work. She filled in for whoever needed help—drivers, cooks, doctors, nurses, even undertakers. Later, the New Mexico writer Erna Fergusson summed up Sadie in one concise sentence: "For a bad woman, Sadie was one of the best." Sadie also carried on with the daily business of the Ocean Grove Hotel and the Orchard Hotel. During the 1920s, she often did the marketing, paying in 1927 a mere thirty-five cents for a pound of pork chops. A few years later, in 1930, Tom Ying was still cooking at the Ocean Grove Hotel, where he offered a cup of coffee for five cents and a full dinner for fifty cents.

Around 1930, Sadie received a visit from her sister, Mae Creech Soldway (also spelled Saldway or Salway), and from her niece, Martha M. Creech Noland, who either had no knowledge of Sadie's real occupation or did not care. Photographs from the stay show a variety of scenes of Sadie with Mae and Martha: standing in front of the Orchard well; with cows; perched on rocks. Although no letters exist, Sadie seemingly kept contact with the folks at home during her years in Hillsboro. It is doubtful, however, that Sadie ever informed family members that she ran a sporting house. Neither did her relatives report this fact when they returned home. Thus, Martha's daughter, Oleta Mae Nelson, was surprised when she later stopped in Hillsboro, only to be told that Sadie had been a notorious and colorful madam.

During the late 1930s, Sadie had become a much-loved local character. Edward Montoya, who as a child lived across the street from the Orchard Hotel, said that his father cleaned the rooms for Sadie's "girls" every morning.

The ruins of Hillsboro's once grand Sierra County Courthouse, built in 1892, often visited by Sadie Orchard. (Courtesy of Glenda Riley.)

In Montoya's memory, Sadie stood out as a kind person who always had a word and sometimes a bit of candy for him and the other children. For him, Sadie was simply a nice neighbor lady.

When Sadie died on April 3, 1943, she was buried in nearby Hot Springs (the town that now is named Truth or Consequences). Sadie's death certificate gave the cause of death as paresis, or partial paralysis, which is often caused by syphilis of the central nervous system. Before her death, Sadie saw a Hillsboro physician on a fairly regular basis. Although this cause of death would have been consistent with Sadie's life story, she was nearly eighty-three years old at the time of her death and had lived through a raucous frontier mining era. It appears that Sadie had what was called in her day a "strong constitution."

Even though Sadie Orchard's legend says she died in poverty, there is evidence to the contrary. An unidentified record book in Hillsboro's Black Range Museum shows Sadie owning and residing on lot, or perhaps section, 59. In addition, Sadie's 1937 will directed that medical bills, other debts, and funeral expenses be paid out of the proceeds from her estate. She gave her clothes and fur coat to Marguerite W. Worden, perhaps another niece. Any additional funds were to be split between her sister Mae Creech Soldway, then of Inglewood, California, and her brother Phil Sheridan Creech. Both attended the funeral. Apparently enough money came out of Sadie's estate for a nice funeral, which took place at a Hot Springs chapel with a minister presiding, and to bury Sadie in what was then a new section of the French Mortuary and Cemetery on North Cedar Street. Because this was a private cemetery, someone — Sadie's executor or a member of her family — must have paid for the plot. Six pallbearers, including the attending physician, A. E. White, lowered Sadie's casket — which was of "English Crepe" style and cost $130 — into the ground.

Even though Sadie was gone, the rumor mill continued to crank out tales. Stories about Sadie were retold and embellished. Whenever an occasional newspaper account appeared predicting Kingston's and Hillsboro's impending comebacks as mineral centers, tales of Sadie Orchard popped up as well. Myths and errors intertwined. Whoever placed the gray granite stone at Sadie's grave gave her birth year as 1865 rather than 1860. More recently, the person or persons who decorated Sadie's gravesite with flowers plucked from nearby graves invoked the ire of the cemetery's keepers, who placed a small notice on the grave asking visitors to bring their own flowers. Thus, even in death, Sadie is shrouded by inaccuracy and controversy.

*Sadie Orchard's gravestone in the
French Mortuary grounds in Truth
or Consequences, New Mexico.
The date of birth should be 1860.
(Courtesy of Glenda Riley.)*

Clearly, few of the facts of Sadie's life match up with the details of Sadie's epic. Like many of the West's prostitutes and madams, Sadie's existence was not as glamorous as outsiders thought. Although Sadie took advantage of the openness of the frontier West to shape her life as she pleased, she endured risk, danger, and instability. In addition, she increasingly withstood criticism from some townspeople. As a woman who flaunted society's mores, Sadie also faced growing legal jeopardy. Yet little of this matters to her fans. Today Sadie remains one of New Mexico's colorful and revealing figures. Morally, it might matter to some that Madame Sadie ran a brothel. For others, however, Sarah Jane Creech Orchard—or Sadie—was a hard-working woman who contributed a lifetime of good humor, energy, and altruism to New Mexico and to the Old West, and for that she is remembered.

Part Three

Showtime Cowgirls

~ 6 ~

Lucille Mulhall

A True Western Cowgirl

CANDY MOULTON

As if every writer who put pen to paper wanted to come up with a new term to describe Lucille Mulhall, she became almost everything in the book: Rodeo Queen, Queen of the Range, Queen of the Western Prairie, Lassoer in Lingerie, Queen of the Saddle, America's Greatest Horse Woman, Ropist, World's Champion Roper. Indeed, she was all of the above, but she was not, as some have said, the first to be called a cowgirl—though she likely was the first who could live up to such a title. She really knew how to sit a horse, and how to throw a rope after a lunging steer and then tie his feet together once she had caught him. She had sucked into her nostrils the smell of singed hair from a red-hot branding iron pressed against the side of a calf. She had experienced dirt blowing in her face and the sun baking down on her head while riding across the Oklahoma prairie knowing she was miles from a drink of clean, cold water.

A New York reporter used the term "cowgirl" in 1905 to describe Lucille, the teenage daughter of Col. Zack Mulhall, Oklahoma Land Rush homesteader turned rancher turned Wild West show promoter, and his staunchly Catholic wife, Mary Agnes. But cowgirl was not a new term. William F. "Buffalo Bill" Cody and partner Nate Salsbury used the word in promotional materials for their show in 1891. Annie Oakley, who shot her way into fame as part of Buffalo Bill's Wild West Show, had been called a cowgirl by Buffalo Bill Cody, though anyone familiar with her background knew that the Ohio farm girl wasn't one.

For his western shows, Colonel Mulhall drew from the wiry young riders who learned their trade on his sprawling Oklahoma ranch, not the least of whom was his daughter Lucille. Lucille more than once dominated the arena as she rode and roped, and then made a mark in the new world of rodeo by wrestling a steer. The skills she used to entertain crowds were those she had learned on her family's ranch; they were demonstrations of the everyday duties of men and women who make their living raising cattle.

Lucille Mulhall throws a lasso around five cowboys on their horses at Cheyenne Frontier Days, Cheyenne, Wyoming. (Courtesy of Martha Fisch.)

Though Lucille could train a horse and rein in the natural fire in its belly, no one ever quite reined in her own fiery spirit. In taking chances and stepping outside the normal bounds of propriety, Lucille clearly followed the course of her father. In determination, she was her mother's daughter through and through.

At Home on the Ranch

Lucille Mulhall, born October 21, 1885, was one of four girls born to Zack and Mary Agnes Mulhall. She had two full brothers. Of those children, only Lucille and her sister Agnes (nicknamed Bossie), born in 1877, survived to adulthood. Brother Logan died at age fourteen of diphtheria, and Marmaduke, along with twins Mildred and Madolyn, died as infants.

There were other children in the family. The first was Georgia Smith, born in 1872, whom Zack and Mary Agnes Mulhall adopted—though Zack displayed his true colors when he took Georgia as a mistress. He had met her at a roadhouse where she worked as a serving girl before Zack and Mary Agnes adopted her. Georgia subsequently bore Zack two children: son Charles (Charley) and daughter Mildred. Raised primarily by Mary Agnes, both Charley and Mildred believed their mother was their sister. Charley learned the truth first; he told Mildred when she was in her teens.

Father Zack, by all accounts, was a hard, demanding man. He expected obedience, cooperation, and loyalty. He never forsook Georgia—as either daughter or mistress—though at times he had to beg Mary Agnes to allow him to return home, consent that she always gave, however grudgingly. Zack, born September 22, 1847, was a dozen years older than Mary Agnes, whom he had married when she was sixteen and he was twenty-eight. He was a full twenty-four years older than Georgia.

As a teenager Lucille performed in various riding events with her full-blood sister Agnes (Bossie), her half-blood sister Mildred (known as The Little Sheriff), and her adopted sister Georgia, as well as her half-blood brother Charley. Lucille's mother, Mary Agnes, treated all of them as if they were her own children, along with others who came to her home through one circumstance or another. Staunchly Catholic, she was the saint of the family.

Raising children in Missouri and then in Oklahoma during the Land Rush days took fortitude, and Mary Agnes, who watched four of her children die when they were young, no doubt learned that it also took a certain amount of grit. She must have had it; daughter Lucille certainly did. As one reporter noted in an undated clipping,

> Miss Lucille…is like other girls in some respects and in others she is as different as day from night. She has all the frankness, and all the reticence that form the antithetical characteristics of the "plains" people. Ask her a question and she replies in as few words as possible, but always to the point, and with simple courtesy. She is averse to discussing her own feats, and if pressed on the subject is apt to hang her head diffidently, and seek to change the subject.
>
> Her voice is soft and low, and she has a marked Southern accent. But she doesn't disregard her Rs, and say "Ah" for I, as some dialect writers attempt to make all Southern girls do. She talks like any educated girl from the South, and she has a musical laugh. But it is rather difficult to provoke that laugh. She appears to view the world seriously—another cowboy attribute—and to believe in doing things rather than talking of them.

The Mulhall homestead began as 160 acres that Zack staked when he rode in the Oklahoma Land Run of April 22, 1889. He chose the site with great forethought; he had been working as the station agent on the Santa Fe Railroad and knew the strategic location of what became the town of Alfred in Oklahoma Territory. The land run itself began just seven miles from Alfred, and Zack quickly rode to a site south and west of the railroad's water tower, driving his ownership stake.

Zack had made sure that he would get the land he wanted: he had some of his cowboys already in place on Beaver Creek before the gun sounded that signaled the start of the run. True, the cowboys had their positions in order to watch a herd of cattle owned by Zack and other men, but their shelters and presence in Indian Territory prior to the land run made them Sooners—people who made their way to claim Oklahoma land before the legal opening of the territory. In June 1890, a post office charter for Alfred was established, and the town changed its name to Mulhall in honor of Zack Mulhall, who was the town's mayor at the time and who was then building a stockyard near town for the railroad. By that time he had a shelter erected on his homestead and had moved Mary Agnes and their children to the area.

Zack continued working for railroads, first the Santa Fe and later the San Francisco, as he expanded his 160 homestead acres to more than 80,000 rolling red-soil acres—both deeded and public range—used by the ranch. On that ground he raised cattle and kids, though Mary Agnes kept track of it all. Adopted daughter Georgia told a newspaper reporter:

> Father is livestock agent for the San Francisco Railroad, so he is away much of the time, and mother runs the ranch.... She is the best educated, the most practical and the cleverest woman in the world. We're all strong and healthy, but mother has more brains than all of us put together. She gets up before daylight and is in her office at dawn. She receives reports and gives instructions for the day, and in the afternoon she drives around to see that all her orders are carried out. There isn't a detail that escapes her attention and absolutely nothing goes on that she doesn't know of. It takes a pretty clever woman to run 80,000 acres.

As children, Agnes and Lucille learned to ride horses along with brother Logan. But Lucille soon displayed her talent with livestock. She learned not only to ride, but also to rope, train horses, brand cattle, and even doctor animals. She had natural ability, the desire to be riding over the hills, and a competitive nature. After Logan's death, Lucille became her father's closest assistant. She built fences, chased cattle, and caught and branded calves. She learned to shoot, and carried a pistol when riding the range for the same reason men did: to kill rattlesnakes and, if necessary, a horse, should the rider get thrown and have a foot caught in the stirrup. Once she asked her father if she could brand any calves she caught. He readily agreed, not realizing her skill. The young girl promptly obtained branding irons of her own and began roping calves on her family's ranch. She had slapped her LM brand on quite a bunch—some reports say two thousand head—before daddy called off the bargain.

"Lucille is happiest when she can ride far out on the plains where there is nothing but sky, earth and cattle. She likes much to be alone out there," Georgia Mulhall told St. Louis reporter Rose Marion.

"I ride because I like to," said Lucille to one reporter, "and I rope cattle because it is fun. I like to do things as well as I can, and it makes me feel nice to know that I can take care of myself in the country. I ride astride because it is the safest and most comfortable way."

Then she added, "I don't know that I can explain how a rider sticks on a pitching horse. I suppose it is by having perfect control of the muscles of the body and limbs, and in knowing more than the horse does—that is, knowing what he is going to do just a little before he knows he is going to try to do."

A Cowgirl's Rise to Fame

On ranches across the West, cowboys liked to compete against other cowboys in contests of ranching skills. At open-range roundups, the Mulhall crews— including the Mulhall children—challenged cowboys from other spreads to determine the best hands. Such roping and branding activities were among those that led to the timed events of modern rodeo. Zack Mulhall took his

Lucille Mulhall, wearing her trademark split skirt, boots, and white shirtwaist, practices with her lariat. (Courtesy of Martha Fisch.)

cowboys a step beyond the roundup when in 1899 he organized the Congress of Rough Riders and Ropers, which gave performances similar to those started in 1883 by Buffalo Bill Cody.

The first exhibitions by Mulhall's Congress of Rough Riders took place under the show name Interstate and Territorial Exposition, in nearby Oklahoma towns like South McAlester, Vinita, and even Oklahoma City. At age fourteen, Lucille was competing with the men. The contests included trick or fancy riding, steer riding, and saddle bronc riding, but she always excelled at steer roping.

Before long the Mulhalls played in St. Louis, and then in 1900 put on a performance in Oklahoma City for Theodore Roosevelt, a candidate for vice president of the United States. When Roosevelt saw Lucille's performance, he urged Mulhall to take her on the road and share her talent with the rest of America. Roosevelt is reported to have said to Zack that "before that girl dies or gets married, or cuts up some other caper, you ought to put her on the stage and let the world see what she can do. She's simply great!"

By the time she was sixteen, Lucille Mulhall had appeared at many venues in Oklahoma and the East, including performances as part of the 1901 inauguration festivities for President William McKinley and Vice President Roosevelt. She displayed her skills roping steers and riding in relay races, among other events.

The Mulhall Wild West Show in 1905 combined with two other Oklahoma shows—The Miller Brothers 101 Ranch Show and the Pawnee Bill Show—to perform at the National Editors' Association meeting near Ponca City, Oklahoma, for a crowd estimated at from thirty thousand to sixty thousand people. In addition to demonstrating steer roping and other riding skills, the performers enacted cattle stampedes and the hanging of horse thieves. At that performance Lucille met Geronimo, the Apache who had led the frontier army on such a chase years before. He subsequently gave her a beaded vest, which she often wore in parades and other performances.

When the show performed in New York City's Madison Square Garden later in 1905, a reporter wrote:

> This is Miss Mulhall's first visit to the metropolis, and horseman are anxiously awaiting her appearance in the Garden arena, where she will attempt to break the world's record, held by herself, for roping steers.... The exhibition will be the first of its kind ever attempted in the East, and the fact that an eighteen-year-old girl is to accomplish the feat has added considerable interest to the events.

In 1903 in Dennison, Texas, Lucille had roped a steer in thirty seconds to win a gold-and-diamond medal and set the world record for steer roping. A follow-up report about the New York performance did not say whether she had broken her own record, but it changed the way reporters would write about Lucille and women horseback riders in the future. In connection with the Madison Square Garden performance, the term cowgirl first became popularly associated with Lucille Mulhall. Newspaper writers had used various terms to describe her abilities, including such descriptions as Female Conqueror of Beef and Horn, and Lassoer in Lingerie. Some had called her Cowboy Girl or labeled her Ranch Queen, whereas others called her a ropist. But then a reporter for the *New York Times* of April 23, 1905, wrote, "The presence of several cowgirls, headed by Miss Lucille Mulhall, Queen of the Range, with her trick horse, called Governor, was a feature of the evening."

Thus was put into popular usage the term "cowgirl," a word that certainly described the abilities of Lucille Mulhall, who had already proven her mettle in competing against cowboys. Of course, the word "cowgirl" had already been in use to describe Annie Oakley and her performances with Buffalo Bill Cody's Wild West Show, so the word itself wasn't newly coined in 1905. But soon it would be used universally to describe Lucille and other women with riding and roping skills.

Lucille and other female riders captured the American press in much the same way they roped steers or leaned from their saddles to sweep up a hat or scarf lying in the middle of an arena. Wherever they performed they gave interviews, oftentimes talking about the reality of their lives, and occasionally embellishing for the reporter's benefit. But one reporter had the opportunity to observe Lucille and her father. Though the publication and the reporter's name aren't known, nor even the date the article first appeared, the reporting is as honest as anything written about Lucille Mulhall:

Probably her most striking characteristic is her absolute devotion to her father. She obeys him with the same unquestioning faith that the religious devotee obeys a priest. They are great chums, but there is no question as to who is the ruler.

"Pappy, may I go down and sit on the front steps?" said the young lady the other night.

"No, stay up here and keep your old daddy company," was the reply.

The girl walked over to her father and kissed him, then went to the piano and began to play an air from *El Trovatore* [sic].

Lucille Mulhall jumps into the air and raises her arms above her head to signal the successful tying of a steer she has roped. She became the World's Champion Steer Roper in 1913 in Winnipeg, Canada, but had won similar titles at competitions in Texas as early as 1903. (Courtesy of Martha Fisch.)

It was a small thing in itself, but as there was a party of young people on the front steps, and Col. Mulhall was talking with men on subjects in which Miss Lucile [sic] had no interest, it would seem that she is a pretty good little soldier to obey orders so unflinchingly.

Lucille always wore skirts—long, though divided so she could ride her horse—and was never one to don pants. In that sense she was like other cowgirls of her day and certainly like the best-known Wild West show woman, Annie Oakley. Even in skirts, Lucille competed with the men, often scoring a successful catch when they had failed, or roping a steer more quickly than they could. As one reporter put it: "Every man and woman of the thousands who visited the Garden expected to see a rawboned daughter of the Western plains, seared and yellow from exposure to the elements, but instead they were surprised to see a fair, young red-cheeked womanly woman with long flowing golden tresses."

Will Rogers, who rode with the Mulhall show, said Lucille "never dressed like the Cowgirl you know today, no loud colors, no short leather skirts and great big hat, no sir, her skirt was divided, but long, away down over her patent leather boot tops, a whipcord grey, or grey broadcloth, small stiff-brim hat and always a white silk shirt waist."

Most often her long auburn hair was swept back and away from her face, falling down her back in long curls, or sometimes held back in braids. At one moment she appeared demure, the daughter of successful cattle-ranching parents, student of a convent; the next she showed that she was a rancher's daughter who had spent time around the bunkhouse and out on the range.

Lucille was quoted by one reporter as saying: "Eight months of each year of my life I have spent on the Visitation Convent at St. Louis, where I am compelled to comply with every formal propriety that is expected of a debutante of the smart set. Then for four months I live a free and easy life on my father's ranch, riding and punching cows with the roughest of the rough."

Lucille made her comments while seated on the panting horse that had carried her to victory. The reporter continued, "Suddenly the horse shied and balked. Just as quickly did the entire demeanor of the young woman change. An ugly, determined scowl spread over her face, and in a rough, uncouth voice, she heaped objurgation upon the horse."

Of course, she also embellished. She didn't attend the Visitation Convent at St. Louis eight months of each year. She attended some courses there, but most of her schooling took place at a Catholic convent in Guthrie, Oklahoma. Even there her attendance was intermittent at best, often interrupted when her father, Zack, pulled her out of classes to participate in a performance.

In an interview with a reporter in Wichita, Lucille wore a short jacket and blue skirt and her hat was trimmed with blue. And she spoke of roping horses:

"Yes, I am going to ride in the roping contest this afternoon," she told the reporter.

"Aren't you afraid your horse will slip and fall this afternoon?" she was asked.

"Oh, I expect that,'" she replied. "I'm not afraid of getting hurt."

By the time she was seventeen, Lucille had won wide recognition and prizes. A 1903 newspaper report noted:

At seventeen she has the unique distinction of being the only professional woman ropist in the world, with sparkling jewels, by way of medal testimony, to bear witness to the fact. She has won these medals fairly and squarely in roping contests with the most skillful knights of the spur and lariat in Texas.

Lucille possessed two medals. One of solid gold was a Lone Star State Emblem with the date 1902, signifying her roping success at San Antonio, Texas. The second was the one she was awarded in Dennison, Texas, when

Looking every bit the schoolgirl that she was, Lucille Mulhall in a publicity photo. (Courtesy of Martha Fisch.)

she roped a steer in thirty seconds. The top piece of the heavy gold pendant had her name on it along with the year — 1903 — and a diamond set in a center of blue enamel showing a reproduction of the scene in which she roped the steer.

But she didn't always have the best of luck; not every rope went straight and true. She ran into trouble trying to rope a steer in competition at El Paso on April 26, 1903 — and the way she handled the difficulty was tribute to her spirit and determination. A reporter described it this way:

> The fair contestant looked the queen she is.... Miss Mulhall does not ride in prim military style, but with the easy, relaxed grace of cattle men. No favors were shown her. The stakes were high and it was everybody for himself.
>
> When it came Miss Mulhall's time to show her skill a big wild setter was turned into the park and chased in a lively manner across the "dead line," about 100 yards distant from the roper.
>
> The little "queen" was after him like a flash the instant the flag fell, with hat off and curls flying in the wind.

But when Lucille cast her loop, she missed. So she gathered her rope and again raced in pursuit of her quarry. She sailed the loop over the steer's horns, and as her horse braced for the steer's impact, Lucille jumped from her saddle to tie the steer. However, the steer recovered too quickly and escaped the loop. Still Lucille didn't quit. She remounted her horse, gathered her lariat, and made another dash, catching the steer and throwing him to the ground. The reporter continued:

> Once more the rope was taut. Miss Mulhall disappeared from the saddle and again ran to the fallen captive. There was a magic twist and tie of the rope about the animal's hind legs, a kicking foreleg was mysteriously looped to these, and up went the young woman's hand as a signal that the deed was done.

The headline over the reporter's article had called Lucille a Texan. Perhaps that claim was understandable: after all, she had already bested many of the Texas men in roping. The reporter added:

> The Texan trails are literally alive with manly hearts in manly breasts that she can have her choice of any day. But little Miss Lucille is not bothering her independent young head—as yet—about matrimonial problems. She is too much in love with lariat sport to give serious attention to her cavaliers. Medals are dearer to her just now than proposals of marriage.

Life Outside the Arena

Four years later Lucille fell to the matrimonial loop, though it's not clear who threw it—she or her future husband.

From 1905 to 1915 the Mulhall show performed under various names across the country, riding in stock arenas, pastures, and on the stages of theaters known as orpheums. For those orpheum programs from 1907 to 1909, which were billed as horse operas, the performers did a shortened version of the Wild West show. They wore elaborate costumes and used their horses to perform trick riding and other acts, usually on indoor stages. Lucille's brother Charley would demonstrate riding a bucking bronc.

Vaudeville singer Martin Van Bergen, billed as a cowboy baritone, was a part of the show then known as Lucille Mulhall and Her Ranch Boys, singing "My Lucille" as Lucille rode across the stage with a spotlight following her. The show was booked into Keith's Theater in Philadelphia, the Majestic in Chicago, the Grand in Pittsburgh, and other theaters in Memphis, St. Louis, Louisville, Minneapolis, and Omaha. And somewhere among all of the performances, Lucille found time for romance, and the opportunity to defy her father.

By October 1907, the *St. Louis World* reported on rumors that she had married Martin Van Bergen. She denied the report, but in early 1908, when she was in Topeka with Van Bergen, she admitted the marriage had indeed taken place in Brooklyn, New York, on September 14, 1907. To avoid publicity, she gave her name on the civil marriage certificate as Lucille Vandeever, using her father's birth name (he had changed his name to Mulhall after being adopted by an uncle). She told reporters that because of her Catholic upbringing, she intended to have a second ceremony in a church. Such a church ceremony apparently never occurred.

Lucille, her waistline obviously changing, performed through the show season of 1908, and on January 29, 1909, gave birth to a son, William Logan Van Bergen—his middle name honoring one of her dead brothers. The child did not find a true welcome from his parents. Almost immediately after the baby's birth, Lucille returned to the show circuit, riding with the 101 Ranch Real Wild West Show in Ponca City, Oklahoma, in the spring. By fall Lucille had deposited her infant son with his paternal grandparents and was on the road to the Horse Show and Interstate Livestock Show in St. Joseph, Missouri.

William Logan was the one child of a Mulhall who did not find a home with Mary Agnes on the Oklahoma ranch, perhaps because Mary Agnes was tired of child rearing. Almost certainly Zack didn't want the child to divert Lucille's attention from her work as a show performer. Furthermore, the child's father clearly wanted the little boy to be with his paternal grandparents, the Van Bergens of DeSoto County, Kansas. The boy spent much of his childhood living with them.

In all likelihood, William Logan Van Bergen was Lucille's second child. There had been a baby girl born around 1906 after a time of seclusion for Lucille and her mother. As she had done so many times before, Mary Agnes took the child into her home, naming her Margaret and raising her as a daughter. Most members of the family figured she was really a granddaughter, the firstborn of Lucille Mulhall. The name of the father remains one of speculation.

In 1914 the marriage to Van Bergen that had started in secrecy apparently ended. Van Bergen filed for divorce from Lucille in Olathe, Kansas, although there is no record with the court there that the divorce ever became final.

Lucille didn't remain alone. On April 14, 1919, she wed Tom Burnett, the son of Burk Burnett, a Fort Worth multimillionaire stockman and oil operator. The marriage ended in divorce by 1922. There were conflicting reports of the divorce settlement. The *Daily Oklahoman* reported that she "received $200,000 in

With quirt in hand and spurs on her boots,
Lucille Mulhall poses for a publicity photo
used to promote her family's Wild West
show. (Courtesy of Martha Fisch.)

cash and a deed to 5,000 acres of Texas land thought to have a large oil value."
The paper later amended its figures, saying that Mulhall received $20,000 in cash
and a deed to 15,000 acres of land. Yet another report indicated that she received
$10,000 in cash and a deed to 15,000 acres, along with $6,000 a year for ten years.

In reality the only settlement she received was a deed to land in Logan
County, Oklahoma, which included the small portion of the Mulhall ranch the
family still owned. Apparently Burnett had loaned money to Zack Mulhall in
order to clear a mortgage on the property. The divorce settlement provided
for transfer of that same land to Lucille.

There were reports of other relationships—possibly even marriages—with
Bud Ballew and J. W. McCormick, but for the most part Lucille maintained
allegiance to only one man—her father. He was a tyrant, yet she remained
devoted, perhaps because she realized she held the place in her father's life of
his dead son Logan. She was loyal to her father throughout her life.

Her divorces flouted her Catholic upbringing, no doubt shocking her
Catholic mother, who had stood by Zack through some good, lots of bad, and
much heartbreak. Lucille's experiences with motherhood appeared to be no

better than her experiences with marriage. She seldom saw her son, William Logan, because she spent so much time on the road, and he grew up not really knowing his mother or her family. Meanwhile, the girl Margaret—who may well have been Lucille's daughter—drank poison when she was twenty-two and died June 3, 1928, after five days in a hospital.

The End of the Show

If she could not hold a relationship or a family together, at least Lucille could maintain her success at roping and riding. She performed at all the major rodeos: the Calgary Stampede, Cheyenne Frontier Days, the Pendleton Round-Up, and dozens of minor shows. She won the title of Champion Lady Steer Roper of the World, at the Winnipeg Stampede in 1913.

At times Lucille rode in her father's shows, and at times she rode for other Wild West companies. For a time, a show in her own name, Lucille Mulhall's Round-up, played in such venues as the American Royal Live Stock Show in Kansas City, in Milwaukee, and in El Dorado, Kansas, at the Round-up and Oil Celebration. The final performance of that show took place in Vernon, Texas, in a three-day run over the Fourth of July 1917. The end came not because Lucille sought to quit as the first woman to produce rodeos, but because the United States had entered World War I and national attention then centered on world security rather than rodeo and Wild West shows.

During her years of performing, Lucille had exhibited a natural ability with animals, particularly horses. She could make them do what other people had no success at. Though she rode many horses through her life, no doubt the one she trained the best was Governor. She said:

> My system of training consists of three things—patience, persever-ance, and gentleness. Gentleness I consider one of the greatest factors in successful training.... Governor, the horse I ride in our exhibitions, was raised and trained on our ranch. He has nearly forty tricks (as we call them), and is capable of learning many more. He can shoot a gun; pull off a man's coat and put it on again; can roll a barrel; can walk up stairs and down again—a difficult feat; is perfect in the march and the Spanish trot; extends the forelegs so that an easy mount may be made; kneels, lies down, and sits up; indeed, he has received a good education, and does nearly everything but talk. He often utters sounds that would seem to indicate his desire to talk. "Grunts of satisfaction," we call the sounds!

Though Lucille rode the horse Sam for roping and used Governor as her trick horse, she rode other Mulhall ranch mounts as well, including Tinkle and Edy-Cee, a horse trained by her younger sister Mildred.

As might be expected, Lucille had her share of mishaps and injuries. Some no doubt occurred out on the ranch or in practice arenas, far from the pencils and notepads of reporters, but others happened in full public view. At a show in 1905 in Madison Square Garden in New York City, Lucille raced her horse across the arena, leaning from the saddle to snatch a handkerchief from the ground. In this case, however, she missed the handkerchief, lost her balance, and was dragged by her horse before throwing herself free. The incident didn't keep her down for long. She soon had her horse in hand, was remounted, and performed the trick with success.

When the show played at Keith's Theater in Philadelphia in 1907, reporter Hildebrand Fitzgerald wrote of Lucille's background, including information about one accident when she was sixteen:

> The accident occurred in a relay race, at the end of the first quarter. As she jumped from one horse to mount another, a rider back of her swerved suddenly and ran her down, inflicting very painful injuries, compelling her to remain in plaster casts until torn ligaments had properly united again. By careful and skillful attention, she was completely restored.

In that same interview, Lucille is quoted as telling Fitzgerald: "Some people...thought I would never ride again, but they failed to properly estimate the kind of material that constitutes the make-up of a girl reared on a great ranch of the boundless West!"

In yet another incident, Lucille stunned women and children in the audience at a performance in Chicago when she accidentally killed the steer she roped, gaining her notoriety—and criminal charges—from the Society for the Prevention of Cruelty to Animals. One paper reported: "Several hundred men, women and children saw a badly frightened steer killed yesterday at the Coliseum by the woman roper, Lucille Mulhall. When the animal, struggling feebly as it was dragged about the ring by the young woman, gave a convulsive gasp and became unconscious, a cry of disgust and horror arose from the audience...."

Charges were filed against Lucille, Zack, and one of the cowboys involved with the show. A judge fined Zack and the cowboy, but dismissed charges against Lucille, not believing the small woman — she stood only a little over five feet tall and weighed around one hundred pounds — could have caused the steer's death.

After the demise of her own company, Lucille Mulhall's Round-up, Lucille continued to perform in various shows along with brother Charley, who eventually made his way to Hollywood along with other Wild West show riders like Tom Mix, who had been a part of the Mulhall operation. Meanwhile, her sister Bossie (Agnes) and then later Bossie's husband had died, leaving another child — a young son — for Mary Agnes to raise. Georgia and her daughter Mildred were living in Florida.

Even though Charley was involved in films, he performed with Lucille through the 1930s when he returned to Oklahoma to produce rodeos. She made her last public appearance — riding in a car and not on a horse — in September 1940 at the Cherokee Strip Parade in Ponca City.

Lucille's parents had died within months of each other in 1931, Mary Agnes on January 30 and Zack on September 18. The hard times that hit the United States during the Depression struck the Mulhall ranch and family as well. Finances had been drained by show performances and then by Mary Agnes's illness, so by the time her parents died, Lucille found she owned a ranch that was only a fraction of its original size. She rented the land to farmers, and when Charley (who had already been married and divorced once) again said vows — with Esther Childers of Guthrie, Oklahoma — Lucille, Charley, and Esther raised milk cows and hogs and sold produce to bring in money from the ranch.

Perhaps she had always imbibed a bit, but without her father to lean on, and facing poverty, Lucille began drinking heavily. At times she found herself back in the spotlight, as in 1935 when she and Pawnee Bill Lillie led the 89'er Parade in Guthrie. But such appearances soon ceased. On December 21, 1940, Lucille Mulhall, the Queen of the Range, died in an automobile accident at age fifty-five.

Lucille Mulhall's renown continued after her death. She was inducted into the Rodeo Hall of Fame at the National Cowboy Hall of Fame (now the National Cowboy and Western Heritage Museum) in 1975 and is also an honoree of the National Cowgirl Hall of Fame in Fort Worth, Texas.

Although her performances in western shows across the nation put Lucille Mulhall in the spotlight and made her a famous name in the world of rodeo, at heart she was a devoted rancher's daughter. She learned how to work on the range, perhaps to live up to the expectations of her father or in an attempt to somehow fill the void caused by the death of her brother Logan. She learned the skills that gave her fame while roping and branding calves for her father, and for herself. Along the way she gained the respect of cowboys, both on the ranch and in the arena, and she clearly earned her reputation. With her superlative abilities in riding and roping, moving cattle, branding, and other ranch skills, she set the bar exceedingly high for all women who followed her and aspired to the title of cowgirl.

Bertha Kaepernik Blancett

The Woman Who Stayed Aboard

M. J. VAN DEVENTER

W hat was it that pushed Bertha Kaepernik Blancett to pursue a career in a man's world at the turn of the twentieth century? What driving force motivated her to perform heroic stunts on horseback and fearlessly ride bucking broncs?

Was it her early upbringing on a Colorado ranch, living in a house that was part soddy, part dugout, working alongside her German immigrant parents and six siblings? Or was it some innate determination to escape the back-breaking rigors of ranching and carve a name for herself outside the boundaries imposed on women at that time? Did she have a natural-born sense of courage, or did she find and nurture that courage in the face of challenge?

Some believe her incredible drive to succeed began on a warm summer day in 1888 on the Great Plains of eastern Colorado when William Kaepernik placed his five-year-old daughter on the back of a horse. "Now Bertha, be sure you stay aboard," he commanded. "If you get off, there may not be anyone around to put you back on." He gave her the job of riding an old horse along a path to keep the cattle from straying into the garden—a daunting job and a good lesson in self-reliance for any five-year-old.

William Kaepernik could not know that simple act of telling Bertha to "stay aboard" would be one of the defining moments of her life—a moment that would carry her through a spectacular rodeo career and into the arena of the country's top Wild West shows. From then on, whenever the family could not find her, they looked for the old horse. Even when she had advanced to more spirited horses, she was never afraid. There was not a horse she could not or would not ride. She was a true pioneer in women's rodeo competition and one of the greatest of all women riders.

The Cheyenne Surprise

Bertha's parents, German-born William and Federico Kaepernik, had emigrated from Germany to Cleveland, Ohio, and then moved west in 1886 with their seven children to begin a new life near Atwood, Colorado. It was a hard life on that one hundred sixty acres, and Bertha—the youngest of the seven children—learned the meaning of the word "toil" when she was barely out of diapers.

Bertha's youth was spent working on the family's ranch and trailing her father, helping him work the cattle. She was riding after the cattle, gradually learning about horses and their ways, and how to break them—how to train them to accept riders. She was strong and healthy from an almost constant life in the saddle between days at school or between school terms. She rode with the same ability, and all of the confidence, exhibited by the men she knew.

When Bertha had leisure time, she competed with men in local rodeos, a pastime then uncommon for girls. These were casual riding and roping contests held at roundups. These informal tournaments had no arenas, no paying spectators, no entry fees, no rules, and no prizes. This was considered cowboy fun, a way for cowboys from neighboring ranches to get together and show off their horsemanship and ranching skills.

By the time she was twenty-one, in 1904, Bertha had matured into a very attractive young woman, with pretty brown hair, bright brown eyes that sparkled, a cheerful smile, and the firm, quick step of an athlete. She was also full of spunk and ambition, determined to prove to the world what an expert horsewoman she was and that she could ride not just a horse, but any horse. She had mastered the art of knowing horses and being athletic on them, standing up or sitting down.

Bertha's opportunity came when the promoters of Cheyenne Frontier Days announced that women would be allowed to compete in the upcoming celebration—a first in rodeo history. It is doubtful the promoters were feeling any pressure from women to compete. And did they even know of any women who would want to compete? Did they really expect any takers? Both questions yield doubtful answers. More than likely, it was merely a publicity stunt to round up interest in what was then a fledgling rodeo.

Cheyenne Frontier Days at that time was only eight years old, a mere infant of a rodeo that suffered competition from other rodeos in the region. It would be a long time before Cheyenne Frontier Days earned the slogan "The Grandaddy of 'em All." The announcement welcoming women riders did serve its purpose. It aroused a stir of interest—especially in Bertha.

She took the promoters' dare. She would compete in bronc riding—roaring into the rodeo arena aboard an ornery horse whose only goal was to throw her off. Competitors had to provide their own stock at that time, so she needed to

Portrait of Bertha Blancett, undated.
(Courtesy of the Donald C. &
Elizabeth M. Dickinson Research
Center, National Cowboy and
Western Heritage Museum.)

find an intense, unbroken animal that would give her a challenging ride. She talked Len Sherwin, a well-known Colorado rancher and horse trader, into lending her the bronc she needed.

Why did Sherwin say yes? Perhaps it was because he had been a romantic about the West ever since 1883, when he came to the wild prairie of Colorado with his parents, the Augustus Sherwins. He also had a penchant for the thrills and adventures the West of his era provided. Sherwin loved horses as much as Bertha did, and maybe he wanted to live vicariously through Bertha's desire to perform in a man's world. According to Nell Brown Propst (writing in *The Ketchpen,* published by the Rodeo Historical Society), Sherwin told Bertha, "You can take Tombstone. He's my best. You'll get a hell of a ride on him."

Going to Cheyenne was a bold undertaking for Bertha, who had to counter the objections of her parents, worried about the dangers to a young woman traveling alone on the prairie. Bertha's defenses were solid. She had tamed a number of wild horses. She knew she could ride a bucking horse as well as anyone, and she was eager for the opportunity to prove it.

It was an arduous trip. There was no road or path to guide Bertha across the plains on her way to Cheyenne, which was more than one hundred miles from Atwood. She followed the tracks of the narrow-gauge railroad, the

Prairie Dog Special, from Sterling, Colorado, to Cheyenne. Mounted on a riding horse, Bertha led the unbroken Tombstone across the high, open country.
She packed food for herself, oats for the horses, and a bedroll. She slept in a
railway depot her first night, tying the horses outside. On the second night, she
begged shelter from a farm family when she was caught in a horrific rainstorm.

The Ketchpen article notes, "The prairies of eastern Colorado get only fourteen or so inches of moisture a year, but sometimes it comes in big batches,
accompanied by life-threatening hail and lightning. Seasoned plainsmen hope
to avoid being caught in the open." Bertha was definitely in harm's way when
the storm boiled off the eastern slope of the Rockies.

Out in that open country, with wind and rain beating down on her,
Bertha may have found encouragement in thinking of other women who
were following paths of independence. Some women had come alone to
homestead on the frontier. Others pursued occupations unusual for women
of the day. One, Sarah Ayres, drove a team to deliver mail, and she did it in
all kinds of weather.

When Bertha reached Cheyenne, she was met with great surprise. The
rodeo promoters had not expected any women to actually enter. She was the
only woman who had answered the call. She was also met by a torrential
downpour. The rain turned the arena in front of the rodeo stands into a quagmire,
and the cowboys at first refused to compete, claiming it was too dangerous to
ride bucking broncs in the deep mud. Bertha said she would ride.

A newspaper account told what happened next:

The Frontier Days crowd may have laughed at the pretty girl mounting
her horse in the chute. They undoubtedly made dire—and perhaps
ribald—predictions. No doubt, the crowd laughed and scoffed at her
as she mounted her bronc in the chute. But their laughter quickly
turned to awe, and ultimately admiration, as she catapulted into the
arena on the back of Len Sherwin's horse. They watched intently as
she performed.

Tombstone gave Bertha, and the crowd, a wild performance to remember.
He could not buck Bertha off. When he failed to do that, he reared on his
hind legs, a move fraught with danger for even a seasoned rider, and plunged
into a bucking frenzy. Then the worst happened. He fell backward, pulling a
widow-maker, as old-time cowboys called the move. The fun was gone in the
stands. A collective groan emerged from the crowd.

Determined to "stay aboard" as her father had commanded, Bertha slid to one side as the horse went down: she was still aboard as Tombstone exploded to his feet. The crowd screamed, amazed at the feat they had just witnessed — and astonished it was performed by a young woman.

Candy Moulton, a Wyoming writer and historian, continues the story: "When offered a second chance to ride, Bertha quickly claimed it. The horse bested her, tossing her over its head and into the dirt. But Bertha had tenacity. She stepped back up to Tombstone, climbed aboard, and rode until the horse finally bowed in exhausted defeat."

A report in the *Denver Post* noted Tombstone was a bronc few would have mounted in fun. The reporter observed that "Bertha sat straight in her saddle while she rode him to a standstill. The crowd cheered themselves weak at the sight of a woman riding as they had not conceived that a woman could ride." He added that Bertha left the arena in triumph "without a glance at the howling mob."

Warren Richardson, an early-day Cheyenne Frontier Days chairman, recalled the performance: "Undaunted by the rain and mud, Bertha saddled her wild horse, then stepped aboard. Bertha rode one of the worst buckers I have ever seen, and she stayed on him all the time. Part of the time he was up in the air on his hind feet. She rode him to a finish and the crowd went wild with enthusiasm."

As Bertha made the one-hundred-mile trek home, again mounted on her riding horse, she wondered why she was leading Tombstone. He was now broken. So instead, she rode the bronc all the way back to Sterling, delivering the horse to Len Sherwin, who was astonished at her ability to tame Tombstone. One of the hands on Sherwin's ranch looked at Bertha and complained, "You've spoilt him. Now he will never be any good for bucking."

Showing Her Stuff

It seems fitting that Bertha would have had such a triumphant epiphany in Wyoming, which calls itself the Equality State because it was the first to grant voting rights to women (on December 10, 1869, when it was still a U.S. territory). When Bertha made her historic Cheyenne ride in 1904, Wyoming women had had the right to vote for thirty-five years. The suffrage movement was gaining national momentum, leading up to passage of the Nineteenth Amendment to the Constitution in 1920, which granted voting rights to all women in the United States.

In spite of Bertha's desire to compete on an equal basis with men, it seems doubtful that this national suffrage campaign was ever an issue that spurred her, or other cowgirls, to make a name for themselves in rodeo. More likely, her internal drive to excel on a horse and in an arena pushed her harder than any desire to make a social or political statement. She just loved the thrill of competition.

Mary Lou LeCompte, in *Cowgirls of the Rodeo: Pioneer Professional Athletes*, writes, "Women like Dorothy Morrell, Lucille Mulhall, Prairie Rose Henderson, and Bertha Blancett felt they had already achieved feminist goals such as Crystal Eastman expressed: 'How to arrange the world so that women can be human beings, with a chance to exercise their infinitely varied ways, instead of being destined by the accident of their sex to one field of activity, housework and child raising.'"

Bertha realized, with Len Sherwin's advice, that if she intended to continue in rodeo, she would need to concentrate on making a good ride, and she gave up breaking horses. She rode in shows in Colorado—at Loveland and Fort Collins—in 1904, and she was well received by the crowd when she returned to Cheyenne in 1905 and competed in one of the cowgirl bronc-riding contests.

Bertha achieved another milestone in 1905 when Sherwin, his brother Claude, and a friend, Joe Baker, organized the Sherwin Wild West Show. The trio lined up an impressive array of talent, riders who pitted their skills against local challengers wherever the show played. The Sherwin crew included champion riders Sam Brownell and Irvin Monette, and Bertha Kaepernik, with a title bestowed on her by the Sherwins: champion lady rider of the world. Bertha was the only woman in the show.

Sherwin's show, though popular, lasted only a few months. It was plagued by bad weather. Winds blew down the tent, torrential rains kept the crowds away, expenses piled up, and the show was forced to close. But people never forgot the show, and they never forgot Bertha Kaepernik. Her rodeo career was under way.

In late 1906, she joined the Pawnee Bill Wild West Show, which originated in the small rural town of Pawnee, Oklahoma. The show was the brainchild of Major Gordon "Pawnee Bill" Lillie, one of the most colorful men to ever live in Oklahoma.

Lillie's interest in the West was sparked early in his youth by a visit from his Kansas cousins, and he began reading pulp fiction extolling the exploits of William F. "Buffalo Bill" Cody and James Butler "Wild Bill" Hickok. In 1883, the year Bertha was born, the federal government appointed him as an interpreter and escort to a group of Pawnee Indians performing with Buffalo Bill's Wild West Show. Thanks to his good working relationship with the Indians, he acquired the nickname Pawnee Bill.

In 1888 — the same year Bertha's father hoisted her onto a horse and said "stay aboard" — Pawnee Bill broke with Cody and organized his own Far East show, featuring an Oriental theme, which eventually evolved into his historic Wild West Show. Lillie was a great showman, and his fame was further enhanced after he became the subject of several dime novels.

From 1855 to 1930, at least one hundred fifteen different Wild West shows came into being in the United States, ranging in size, talent, and extravagance. Buffalo Bill and Pawnee Bill and the Miller Brothers from the 101 Ranch were the best-known producers of these shows, most of which included cowgirls like Bertha, who was becoming increasingly comfortable, and famous, in this life.

Bertha left the Pawnee Bill Wild West Show after one season and signed on with the newly formed Miller Brothers 101 Ranch Wild West Show, which had its headquarters near Ponca City, Oklahoma. The 101 Ranch was founded in 1892 by George W. Miller, and he and his sons, George Lee, Joseph, and Zack, built it into a 110,000-acre diversified commercial empire. The show toured for many years across the United States and Europe, and the ranch became the setting for a number of western films.

At the 101 Ranch, Bertha was performing in an environment that provided a unique blend of myth and reality. The Millers believed that by memorializing

Bertha Blancett riding Snake in a bucking contest in Pendleton, Oregon, undated. (Courtesy of the Donald C. & Elizabeth M. Dickinson Research Center, National Cowboy and Western Heritage Museum.)

Bertha Blancett and her husband, Dell, at an Oregon rodeo in 1911. (Courtesy of the Donald C. & Elizabeth M. Dickinson Research Center, National Cowboy and Western Heritage Museum.)

their riders and ropers on film, they could keep alive the old traditions their father had instilled in them. In his book *The Real Wild West,* writer Michael Wallis says that "by producing their own creative concoction, the Miller Brothers ensured the 101 would endure as one of the last links with the Old West." And it did endure longer than most. After a break to raise livestock for the government during World War I, the Wild West show reopened in 1925, embellished with ballet, Ziegfeld dancers, and elephants. But in 1931, the 101 Ranch fell to bankruptcy, a victim of the Depression.

Sources are conflicting about the turning point in Bertha's life when she met a young man named Dell Blancett. Willard Porter, author of *Who's Who in Rodeo,* indicates she met Blancett at the 101, where he was a world champion steer wrestler and bulldogger who had even replaced the famous African American bulldogger Bill Pickett for a season when Pickett was injured. Mary Lou LeCompte, however, writing in *Cowgirls of the Rodeo,* says they met at the Pendleton Round-Up in Oregon in 1910. Bertha lists 1909 as the year of their meeting and marriage, according to Rodeo Historical Society records at the National Cowboy and Western Heritage Museum.

Bertha was attracted to the tall, nice-looking man with the affable personality that endeared him to others. He was as gentle with horses as he was with Bertha, a trait she strongly admired in him. They were wed in Detroit, their marriage signifying the pooling of two considerable talents.

In a ball park in Endicott, Washington, Bertha and Dell began regularly staging trick riding, roping, and bulldogging events. Bertha became Dell's hazer in bulldogging—the person who rides on a second horse from the chute in order to keep the steer in a straight line, preventing it from turning away from the bulldogger's horse. Bertha was excellent at controlling the steer so that Dell had the best chance to plunge from his horse and wrestle the animal off its feet in winning time.

In 1910 the couple began working as trick riders for the Bison Moving Picture Company in Los Angeles, with Tom Mix, Bebe Daniels, and Hoot Gibson. Bertha and Dell had known Mix and Gibson in the rodeo world— Tom Mix when they worked together at the 101 Ranch, and Hoot Gibson when he had been a world champion cowboy.

Rodeo promoter Foghorn Clancy noted in an article in the May 1942 *Hoofs and Horns,*

> Old timers will remember those Bison pictures. They were plenty rough. The actors really did some real riding in those thrillers. It was a common occurrence to put a rider on a horse, rig up a running W, a piece of equipment designed to trip up the steed, start them off at breakneck speed, and then turn the horse out, the steed turning flip-flops and the rider looking out for himself as best he could.

One can easily see Bertha and Dell in this challenging, exciting environment, with Bertha ever-hungry for new adventure.

In *Cowgirls of the Rodeo,* Mary Lou LeCompte wrote,

> At the time, the western films depicted remarkably authentic western women, who were self-reliant, athletic, and also appealing. Rodeo stars like Dorothy Morrell, Mildred Douglas, and Mabel Strickland also portrayed these roping, riding, robust cowgirls. They sometimes captured bandits at gunpoint, or galloped wildly across the plains with the cowboys. Their films helped publicize rodeo and maintain the image of true cowgirls in the public imagination. While in Hollywood, Bertha issued a $10,000 challenge for any cowgirl who could beat her in a bronc riding contest. She had also developed quite a local reputation by winning steer roping matches against the cowboys.

LeCompte doesn't mention if any cowgirl accepted Bertha's challenge.

Championship Days

While Bertha and Dell were busy making movies, rodeo had been slowly changing from casual contests at annual roundups to a serious competitive sport. Rodeo cowgirls were among the first women in the United States to achieve recognition as professional athletes.

In 1911, the first year women officially competed at the Pendleton Round-Up, Bertha entered the bucking horse, trick riding, fancy roping, and relay racing competition. Foghorn Clancy wrote of those relay races: "For the girls in those days, these were by no means child's play. They were for a distance of two miles, and they had to change horses each half mile."

A member of a relay team had to be tough to turn a spirited horse into the change station and bring it to a stop because after one of these horses was warmed up, it was eager to run. Then the contestant was required to take the saddle off the horse she had just ridden and place it on the mount to be ridden by the next relay-team member, and do the cinching herself. The horses were lively, fast, and anxious to get away.

That year, Bertha won the women's bucking horse championship at the Pendleton Round-Up, and returned in 1912 to repeat her victory. She also won day money in women's fancy roping, the maverick race, and the coed

Bertha Blancett posed on horseback, undated. (Courtesy of the Donald C. & Elizabeth M. Dickinson Research Center, National Cowboy and Western Heritage Museum.)

potato race at the 1912 Los Angeles Rodeo. She went to Australia to work with the Atkinson Show for nine months in 1912.

In 1914 she was awarded another saddle for winning the women's bucking bronc contest at Pendleton. This saddle—an exquisite warm brown leather, with richly detailed floral patterns and engraved silver conchos and a silver horn—is now in the permanent collection at the National Cowboy and Western Heritage Museum in Oklahoma City.

That same year she missed, by just two points, winning the Pendleton Round-Up's All-Around Championship—the title that had always gone to a man. That was much too close for the men. New rodeo rules were established in 1915, defining the events in which women could compete against other women and changing the rules by which women competed. Up until that time, the women had competed under the same rules as the men.

During this time, there were few places where women's bronc riding was a competitive event; it was usually presented as an exhibition. Bertha practically quit riding at the competitive events, choosing instead to ride buckers in exhibition as a way to show that women could give a good performance in this category. Her reputation, and the fact she was so well known to the rodeo public, made her an attraction that helped the box office. She was engaged to ride exhibition and perform at scores of rodeos in the United States and Canada.

Most women bronc riders of the day rode with their stirrups hobbled—that is, tied together beneath the horse in the interests of stability and safety. But Bertha was one of the few who rode "slick"—with the stirrups allowed to move freely. Women who rode with hobbled stirrups were actually likely to be at greater risk for injury when a horse fell, and they were generally not judged or scored as well as those who rode slick. Perhaps Bertha never hobbled her stirrups because of the possible danger. Also, Bertha's adventurous spirit, the need to conquer new challenges, seems to have been a strong motivation for riding slick.

According to Richard Rattenbury, curator of history at the National Cowboy and Western Heritage Museum, the Cheyenne Frontier Days Rodeo and the Calgary Stampede were important in establishing women's place in rodeo and creating the first cowgirl superstars. By 1916, more than twenty rodeos held cowgirl contests, and as many as one hundred women were pursuing the sport professionally. Although World War I diminished arena competition for a time, these pioneer cowgirls already had proven their athletic ability, showmanship, and determination.

During the World War I lull in bucking contests, Bertha took on Roman race riding, a dangerous routine where the rider stands atop two horses while they are racing in tandem around the arena. Bertha made the fastest time ever recorded for a female Roman rider for a half-mile in the Walla Walla, Washington, rodeo, and for a quarter-mile at the Pendleton Round-Up. Roman racing was one of Bertha's favorite and most exciting events and illustrates her continuing quest to succeed and master other aspects of the rodeo sport.

Amazed audiences must have felt she had each foot in a separate world. She would stand upright, urging her galloping horses forward, her left leg braced on the back of one, her right leg bending with the movements of the other horse. The crowds did not believe this daring competitor was a young woman. But they admitted she was good—so good she often gave her competition a huge advantage by facing her mounts in the opposite direction at the moment of send-off. And still, she won.

Bertha never competed in regular straightaway racing because of her weight, a solid 165 pounds. But in Roman racing, straddling a pair of horses, she was able to shift her weight on the backs of her mounts. She won the Roman relays at Pendleton three years in a row.

Last Miles of a Long Ride

Then the war changed her life forever. Both Bertha and Dell had strong patriotic feelings for the country that had given them a life they loved. At the Pendleton Round-Up, Dell helped organize a cowboy cavalry troop to join the U.S. forces in World War I. On the morning the cowboys were to take their physicals, Dell kissed his wife goodbye and announced, "When you see me next, I'll be a soldier in the U.S. Cavalry."

Dell was a strong and vigorous man. He could ride bucking horses and wrestle an eight-hundred-pound steer onto its back. Like other rodeo contestants, he was athletic and spent a great deal of his time outdoors. He believed he had a lot to give to his country at war, and it never occurred to him he might not pass the physical. Perhaps Bertha felt a secret relief when he failed the physical. But she had faced danger most of her life to do what was important to her, and she could understand how Dell would want to do the same.

And so she kissed her husband goodbye again after he enlisted in the Canadian Cavalry, which had less stringent physical requirements. Dell served with the prestigious Lord Strathmore Horse Unit. While Dell was away, Bertha took the quietest, tamest job of her career, working in a print shop. It was as if she had put her life—her career, and her determination—on hold until Dell came home from the war.

*Bertha Blancett with General de
Gaulle of France after working out
her horse for the Indians Field Days
in Yosemite National Park, undated.
(Courtesy of the Donald C. &
Elizabeth M. Dickinson Research
Center, National Cowboy and Western
Heritage Museum.)*

Dell Blancett, the only love of Bertha's life, never came home. The man who could face all the open dangers of bucking horses, angry steers, flailing hooves, and horns of wild bulls in the arena was as vulnerable as any other man to the unseen menace on the Western Front. Bertha was widowed in 1918 when a German sniper shot her husband to death in France. Bertha never remarried. When she returned to the Pendleton Round-Up in 1920 and 1921 as a guest of the rodeo committee, she wore a gold star on her sleeve in memory of her beloved husband.

Rodeo had been her whole life, so Bertha continued in the rodeo world, serving as a pickup rider—snatching riders from the backs of pitching broncs—on her favorite Morgan horse, Yuma. (She helped now and then as a pickup rider until she was sixty years old. That cowboys would trust this sixty-year-old woman to rescue them at the end of a ride was further proof of her expert horsemanship.)

In 1922, when she was thirty-nine, Bertha went to Yosemite National Park to guide on the horse trails, a job she held for nine years. Bertha once told a newspaper reporter, "I didn't mind the novices on the Monday to Saturday expeditions there, but I cared little for the people who considered themselves 'experienced' in the high country. They think they know it all."

Bertha Blancett, Champion Lady Rider of the World, Pendleton Round-Up, Oregon, 1914. (Courtesy of the Donald C. & Elizabeth M. Dickinson Research Center, National Cowboy and Western Heritage Museum.)

It was during those years at Yosemite that a young army colonel named Dwight D. Eisenhower told her he had never seen anyone ride as she did. He had watched her as she straightened out a balky tourist horse on a rocky, backcountry trail and was extremely impressed. Years later, Bertha relished that compliment with pride when the colonel became a general, a hero of World War II, and later, president of the United States.

Bertha spent a total of forty-two years in the world of rodeo, ending her career as a pickup rider at the close of the 1934 season and then retiring to a modest duplex in Porterville, California. After a lifetime of thrills, daring stunts, and the applause of thousands, she was comfortably ready to leave the rodeo arena.

Foghorn Clancy, who covered her career with more diligence than any other reporter, wrote of her retirement years:

> She has had her day, her career, and she is not sorry. She is content to
> live a quiet life and she loves to let her memory run back over the days of
> the thundering hoofbeats of the rodeo, and likes to talk about the old days
> when she and Dell used to travel the rodeos together with their friends.

Retirement brought Bertha new achievements. In 1958, when she was seventy-five, she was still agile enough to serve as the grand marshal of the Porterville Round-up Parade. Then in 1975, at the age of ninety-two, she received what she considered the highest honor of her life. She was inducted into the Rodeo Hall of Fame at the National Cowboy and Western Heritage Museum as one of the country's foremost pioneer rodeo cowgirls. The occasion in Oklahoma City included a luncheon in her honor and box seats at the National Finals Rodeo. The following year, at the age of ninety-three, she visited Sterling, Colorado—the home of her youth in Logan County—and gave advice on the care of horses to admiring 4-H girls.

With her spurs put away and her beautiful championship saddle showcased in the museum, Bertha lived quietly and savored the sweetness of her memories. She was an enthusiastic member of the Emblem Club, a women's social organization, missing only three meetings during her many years in Porterville. Her hearing remained keen, and her eyesight was good enough to allow her to read her favorite magazine, *Persimmon Hill*, published by the National Cowboy and Western Heritage Museum. She loved dressing up in her Sunday finery, which usually included a flamboyant hat, and driving herself around in her 1958 Plymouth, almost up until the time of her death in 1981 at age 98.

Legacy of a Strong Woman

Was Bertha Kaepernik Blancett a "wild woman" of the Old West?

Occasionally there were instances in which a man tested her values. But cowboys quickly learned that even though she followed an unconventional dream for a woman, she was nevertheless always a "good girl," upholding the standards and traditions instilled in her by her German parents. "I was always a lady," she said many years after her rodeo career ended, "and they always treated me as such."

Still, when a Wild West show pulled into town, men on the lookout for girls figured that one riding with the show would be appropriately wild. In that sense, Bertha was not wild. She was strong. Most of the time, she did not even need to worry about protecting herself. Her teammates in the rodeos and the shows saw to it that no local Romeo bothered her.

Everyone liked Bertha. Billy Armour, who traveled with the Sherwin Wild West Show and was a real-life cowboy as well, said that during his long years in the business, one girl stood out as a dancer. "It was Bertha," he said, "the best dance partner I ever had. She was very much a girl, a lot of fun."

Bertha Blancett followed her ambition to be an expert horsewoman and rodeo rider when it meant stepping into a world that belonged to men. In so

Bertha Blancett in her later years, no date. (Courtesy of the Donald C. & Elizabeth M. Dickinson Research Center, National Cowboy and Western Heritage Museum.)

doing, she was courageous and determined, carving out an action-packed career filled with high drama and danger—in a most important sense, she was a true "wild woman." It's easy to imagine that the thread of motivation that ran through her life was the childhood memory of being placed on a horse by her father and being told to "stay aboard."

Her daring performances thrilled thousands of people throughout the country, and she mastered riding some of the toughest horses ever placed into women's competition in the largest rodeos in the United States and Canada. More than that, she helped pave the way for other women to step into the rodeo arena and win. She was among those early cowgirls who earned their spurs and buckles through hard work and a gritty resolve to win, often competing with men who had advantages in size, practical clothing, and the ability to ride astride without censure. Women, on the other hand, Bertha included, often wore blouses and wide, split skirts—hers were usually of leather—and sometimes rode sidesaddle, even while chasing cattle.

Bertha was a fine role model for the women who followed her, in that she was willing to challenge the accepted gender roles of her time. Her story became an inspiration to many riders: rodeo champions like steer roper Lucille Mulhall, trick riders Tad Lucas, Lorena Trickey, and Florence Randolph, bucking horse champion Fannie Sperry Steele, relay riders Mabel

Strickland, Fox Hastings, Bea Kirnan, and Vera McGinnis, bronc rider Alice Greenough, and barrel racer Charmayne James.

Bertha followed the careers of those who came after her, taking pride in their accomplishments. She reveled in the 1920s and 1930s, which marked a "golden age" in women's participation in rodeo. She watched with sadness, too, as the place of female contestants virtually disappeared in the 1940s with Gene Autry's monopoly of big-time rodeo. Autry introduced glamorous "ranch girls" dressed in flashy western-style costumes—women with little or no rodeo experience—at Madison Square Garden and other major rodeo venues in the 1940s, encouraging male-dominated rodeo organizations to ignore women as serious participants. Bertha said of this switch, "I was always grateful I had the opportunity to perform and compete before times changed."

In 1948 the Girls Rodeo Association was founded to ensure women's future participation in legitimate rodeo competition. "All-girl" rodeos gained prominence in the 1950s and 1960s, but are now less common. Today, under the auspices of the Women's Professional Rodeo Association, female rodeo athletes concentrate on barrel racing, a timed event with more than $2 million in annual prize money. Second only to bull riding in popularity among today's rodeo fans, this timed event combines superb horsemanship with all-out speed.

Looking at Bertha's legacy, Richard Rattenbury said:

Certainly, Bertha's greatest symbolic contribution to rodeo sport involved her bold challenge to compete against the men in bronc riding at the 1904 Cheyenne Frontier Days. Although her stalwart performance on a dangerously muddy field was only an exhibition, it clearly broke the gender barrier in rough stock competition and opened the door to other female bronc riders and steer wrestlers in what would become the golden age of women's rodeo during the 1920s.

Bertha stayed the course her father had directed. That compelling command to "stay aboard" served her well throughout her career. She was, in the term coined by western writer Wallace Stegner, a "sticker"—a pioneer with the guts to stick to a goal and succeed. Bertha seemed driven to succeed by that seed planted so early in her life. She had the gumption and the determination to place herself firmly in the man's world of rodeo competition and "stay aboard."

Part Four

The Almost Outlaws

⚬ 8 ⚬

Cattle Kate

Homesteader or Cattle Thief?

Lori Van Pelt

On a sunny summer Saturday in 1889, Ellen Watson and her fourteen-year-old employee, John DeCorey, walked to the nearby Shoshone Indian encampment not far from the Sweetwater River. While there, Ellen, a tall, square-faced woman, purchased a pair of intricately beaded deerskin moccasins. So pleased was she with the beautiful design, she wore the shoes home. But she would not be able to enjoy her purchase for long. When Ellen and John arrived at her homestead, they discovered that her recently branded cattle had been driven from her corral. Six angry stockmen confronted Ellen.

Cattle rustling had been rampant in Wyoming Territory. Ellen's newly branded animals had piqued the suspicions of a local stock detective, who told the stockmen that she had stolen and branded their missing mavericks—unbranded calves—as her own. As a homesteader living in the midst of prime grazing ground, Ellen, who was also known as Ella, had earlier risked the ire of her cattleman neighbors by settling on what they considered range open for their exclusive use. Her stubborn refusals to move and her conspicuously growing cattle herd further fueled their anger and mistrust.

Now, Albert Bothwell hollered at Ellen, as DeCorey recalled, telling her he'd "rope her and drag her to death if she made a move." Frightened, DeCorey watched as the stockmen made Ellen, her blue eyes fixed in fierce expression, get into Tom Sun's buggy. The gang, which also included stockmen John Durbin, Ernest McLean, Robert M. "Captain" Galbraith, and Robert Conner, then headed off to the house of James Averell, Ellen's longtime lover. DeCorey followed the buggy to Averell's place, where he witnessed Bothwell threaten Averell at gunpoint. Bothwell saw DeCorey, threatened him, too, and told him to get inside the house, and the cattlemen took off with both Ellen Watson and James Averell.

When the group left, DeCorey raced to the roadhouse that Averell owned, giving news of the kidnapping to Averell's friend Frank Buchanan and to Averell's nephew Ralph Cole. Buchanan gave chase to the abductors.

*Photograph of Ellen L. Watson with her
first husband William Pickell, taken in
Red Cloud, Nebraska, probably near the
time of their wedding, November 24, 1879.
(Courtesy of Lola Van Wey.)*

DeCorey returned to Ellen's house to comfort her unofficially adopted son, Gene Crowder, who had stayed there during the whole startling affair. The boys waited anxiously for Buchanan's return.

Hours later, Buchanan returned to the house with tragic news. The stockmen had lynched Ellen and Averell. Buchanan had shot John Durbin, a member of the lynch mob, and he himself had taken return fire but had not been hurt. His gunshot volley had not stopped the stockmen. Bothwell pushed Averell from a boulder while Ellen watched, Buchanan said, then McLean shoved her from the same rock. Her auburn hair glowed red in the afternoon sunshine as she met her fate. The pair dangled from the same limb of a pine near the Sweetwater River, grabbing for purchase on the very ropes that choked them. They didn't fall far enough to break their necks and slowly strangled to death. Struggling to breathe, Ellen kicked off her pretty new moccasins.

Ellen Watson, often referred to as Cattle Kate, was the only woman ever hanged in Wyoming. The grisly deed occurred July 20, 1889, ironically while Wyoming Territory pressed to gain statehood and faced a controversy over whether or not women's suffrage should be made part of the deal as it had been when the territory was created. Ellen Watson and James Averell became symbols of the societal contempt raging against rustlers during the latter part of the nineteenth century.

Following their deaths, factual mistakes and a healthy dose of conjecture mixed to create a legend that still survives. Gaps in the factual information—widened by Ellen's own sloppy paperwork—and numerous unresolved questions remain. Historians continue to make educated guesses about what really happened. The early story argued that Cattle Kate accepted calves in payment for sex and died because of her sexual misdeeds. However, it's likely that she was the victim of mistaken identity—at least as far as the prostitution story goes. Whether she stole cattle from her neighbors cannot be conclusively proven, begging the question of why six reputable stockmen decided to take the law into their own hands on that July afternoon. Something deep had to have been astir in the Sweetwater country to prompt such shocking behavior. Hanging a man in the name of vigilante justice was one thing, but murdering a woman was unprecedented.

Ellen did not adhere to the norms of behavior for a woman during her era. She left her first husband and is said to have lived with Averell, her employer, although they secretly married. She possessed a strong will and flaunted this in a region where the opinions of men dominated the landscape, both geographical and political. Despite the fact that Wyoming Territory granted women suffrage in 1869, men continued to wield primary influence in the political arena and through land ownership. But Ellen, a divorcée, claimed land, refused to allow her male neighbors to buy her acreage, and applied for her own cattle brand. She also kept sloppy records, retaining some important legal documents while ignoring others. All these factors contributed to her murder.

Newspapers carrying reports of the lynching confused her at first with a prostitute, Kate Maxwell, from Bessemer Bend, more than twenty miles from Ellen Watson's homestead claim. Because Ellen had been accused of rustling cattle, newspapers affixed the moniker Cattle Kate, and the name stuck. Nearly a century later, composer George Hufsmith, doing research for his tragic opera *Lynching on the Sweetwater*, discovered this error in identification. His book, *The Wyoming Lynching of Cattle Kate, 1889*, was published in 1993 and contained new information provided by Ellen's family, who had finally begun to speak about their infamous ancestor.

Much of the primary evidence about Ellen's life went up in flames when her father, Thomas Watson, burned her letters to him. Heartsick over the ruined reputation of his daughter and her gruesome demise, Watson destroyed the letters and most of her personal belongings when he returned to Kansas following the lynching.

The Education of Ellen Watson

Ellen Liddy Watson, of Canadian heritage, was sometimes called Ellie or Ella by family members. The 1861 census for Bruce County, Ontario, Canada, indicates a one-year-old child, probably Ellen, lived with Frances (Fanny) Close and Frances's single brother Andrew. Birth certificates were not given out at that time in Canada, so Ellen's birth is not recorded in the local district office. Other sources list Ellen's birth date as July 2, 1861, but this is not possible, because her brother John was born only about four months after that date.

Ellen's grand-nephew Daniel Brumbaugh extensively researched the family history and concluded that Ellen was born out of wedlock in July 1860 to Frances Close, who later married Thomas Watson, probably Ellen's father. The Watson family lived two farms away from the Close home, and records indicate Thomas Watson married Frances Close on May 15, 1861, in Grey County, Owens Sound, Canada—the wedding taking place over the objections of Thomas's father. The wedding date is listed as May 6, 1859, in the obituaries of both Thomas and Frances, but this undoubtedly represents a backdating done to protect their reputations. Frances had become pregnant out of wedlock twice, with both Ellen and John.

In March 1865, Thomas enlisted in the Union Army with the 96th New York State Volunteers, but after serving a short time he returned to Canada, a deserter. His dream of living in the United States lingered, however, and in 1877, Thomas moved his family to Kansas. They homesteaded 160 acres a few miles northwest of Lebanon in Smith County. Ellen, the first of ten surviving children, attended a one-room school and helped care for her siblings, cooking and cleaning and doing farm chores. Although she was not highly educated, she could read and write. When she was sixteen, her family sent her to Smith Center, Kansas, to work as cook and housekeeper for banker and farmer H. R. Stone, a position she held for about a year.

On November 24, 1879, Ellen married William A. Pickell, a farm laborer who owned a small acreage. Her wedding photo, one of only three known photographs of her, depicts a stout, somewhat stern-faced and respectable-looking woman in a fine dress. The marriage was not a happy one. Pickell was abusive and drank heavily. Ellen escaped. In 1883, she moved to Red Cloud, Nebraska, twelve miles from her family, and worked as a cook and domestic at the Royal Hotel. She remained in Red Cloud for a year to establish legal residency and then filed for divorce in February 1884, claiming Pickell horse-whipped her, called her names, and drove her away from their home.

Ellen then traveled to Denver City to visit a brother before moving to Cheyenne, Wyoming Territory. Ellen may have moved to Cheyenne because there was not much work available in the places she had been and because she wanted to get away from memories of her failed marriage. She disliked Cheyenne. Daniel Brumbaugh believes that the town was "too wild of a cattle town" for her. According to Brumbaugh's research, Ellen moved to Rawlins, Wyoming, in either late 1885 or early 1886, where she worked as a cook and domestic at the Rawlins House.

Ellen met James Averell, a widower and fellow Canadian, at the Rawlins House on February 24, 1886, when Averell journeyed to Rawlins to file on his third homestead claim, according to John Fales, a friend of the couple. Averell, a former military man, had been arrested on charges of murdering a Buffalo, Wyoming, rancher in 1880, while still serving in the United States Army. His case had been dismissed because a civilian court decided it did not have jurisdiction. Averell ate at the Rawlins House and enjoyed Ellen's cooking. Fales said Averell offered Ellen a job at his own roadhouse—a place that included a dining room, general store, and bar—fixing meals for customers at fifty cents each. The meeting of the two was providential, leading to a whirlwind romance and perhaps a chance for both of them to improve their opportunities for land ownership.

Averell's third claim appeared suitable for his roadhouse business because it was situated within a mile of the Oregon, California, and Mormon Trails. Even as late as 1886, some travelers still journeyed along those routes. The next nearest roadhouse to Rawlins was at Sand Creek, about twenty miles to the south, while Bessemer was about twenty-five miles north. A spur of the Central Pacific Railroad was planned to run nearby, but it was never built.

Averell's first claim was filed in 1881 under the Desert Land Act for a one hundred sixty-acre homestead on Cherry Creek near Ferris Mountain. The Desert Land Act of 1877 allowed settlers to secure sections of nonirrigated land for twenty-five cents an acre and, after residing on the land for three years, to gain title by paying an additional dollar per acre. The catch was that water had to be brought to the land, and it had to be irrigated. This experience undoubtedly taught Averell much about the importance of water in growing crops and raising livestock. In the years between his first land filing and his second, Averell married. Their child died on the day it was born, and Averell's wife succumbed to childbed fever soon after. Averell apparently abandoned this first claim, located fifteen miles south of his second claim, which he filed in 1885.

By the time he met Ellen in 1886, Averell had also filed for U.S. citizenship, and intending to raise cattle, he had attempted to secure a brand. Brands, then as now, were of the utmost importance as they denoted ownership of cattle. With cattle thefts taking place throughout the territory, often resulting in rustlers going unpunished, cattlemen relied on accurate brands to easily identify their cattle, prized assets for stockmen. Cattle sold in the mid-1880s at an average of twenty-seven dollars per head. Estimating a herd of about three hundred animals, total value could be more than eight thousand dollars—a great deal of money in a day when homesteaders could buy one hundred sixty acres for only two hundred dollars and when an entire ranch might be purchased for two thousand dollars. Theft of just a few cattle could cost a rancher a significant amount of money, so brands were revered as helpful and protective tools.

Averell applied to the Carbon County Brand Commission for a quarter-circle keyhole brand on April 16, 1885. Of the fifteen applications considered at the commission's meeting, eight were turned down—including that of Averell. No reason for Averell's rejection was listed. Brands already used in the county or in neighboring counties were not allowed because they could lead to confusion over ownership of cattle, and Averell may have unwittingly chosen a brand already in use. But the commission's action did not bode well for Averell and his new love.

In May 1886, Averell and Ellen traveled to Lander, more than one hundred miles from Rawlins, and filed an application for marriage and a marriage license. Ellen, who had been told by her parents that she was born in 1862, listed her age as twenty-four, although she was probably twenty-five. Averell, who is believed to have been born in 1851, apparently fudged on his age, listing it as thirty-one. All indications are that the couple did not want their union known. Ellen's name is given on both the marriage license and application as Ellen Liddy Andrews. The reason why remains in question. Her family believes she listed a different name so that she could still purchase a homestead under her true name, Ellen L. Watson. She later did so, but did not complete the homestead application paperwork until two years after this marriage. She may have married someone named Andrews in the interim between her marriage to Pickell and to Averell, but no documentation of such a marriage has been discovered.

Another possible reason that Ellen listed an alias stems from her failed first marriage. Even though she filed for divorce from William Pickell in 1884, it did not become official until March 1886, only two months before her marriage to Averell—so it is possible she did not know she was divorced. Perhaps the mail carrying such news from Nebraska had not yet reached her, or the court clerk there simply did not know how to contact her. Ellen kept in touch with her family, however, and it seems likely that they would have informed her of the final decree. Perhaps she used an alias to protect herself in case her former husband returned to claim her.

Some sources emphasize the fact that courthouse documents recording the marriage are incomplete, but they still conclude that Ellen's marriage to Averell took place legally. The unfinished portion of the marriage license is most likely the part usually completed by the officiating minister. It appears that the couple were married in the courthouse, so no minister's signature was necessary. Also, courthouse records of the time were copied by hand by clerks who made a mark designating that the official seal had been affixed, thus increasing the likelihood of error. The courthouse record of the document is dated May 17, 1886, although in one place it looks as if the clerk wrote May 11. Since Ellen and Averell journeyed more than one hundred miles one way to marry, it is doubtful that they spent six days—from May 11 to May 17—in Lander awaiting the application's approval, especially since they intended to keep their marriage a secret. They presumably got the marriage license and immediately tied the knot. It's unlikely that any clerical error was made in Ellen's last name, however, since it was listed twice on the form as Andrews.

Trouble on the Land

Things looked bright for the newlyweds. In late June 1886, Averell was appointed postmaster of the new Sweetwater Post Office, helping him gain extra income. Ellen filed squatter's rights August 30, 1886, as Ellen L. Watson, under the Preemption Act on a claim that was north and adjacent to Averell's. The Preemption Act of 1841 allowed squatters to purchase one hundred sixty acres of public land that they improved, at a price of one dollar and twenty-five cents per acre. Altogether, homesteaders could gain as many as four hundred eighty acres if they used the Preemption Act (one hundred sixty acres), the Homestead Act of 1862 (one hundred sixty acres), and the later Timber Culture Act of 1873 (one hundred sixty acres). Ellen may have planned to eventually obtain four hundred eighty acres in her own name, and that may have been why she listed a false name on her marriage license and why she and Averell kept their marriage secret. Then Averell could also obtain that much property under his name. Together, they could own a fairly large spread and become cattle ranchers.

Trouble lurked in this land policy, as Ellen and Averell would soon discover. During the 1880s, land entries in Wyoming soared to 10,962, but most of the claims were not proved up—the claimants failed to meet requirements to improve the land—so patents, or deeds, were not issued. Only about 10 percent of the state's land was patented when the territory gained statehood in 1890. In the meantime, land speculators took advantage of the homestead laws, which were not strictly enforced, by creating false entry applicants to acquire large areas of public land. The one hundred sixty acres allowed to homesteaders often was too much for them to improve on their own, while ranchers needed much larger acreages to run cattle. One rancher, Albert J. Bothwell, lived only a mile or two from Ellen's claim. The son of a wealthy Iowa merchant, Bothwell came to Wyoming Territory in 1883 and was said to have an incendiary temper. He had used the area regarded as open range near Ellen's and Averell's claims previously to graze his cattle herd. Their claims undoubtedly irked him.

Bothwell had also fenced in public lands, not an unusual practice in those days. For example, persons who owned alternate sections among the checkerboard areas reserved for railroads often fenced in the checkerboard property rather than suffering the additional expense to fence the alternate sections separately. In the early 1880s, ranchers started fencing as a boundary to discourage competitors and to protect their herds from disease. The federal government began legal actions in early 1883 against those who fenced illegally, but the fencing issue remained a sore spot well into the 1900s.

By improving their lands with irrigation ditches using water from Horse Creek, Ellen and Averell probably further annoyed Bothwell. Averell filed claim for the Averell Homestead Ditch on September 22, 1886, proposing to use water from Horse Creek for irrigation. The filing gave him the right to begin construction of a ditch that would control more than a mile of the creek's water. Water was extremely important to the open-range cattle owned by Bothwell and other cattlemen. Open-range cattle often died from thirst because they were unable to locate sufficient water sources.

Weather, too, played a part in livestock raising and increased the pressure on ranchers. The winter of 1886–1887 was one of the harshest in Wyoming history. Livestock losses in Carbon County were estimated as high as 23 percent. Surviving animals were in poor condition, and the calf crop was less than expected. Prices, instead of rising because of the slashed cattle supply, actually dropped. Ranchers had gambled that low prices in 1886 would rise and so held onto stock rather than selling. This decision proved disastrous, and in 1887, many were forced to sell because the severe winter depleted their resources. Another profound effect of the hard winter revolved around hay. For the first time, cattlemen began to "put up hay"—cut hay and pile it in stacks in the summer months—to feed cattle during the winter. This process increased the importance of access to large acreages of natural hay meadows. Homesteaders choosing these vital sections of land, like Ellen and Averell, became obstacles to a survival necessity for cattle and for the ranchers who raised them.

Averell still dreamed of raising cattle, but his inability to secure a brand hampered his efforts. He continued his efforts to earn permission for a brand and applied a second time to the Carbon County Brand Commission, but his request was again rejected at the commission's November 26, 1886, meeting, even though he asked for a slightly different brand. Six of thirty-six applicants were refused. Averell may have thought he would easily earn a license for a brand the second time, but this was not the case. Debt records, which placed a lien on Averell's property, including two mules and one horse, indicate some of his animals already bore this brand. The fact that his animals already sported a brand he had just applied for most likely did not endear him to the brand commission. In February 1887, Averell was forced to extend his mortgage note, and he continued to slide further into debt.

As Averell's debts mounted, Ellen discovered that retaining her own claim could involve more than just the physical maintenance of the land. In May 1887, E. P. Schoonmaker filed a one hundred sixty-acre claim, using the Timber Culture Act, on the same piece of land she had claimed under the Preemption Act. Even though her formal filing of squatter's rights the year before provided no guarantee, she did manage to retain ownership of the property. Schoonmaker was known as a friend and neighbor of Bothwell, and his unsuccessful filing may have been an attempt on their part to get Ellen quietly to leave her property. Ellen must have decided to strengthen her position by applying for U.S. citizenship. She filed her application on May 25, 1887, in Carbon County. The clerk listed her name as Ella Watson on the form; she signed as Ellen L. Watson.

Averell continued to seek improvements by trying to obtain a brand and through new irrigation plans. In September, Averell applied to the brand commission for the third time, with a brand altogether different from the first two. The commission again rejected him. The next month, Averell filed a statement of another proposed ditch, the Horse Creek Upland Irrigating Ditch, which would stretch south for four miles.

Presumably during this whole time, Ellen lived with Averell and assisted at his roadhouse by cooking meals for customers. If she did live with Averell, this situation may have sparked rumors that she was an indecent woman of ill repute. Ellen and Averell had kept their marriage secret, and people at that time would have taken a dim view of a woman living with a man who was not her husband. The fact that she sometimes mended the clothes that cowboys damaged during roundups may also have worked against her reputation. She owned a sewing machine and made her own clothes and helped repair those of others to earn extra income. Although seemingly innocent, these efforts may have led to rumors that she serviced cowboys in other ways during their stopovers at the roadhouse. And if they gave her calves in payment for sewing, that could have prompted a rumor that she exchanged sexual favors for calves. No evidence supports this theory, but Ellen did own livestock at the time of her death.

Although Averell stated a wish to raise cattle, it doesn't appear that he ever owned a herd, and probate files don't show that he owned any cattle at the time of his death. This lends some credence to the traditional tale, as reported by Duncan Aikman in his 1927 book *Calamity Jane and the Lady Wildcats,* that Averell hired Ellen to establish a brothel near his business and planned to use the store as a cover for a cattle rustling venture. Again, there is no evidence for this conjecture. John Fales, who built a log house for Ellen on her claim, denied that either Ellen or Averell stole cows; he also said that "those who say that Ella Watson slept with the cow-punchers, are slandering a good woman's name."

The couple did not command the respect of the entire community, but not everyone considered them indecent. Harry Ward, of Lake Ranch Stage Station, located halfway between Rawlins and Ferris, claimed Averell had a reputation as a "roughneck" but said he "was no hillbilly. He was a well edu-cated man and of gentlemanly appearance." Of Ellen, Ward wrote that she had once brought him a pair of striped socks from Rawlins. He called her "a fine looking woman. Other women looked down on her in those days, but no matter what she was or did she had a big heart. Nobody went hungry around her." Ward wrote that Ellen and Averell "may have been bad in some ways but they had their good points."

In early 1888, the couple took steps to document important paperwork. On March 24, 1888, after living with Averell for nearly two years, Ellen filed Homestead Entry Number 2003 at the U.S. Land Office in Cheyenne. This was another important step in gaining ownership of the land she had claimed in 1886 under the Preemption Act. She explained that the great distance to Cheyenne and the expense of travel precluded her from filing the claim entry sooner. Meanwhile, Averell had tied up the use of water from Horse Creek with his irrigation ditches. On May 14, 1888, he sold a ditch easement to cat-tleman Bothwell for thirty dollars. This transaction granted Bothwell use of a strip of land for building a ditch and was "confined exclusively to the owners of Bothwell Sweetwater Ditch No. 2." In this act, at least, it appears that the

Photograph of Ellen L. Watson taken at a studio in Rawlins, Wyoming, probably in the mid-1880s. Ellen sent the photo to her mother after it was taken. (Courtesy of Lola Van Wey.)

neighbors were trying to cooperate with each other. It may have irritated Bothwell to have to purchase the right from Averell, but all appears above-board in this case. Bothwell probably needed the water badly enough to obtain it, even if he had to conduct business with Averell to do so.

Brumbaugh states that Bothwell approached Ellen and Averell several times, offering to purchase their land, but they refused his offers. Bothwell, it is said, offered to lend Ellen money to prove up on her homestead but she declined. She most likely did not want to be indebted to him. The homesteaders' stubborn-ness might have been their fatal mistake. The sale of the property might have allowed them to move on and homestead elsewhere, in a place where escalating tensions like those in the Sweetwater country did not exist. Such a sale would at least have helped Averell pay his debts. Instead, Averell and Ellen appar-ently had adopted the attitude that they had claimed their lands and they would homestead there no matter the consequences.

Versions of Ellen's whereabouts during the summer of 1888 differ. Thomas Watson said his daughter visited Lebanon, Kansas, in June and July. Brumbaugh corroborates this family visit by explaining that Ellen's brother John took her to the train depot in Red Cloud, Nebraska, for her return trip to Rawlins. Ellen offered to pay John for the ride, but he refused, so she gave him a brooch and told him to give it to his future bride. Later, Mrs. John Watson wore the brooch several times, and the family owns photographs depicting it. Some historians, though, have argued that Ella Watson was arrested for drunkenness in Cheyenne on June 23, 1888. Ellen could not have been in two places at the same time, so this must have been another Ella Watson.

The Disputed Herd

Questions invariably arise over the issue of how Ellen acquired her cattle. In the fall of 1888, she supposedly purchased twenty-eight head of cattle at the incredibly low price of one dollar per head from an emigrant named Engerman at Independence Rock, about five miles southwest of her property. Engerman had trailed the cattle from Nebraska and was heading west, and the cattle were in poor condition from the journey. Ellen is said to have collected a bill of sale and placed it in a safe deposit box in a Rawlins bank, but that bill of sale cannot be located. And Ellen did not record a bill of sale in the Carbon County courthouse. This is odd because only one year earlier she had recorded a bill of sale showing the purchase of several horses from Arthur G. Williams. Considering that Ellen and Averell lived near the temperamental cattleman Bothwell and were aware of the volatile issue of cattle rustling, failure to record a bill of sale on the purchase of cattle does not make good sense. Other people recorded bills of sale for the purchase of cattle in those days. A bill of sale would provide proof of Ellen's purchase, and if she took the time to place it in a safe deposit box, she obviously knew its importance. This gap in Ellen's record-keeping created controversy and allowed for interpretation favorable to both sides.

John DeCorey, the fourteen-year-old who worked for Ellen, wrote to the *Casper Weekly Mail* after the lynching, stating that Ellen purchased most of her stock from emigrants. "She bought them and paid her own money for them and had had them in her possession ever since I had been with her," DeCorey wrote. John Fales, too, defended her, saying he drove the cattle from Independence Rock to Averell's ranch.

Ellen's new herd contained a mixture of bred heifers, cows, and steers. She fenced in sixty acres of pasture using cedar posts and three-wire, four-barbed fence. Cattle need about forty acres per head to thrive, and with twenty-eight head, Ellen would need more than one thousand acres to graze her herd. Her cattle may have grazed on public land that Bothwell considered his, creating yet another sore spot. Or perhaps Ellen did indeed get the cattle illegally and then fenced in the sixty acres as a temporary holding area until she could ship them to market and make her profit. To sell the cattle as her own, she would have to affix a brand, which she planned to apply for. With cold weather approaching, Ellen may have decided not to brand her herd until spring to allow them time to recover from their travels and to not stress them further.

The facts surrounding Ellen Watson's brand—critical to the case of whether or not she rustled cattle—have become muddied throughout the years, in part because of confusion about the location and existence of the official brand book. The Carbon County Brand Book was at one time kept at the Carbon County Museum in Rawlins and was later moved to the Saratoga Museum in Saratoga, where it now is housed. It was thought to be lost for a time. Because of this confusion, some sources claim Ellen applied for brands not supported by documentation. Ellen did not apply for the LU brand in October of 1888, as George Hufsmith asserts. And she did not apply for the WT brand, as the Watson family believed. Instead, the brand book indicates she applied for a variety of different brands on December 3, 1888. Ellen's proposal (listed under the name Ella Watson) stands out because she simultaneously applied for so many brands. Perhaps with her newly acquired cattle, Ellen felt desperate to receive a brand. Knowing Averell's unsuccessful record before the brand committee must have also increased her anxiety. All of Ellen's selections were rejected; she did not seek permission for a brand again.

One week after trying for a brand, Ellen proposed that the Watson Water Ditch be created on her homestead claim for irrigation and domestic purposes, although she didn't officially file the proposal until December 22. Her water right was located just above Averell's and would have taken more water from Horse Creek, a fact that may have angered their neighbors further. Brumbaugh states that Ellen and Averell had threatened to cut off cattleman Bothwell's water supply, which incensed him. Under the circumstances, they had to know such a threat would annoy even a gentle-tempered rancher. If they taunted Bothwell in this manner, they courted danger and surely knew it. Perhaps they claimed the water in retaliation for not receiving brand permits, hoping to control at least one aspect of their homestead dream.

As Ellen and Averell sought irrigation improvements for her land, the brand commission continued to reject Averell. On December 29, 1888, James Averell unsuccessfully requested permission to use an open keyhole brand. Either this brand was already in use—something Averell should certainly have been aware of by this time—or the brand commission simply did not want to grant Averell a brand.

Then, in 1889, the proposal to create Natrona County came to the forefront of territorial issues. To create the new county, some of the land currently specified as Carbon County would be taken. Averell favored creation of the new county. He wrote a letter to the *Casper Weekly Mail*, dated February 7, stating, "It is wonderful how much land some of the land sharks own—in their minds, and how firmly they are organized to keep Wyoming from being settled up." He suggested an improvement, saying, "Change the irrigation laws so that every bona fide settler can have his share of the water; and as soon as possible, cancel the Desert Land Act, and then you will see orchards and farms in Wyoming as there are in Colorado." The letter referred to a "Sweetwater land-grabber" who opposed creation of Natrona County (probably Robert Galbraith) and called the town of Bothwell, the namesake creation of his irritable neighbor, "only a geographical expression." These remarks undoubtedly proved inflammatory. The letter was later reprinted in the Rawlins newspaper, probably further provoking Averell's neighbors.

James Averell's fifth brand application, this time for the J-bird brand, was rejected by the brand commission on February 28, 1889. Writing such a hot letter to the newspaper just prior to applying for a brand was not smart. Averell's obvious reference to cattlemen as "land sharks" and "land grabbers" doubtless drew even more animosity to himself and may have killed his chances to receive license for any brand.

Ellen found another way. A March 16, 1889, bill of sale records Ellen's purchase of the LU brand from John M. Crowder for ten dollars. Researcher George Hufsmith contended this bill of sale was for the purchase of branding irons, but the wording in the document explains clearly that she purchased the brand "LU on the left hip of horses and LU on the left side or right side of cattle." The original bill does not exist, but the document was recorded in the Carbon County courthouse and shows the sale was witnessed by James Averell and Frank Buchanan. Crowder's brand does not appear in the Carbon County Brand Book for that time period, however, and it may have been official only in another jurisdiction.

Crowder was probably the father of Gene Crowder, the boy unofficially adopted by Ellen as her own son. Ellen evidently cared for the boy—a frail child—because she felt she could give him a better home than could be provided by his father, a widower with several children.

Ellen knew the value of a brand's protection. Herds grew rapidly during the mid-1880s, increasing the importance of accurate brands. By 1885, more than one million head were counted in Wyoming Territory. Rustling was rampant throughout the territory and had been for quite some time. As early as 1883, the Wyoming Stock Growers Association was notified of trouble brewing in Carbon County, and a special roundup had been held there in October 1884 to help confirm the thieving. In 1886, trials were held in Carbon County for accused rustlers Ed Lineberger, Jack Cooper, and Tom Collins. The case favored the defendants, and the WSGA had to reimburse Cooper and Lineberger more than $1,100 for wrongfully seized cattle. The lack of convictions sent a message that cattle thieves were appreciated and livestock owners detested. Under the circumstances, cattlemen would certainly have grown suspicious of Ellen Watson—a homesteader with a small acreage, a cattle herd of questionable ownership, a rejected brand application, and a lover whose brand applications had been repeatedly rejected.

Ellen apparently branded her herd in the summer of 1889 with her purchased LU brand. That forty-one cattle were branded LU is mentioned in the estate papers assembled after her death. Researcher George Hufsmith assumed that the herd comprised the twenty-eight head bought from Engerman plus thirteen calves born to this herd.

Hufsmith's theory is convenient, but not necessarily correct. If Ellen slaughtered two, as she reportedly did to help feed neighboring settlers, that changes the numbers. And numerous sources emphasize the poor condition of Ellen's herd because of their time on the trail. How many of them would have survived a rugged winter? Some loss would be expected with a herd in poor condition. Some heifers could have lost their calves, and some calves might not have survived after birth.

So why did Ellen have more cattle in her pasture than she would be expected to have, based on a purchase of twenty-eight head? Rustling certainly provides an easy explanation. Another solution involves mix-ups. If she allowed her herd to graze on open range, as many of her neighbors did, mix-ups could have occurred. Cattle roaming the range could have crossed her fence and gotten mixed in with her herd, although she should have known this and cut them out of her own herd. If the winter was harsh, snowdrifts might have covered a portion of the fence and allowed cattle to mix in and out of the fence. The mix-up might not have been noticed for a while. According to Hufsmith, Sam Johnson, foreman of the Bar 11 Ranch on Pete Creek, knew about Ellen's herd. Some of his cattle broke through her fence once and mixed in with hers. He herded his out and fixed her fence.

In any case, Ellen's herd as of summer 1889 apparently included a number of calves that would have been considered mavericks—that is, unbranded calves born on the open range. At that time, under terms of the Maverick Law passed by the territorial legislature in 1884, mavericks were divided proportionately among stock owners at the spring roundups. Thus, those who owned larger herds were entitled to buy more calves, which translated into more profits at market. Small herd owners received fewer calves and sometimes did not even participate.

The territory's controversial law regulating the branding of mavericks was certainly influenced by the powerful Wyoming Stock Growers Association. The WSGA, strongest in the mid-1880s, wielded power over brands used in the territory and exerted mighty political influence. Foremen of the roundups managed the auctions of these mavericks, earning 10 percent of the revenue. The other 90 percent went to the WSGA to be used for brand inspections and other purposes. Branding was forbidden from February 15 until the spring roundup. Unbranded stock became the property of the WSGA, and neighbors had first opportunity in buying any stock. Ellen must have been anxious to secure a brand so that her cattle could remain her property, and she certainly didn't want her neighbors to be able to buy any unbranded stock among her herd, with proceeds going to the stock growers association.

In late June 1889, the *Cheyenne Daily Sun* reported cattle thievery in Laramie, Albany, Sweetwater, and Carbon Counties. Prophetically, the report stated: "The changes now going on in the removal of large herds to northern ranges and which will rapidly continue as the country settles up, and is devoted to diversified agriculture, will bring the small stockmen and grangers in the ascendant in large sections of the territory. They will be obliged to unite for their own protection.... The settler will certainly protect his property, law or no law, and to this complexion it may come at last." A few days later, the *Daily Sun* carried a report from Saratoga's newspaper stating, "The stockmen of the Sweetwater country are combining and will soon offer rewards for stock thieves or any one found defacing brands."

The lines were clearly drawn. Homesteaders, like Ellen and Averell, would defend their property against stock owners expecting rights to graze cattle on previously open ranges. Stockmen, like Bothwell and others in the Sweetwater country, needed those ranges to produce their cattle crops. Stock raisers united against cattle thieves because it was rapidly becoming obvious that the legal system failed them in this regard.

The *Daily Sun* reported on two rustling cases that illustrated the ranchers' frustrations with the courts. One story told of a ranch hand indicted on a charge of stealing cattle in Fremont County. The rancher who employed the man suspected him and his wife of wrongdoing. He searched their house when they were absent and discovered a fresh beef in the cellar and a hide buried nearby. The ranch hand and his wife insisted the beef was theirs and the hide had been planted to frame them. The jury did not convict, but public sentiment favored the rancher. The newspaper noted that Tom Sun, a prominent pioneer stockman, and a number of other residents of the Sweetwater country had been in Lander at the time of the trial. This case and others in which suspected rustlers were released angered ranchers. If cattlemen in the Sweetwater country already distrusted Ellen Watson and James Averell, the results of this trial likely increased their disdain.

Reporting on an unsettling rustling case in another county, the *Daily Sun* article contained an ominous remark: "The honest ranchman and small stockmen must take these matters in hand…and [stockmen] say if the law does not sustain them this time by prompt conviction, they have another surer and more expeditious method of protection from the unlawful stealing and butchery of cattle, which has been a constant menace to their property and prosperity."

The escalating tension between stock owners and suspected rustlers mounted in the Sweetwater country. A late spring roundup was held in July 1889, centered at Bothwell's north ranch on Horse Creek. Although not documented, several sources indicate that Ellen and Averell found skulls and crossbones at their door, supposedly placed there by cowboys hired by Bothwell. Newspapers of the time tell an opposite tale, reporting the homesteaders had been threatening the stockmen.

Anxious cattlemen searched for clues as to whether Ellen and Averell were stealing cattle. On Saturday, July 20, 1889, stock detective George Henderson, foreman of the Quarter Circle 71 ranch owned by John Clay, looked around Ellen's pasture and found newly branded livestock. Hufsmith's research identifies the former Pinkerton man as "almost certainly the party who announced that Ellen had stolen and branded some of her neighbor's mavericks." Henderson apparently then traveled to Cheyenne to join his employer and thus avoid direct involvement in the affair that followed.

Sources differ on the events of this climactic day, but the main points remain clear. Ellen and her young employee, John DeCorey, walked to the nearby Shoshone Indian encampment, where Ellen bought a pair of moccasins. Her unofficially adopted son, Gene Crowder, had remained at home. When Ellen and DeCorey returned to her home, the stockmen confronted them, first taking Ellen and then traveling to Averell's house to get him. The stockmen forced the couple to go with them to the execution site. There the men proceeded with the lynching, pushing their victims from the boulder and watching as they died.

Aftermath of a Lynching

After the lynching, Averell's friend Frank Buchanan rode toward Casper to fetch the sheriff. Buchanan arrived at Tex Healy's cabin about twenty-five miles southwest of Casper at three in the morning. Healy rode the rest of the way, allowing Buchanan to rest. Deputy Sheriff Philip Watson (no relation to Ellen) assembled a posse, designating Dr. Joseph Benson as acting coroner. The authorities arrived at Averell's roadhouse about two in the morning on Monday. They immediately went to the lynching site, cut down the bodies, and held an inquest at the roadhouse, with Justice of the Peace B. F. Emery of Casper officiating. Buchanan had returned to the roadhouse. The inquest, based on the testimony of Buchanan and Gene Crowder, reported that Averell and Ellen had been lynched by the six cattlemen. This inquest named names. The bodies were buried in a single grave, dug slightly southeast of the roadhouse. As a parting mark of respect, the grave was marked with old wagon wheels.

The deputy sheriff then interrogated the implicated stockmen. He rode to Tom Sun's ranch to question him. Sun readily admitted his participation and named the others involved. He said Buchanan had shot John Durbin in the hip. The next stop was the ranch of Albert Bothwell, who also admitted his role in the killings. One newspaper account said that Bothwell told the deputy sheriff "to take a good look at every tree he came to on his way back to Casper for he would be likely to find six or eight more cattle rustlers hanging by the neck when he returned from jail."

The law officer followed procedure by taking five of the cattlemen to Carbon County Sheriff Frank Hadsell. The sixth cattleman, Durbin, had apparently returned to his home in Cheyenne; he commuted often by train to Rawlins and returned to face the charges. Bond for the five other men was set at a hefty five thousand dollars each. They posted bail and were released.

Public sentiment rapidly polarized into pro-lynchers and anti-lynchers. The Cheyenne newspapers—under opposite political banners—were clearly biased in favor of the stockmen. The *Daily Sun* was owned and edited by E. A. Slack, a Republican, while the *Daily Leader* was owned by a group of local Democrats. On July 23, the *Daily Sun* said, "The lynching is the outgrowth of a bitter feeling between big stockmen and those charged with cattle rustling." The newspaper editorialized, "The heroic treatment must prevail and the gentlemen who have resorted to it are entitled to the support and sympathy of all good citizens." Averell was reported to have had forty-seven head of stolen cattle in his possession at one time. The newspaper also stated that "the ownership of live stock should be as sacred as the ownership of any property."

171

On that same date, the *Daily Sun* misidentified Ellen (Ella) Watson as prostitute Kate Maxwell, dubbed her Cattle Kate, and stated that Averell operated a "hog ranch," one of the lowliest kinds of prostitution houses. The next day, the newspaper attempted to correct its identification error. The article proclaiming "The True Story" stated, "The dime novel literature telegraphed from Cheyenne Monday night regarding the lynching of James Averell and Ella Watson Saturday last is the veriest bosh." The newspaper also contained an editorial on the same day, stating, "No one who knows the gentlemen thus implicated would believe that they would commit an act of this nature without ample justification and except under the pressure of the direst necessity."

It does seem unlikely that six highly regarded ranchers would risk their reputations and their property to hang two innocent people, most especially a woman. Something provoked them to uncontrollable anger, most likely their profound belief that the pair were thieves. The best course of action would have been to seek the sheriff, but rustlers had been enjoying a heyday in the courts. Legal action appeared useless. Considering the bitter attitude toward rustlers at the time, the laxness of the courts in providing convictions, and the fact that local ranchers considered Averell and Ellen to be cattle thieves, the stockmen obviously wanted to send a message to any potential rustlers. Their statement resonated with clarity: no matter what the courts decide, rustlers in the Sweetwater country will be punished for their crimes.

However, their easy admittance of their roles in the lynching can be seen in different lights. The lynchers can be commended for confessing, but they were prominent and well-known, and they probably banked on being treated leniently. Cattle-raising was their livelihood. Rustlers had often gone free when stockmen thought they should not have, and cattle thieves threatened their livelihood. In all likelihood, the stockmen realized they would not be convicted. After all, they were only protecting themselves from danger. The fact that several of them participated perhaps gave them further protection.

The inquests into the deaths of Ellen and Averell created further confusion. On July 27, the *Daily Sun* reported that a second coroner's inquest had been held because the first "was not, strictly speaking, an inquest." In this second go-round, the newspaper said, Carbon County coroner James A. Bennett reported the victims "came to their death by violence by persons unknown to the jury." The newspaper added: "This is more like it." This second inquest, held July 23, 1889, came about because the acting prosecuting attorney in Carbon County decided the first inquest had been held improperly. However, coroner Bennett had also prepared the bodies of Averell's first wife and child upon their deaths. Probably feeling sympathetic toward Averell, he refused to disinter the bodies of Averell and Ellen. Had he done so, the first inquest—the one containing names of the lynchers—would have been rescinded. Bennett's finding in the second inquest thus did not invalidate the first inquest. The lynchers' names were documented.

A grand jury was called to determine whether charges should be brought against the cattlemen. The presiding judge was Samuel T. Corn, who directed the earlier Carbon County rustling trials. The witnesses scheduled to testify before the grand jury disappeared under mysterious circumstances. Ellen's adopted son, Gene Crowder, vanished. Gene's father, John M. Crowder, after hearing of the lynching, reportedly unhitched a wagon he was driving and rode away, leaving the wagon behind. Some people speculate that he took his son with him. Other reports claim Gene Crowder died of Bright's disease, a kidney ailment that usually affects elderly people. Averell's nephew Ralph Cole died in the month after the lynching, at the age of twenty-one. Poisoning was suspected but never proven; mountain fever was decided as the cause of death. John DeCorey moved to Steamboat Springs, Colorado, but sent a report on the lynching to the *Casper Weekly Mail,* also in the month after the killings. He, too, apparently disappeared after that.

Frank Buchanan, who had seen the lynching, was taken to Cheyenne and jailed for his own protection. Bond was set at five hundred dollars; his bail was posted by sympathetic homesteaders, and he was released. He did not appear when the grand jury met, although he was probably still alive. A skeleton found nine miles northwest of Rawlins several years later was thought to be the remains of Buchanan. Meanwhile, George Henderson, the stock detective, had been shot in the head by an unknown assailant. The grand jury, called on October 14, 1889, could not return a true bill because without the eyewitness testimony of Buchanan, the remaining evidence was circumstantial and hearsay. On October 25, the grand jury adjourned without indicting anyone for the deaths of Ellen and Averell.

Attorney George Durant, appointed by the court as administrator of the estates of Ellen and Averell, filed suit against John Durbin and Albert Bothwell for $1,100 in compensation for cattle they had taken from Ellen's homestead. But the suit never came to a conclusion. This result suggests that if attorney Durant had possessed Ellen's bill of sale recording her purchase of the twenty-eight head from Engerman, his case would have been stronger. Without a bill of sale, how could he prove Ellen's ownership? Also, Ellen's father, Thomas Watson, would likely have turned such a document over to the attorney to help clear his daughter's name.

In any event, Ellen's cattle were sold after her death. The *Cheyenne Daily Sun* reported on July 27, 1889, that fifty-three mavericks from Rawlins arrived at the Cheyenne stockyards that day. The report said a portion of them had belonged to Ella Watson, and identified "all of them [as] being the mavericks taken from the rustlers in the Sweetwater country." A separate item in the paper said John Durbin arrived in Cheyenne on the same date from Rawlins. He may have accompanied the mavericks, but that is not documented. Under terms of the Maverick Law, the calves became the property of the Wyoming Stock Growers Association, and neighbors had priority in purchasing them. It is likely that Bothwell and Durbin became owners of these mavericks.

Ellen's other property, listed in her probate file, included eight additional head of cattle. Why these were separated from the others is unknown. She also owned one pony, one mare, and fifteen chickens. The horses bore the quarter-circle open keyhole brand Averell applied for but did not receive permission to use in August 1886. Her property was sold at auction on August 11, 1889, with her father serving as clerk of the sale. He kept only her sewing machine, trunk and contents, one breast pin and earrings, two finger rings, one chain, and one pair of bracelets. He destroyed her letters and most of her personal belongings when he returned to Kansas. Administrator Durant was unable to sell Ellen's land.

Neither Ellen nor Averell left a will, and they carried the secret of their clandestine marriage to their graves. Averell's probate file states he left no wife or children surviving him. Averell was in debt; the sale of his personal items did not glean enough to pay his debts, although a sale on the courthouse steps August 19 satisfied the $430.92 balance he owed on a $600 promissory note. His land was sold at private sale, eventually coming into the hands of one of his killers, the cattleman Bothwell.

Epilogue

Following the lynching and its aftermath, the six cattlemen who carried out the killings returned to their own pursuits. All appeared to lead successful lives until their deaths many years later. In 1889, the same year as the lynching, Albert Bothwell and Tom Sun were elected to the executive committee of the Wyoming Stock Growers Association and served for thirteen years. Bothwell eventually moved to Los Angeles and died in California in 1928. Sun remained in the Sweetwater country, and his family built up one of the largest ranches in the state. He died in Denver in 1909. John Durbin, who operated a butcher shop in Cheyenne with his brother, gave up his position as a

The best-known photograph of Cattle Kate shows her astride a horse in her Wyoming Territory corral. This photo was probably also sent to her family and would probably have been taken in the late 1880s. (Courtesy of the Wyoming Division of Cultural Resources, #4104.)

Wyoming cattle inspector and sold his holdings in 1891. Durbin served in 1894 on the WSGA executive committee. He moved to Denver and invested in slaughterhouses, which proved financially successful. He died in 1907. Robert Conner moved to his childhood home of Mauch Chunk, Pennsylvania, and became successful there. He died in 1921. Robert Galbraith was elected to the Wyoming territorial legislature in 1889, but soon after moved to Little Rock, Arkansas, where he became a prominent banker. He died in 1939. Ernest McLean was believed to have returned to the Chicago area.

For the most part, a veil of silence settled over all involved after the incident. Kathleen Sun, the wife of Tom Sun's grandson, says that people who knew about the event never spoke of it. The Watson family, too, remained mute. Daniel Brumbaugh said that Ellen's father, Thomas Watson, who came west to settle her estate, returned to Kansas in August 1889 so distraught over the events in Wyoming Territory that he told his children to never speak of Ellen again as long as he lived. While settling Ellen's estate, Thomas Watson stayed in Rock Springs, nearly one hundred miles away from Rawlins, because the atmosphere there was still charged with hatred and distrust. He traveled under an assumed name to protect himself.

In 1989, the Watson family broke the silence they had kept so long at the wishes of Ellen's father. At their reunion in Casper, Wyoming, on the hundredth anniversary of Ellen's death, family members discussed the event openly and with local historians to try to find out what really happened to their ancestor. But the incident still provokes intense disagreement. Watson relatives believe Ellen was murdered by rough neighbors, cattlemen so enraged by the fact that she and James Averell homesteaded in the middle of prime pasture near a creek with a good supply of water that the stock owners resorted to their deadly solution.

Ellen's grand-nephew Daniel Brumbaugh says many stories about her were written with little regard for documentation. The lynchers made up the story of Ellen having been a prostitute in order to "cover their butts," he said. "Ellen never sold her body for cattle as they state. In fact she helped the area small ranchers out."

This view angers relatives of at least one of the cattlemen who participated in the hanging. Tom Sun, a respected pioneer, had settled on the Sweetwater in 1872 and had been a government scout at one time. He never denied his participation in the lynching. Kathleen Sun says that the stockmen believed Ellen and Averell were rustlers and saw no alternative in dealing with them. At that time, few suspected cattle rustlers were convicted, even in the face of strong evidence against them. Kathleen Sun once asked her father-in-law, Tom Sun Jr., about the hanging of Cattle Kate. Tom Sun Jr. was about five years old at the time of the lynching. He replied matter-of-factly to Kathleen's inquiry, "She was stealing cattle and they hung her."

Ellen Watson, known always now as Cattle Kate, cannot conclusively be proven innocent or guilty of the crimes she was accused of in the summer of 1889. Only the people who were there know the true story of what led to the death of two people by hanging near the Sweetwater River. Whether Ellen and Averell rustled cattle, the stockmen believed they did and took action to prevent future thefts. The land on which this drama unfolded has long since been settled, and the property once homesteaded by Averell and Ellen is part of the privately owned Pathfinder Ranch in Natrona County. The Bothwell Sweetwater Ditch No. 2 runs along the shoreline of what is now Pathfinder Reservoir. Ellen's moccasins, apparently recovered from the site of the lynching, are now housed at the Wyoming State Museum in Cheyenne. Ellen and Averell's single grave still exists. The Watson family placed a plaque on the grave during the 1989 reunion. But the message sent through the events of that hot July Saturday in 1889 speaks to generations. Suspected rustlers — male or female — are still not welcome in Wyoming.

Calamity Jane

The Making of a Frontier Legend

RICHARD W. ETULAIN

The journalist was puzzled. Arriving for an interview with the notorious Calamity Jane in early 1896 in Deadwood, South Dakota, she expected to meet a bold, brassy western heroine. But once inside Calamity's house, the reporter discovered a middle-aged pioneer wife and mother, more worried about her disarrayed hair and untidy sitting room than her legendary reputation.

The perplexed newspaperwoman soon realized she too confronted the central dilemma in thinking about Calamity Jane: was she a female hellcat of the West, as her widespread billing indicated, or was she a wife and mother who wished more than anything to be free from the exaggerated yarns spun about her? Had the legends about this "wild woman of the West" overtaken the real person, Martha Canary, increasingly obscuring her behind the stories?

The turning point for these two women, Martha Canary and Calamity Jane, occurred between 1875 and 1878. In that three-year period a young frontier woman was transformed into a Wild West celebrity. Once the transformation took place, the pioneer female, just emerging from her teens, never reverted to Martha Canary. From that time forward, Calamity Jane blotted out the earlier young woman. The legend had supplanted the life.

The Disappearance of Martha Canary

Martha Canary's earliest years were neither spectacular nor controversial. Her formative life was largely shaped by events typical in the histories of American families. The earliest known of her ancestors was her paternal grandfather James Canary, a farmer, who was born in 1788. James Canary moved gradually west from Virginia (later West Virginia) to Ohio, Iowa, and Missouri. Each move allowed the expanding Canary family to purchase additional tillable land for James's sons and sons-in-law, most of whom were also agriculturalists.

Martha's father, Robert Wilson Canary, James's youngest son, remains a shadowy figure. So does his wife Charlotte, Martha's mother. Robert was born in 1835 in Ohio, Charlotte perhaps in 1840 in Illinois. Robert and Charlotte were married in Iowa in 1855, and one year later they were residing on a farm near Princeton, Missouri, in Mercer County.

According to the U.S. Census of 1860, their daughter Martha—their first child—was born in Missouri in 1856. It's believed that at least three—maybe five—more children were later born to the couple. Rumors suggest that Robert disliked farming and that Charlotte, often seriously bruising the expectations for virtuous pioneer wives, probably encouraged her husband to leave Missouri.

After Robert's father, James Canary, died in 1862, Robert's siblings accused him and his wife of absconding with James's cash and farm assets; they took the couple to court. Rather than face these charges, the Canarys fled to Iowa. A year or two later they went west. Perhaps hoping to find less expensive land, or catching the gold fever then infecting many midwesterners, Robert and Charlotte joined thousands of others streaming toward the newly discovered mineral strikes in Montana and neighboring Idaho.

Tragedy struck in Montana as the lives of Martha's parents spiraled downward. A story in the December 31, 1864, issue of *The Montana Post* [Virginia City] revealed part of the difficulties. The story said "three little girls, who state their name as Canary" had appeared at the home of a local official, asking for help. They were skimpily dressed and hungry. The report added: "The father, it seems, is a gambler in Nevada [City, Montana]. The mother is a woman of the lowest grade." Charlotte died in Montana in 1866; a year later, after Robert took his motherless brood to Salt Lake City, he too died.

Not yet a teenager, Martha already was an orphan. Without parents, a home, or a familiar, nurturing community, she was on her own. Vague stories and hearsay cloud what happened next. In an autobiographical pamphlet published much later, *Life and Adventures of Calamity Jane*, she says she retreated to Fort Bridger in western Wyoming and shortly thereafter to Piedmont, a small Wyoming hamlet on the recently completed Union Pacific Railroad.

It was at Piedmont that the next census taker caught up with Martha. Although listed as fifteen years of age in the special Wyoming Territorial Census of 1869, she was actually thirteen. Perhaps she added years to her age to match her controversial adultlike actions. Many years later, old-timers recalled Martha's life in Piedmont and also in the booming mining towns of South Pass City and Miner's Delight, about one hundred miles north of the railroad. These faint recollections and other rumors pictured Martha as a lively, sassy young woman already exhibiting her independent, individualistic ways. So unorthodox were her actions that families in Piedmont and South Pass City were said to have washed their hands of her and sent her away to the hell-on-wheels towns recently sprung up along the Union Pacific.

The next five or six years of Martha's life are largely a mystery. The claims in her autobiography about serving as George Custer's scout in Arizona in the early 1870s are clear falsehoods since Custer was not in the Southwest during that period. Other shaky sources place her in military forts or in railroad hamlets between 1870 and 1875, but no dependable information substantiates this hearsay.

Then Martha reappeared in 1875—with a new name. In the late spring of that year, Professor Walter P. Jenny, supported by Lieutenant Colonel R. T. Dodge, led an expedition to the Black Hills to test the rumors of gold there and to consider possible agreements with the Sioux should rapacious white miners flood into the Indian lands. Some way or another Martha became part of the expedition. Discovered as an infiltrator, she was tossed out by Colonel Dodge, only to find her way back among the men the next day. Rediscovered, she was again sent away but surreptitiously returned. After a few days of this hide-and-

Miss Martha Canary ("Calamity Jane"), the Female Scout, in H. N. Maguire, The Coming Empire *(1878). (Courtesy of Richard W. Etulain.)*

seek, she was sent away for good and did not complete the expedition's five-month trip to the Black Hills in the Dakota Territory. By then she had been given the nickname Calamity Jane. A journalist traveling with the expedition wrote in the Chicago *Inter-Ocean* that Martha, now dubbed Calamity, surprised the men with her skills at riding and bull-whacking—and with her salty English, which was "not the Queen's pure." Quite possibly Martha had become Calamity not because of a single, dramatic act, but because of her many untoward actions.

In February 1876, Calamity went north again—this time traipsing along with General George Crook's command into Montana on a brief expedition. She probably went along again with Crook during his second trip north in May. It is unlikely she was a scout with Crook, but she may have been among the bull-whackers or teamsters, or she may have tagged along as a camp follower.

Calamity's social calendar filled quickly during the late spring and early summer of 1876. In the last week of May, she was jailed in Cheyenne, Wyoming, on a charge of stealing clothes and other personal effects. The Cheyenne newspaper reported that when the jury in early June declared her not guilty, Calamity "greatly rejoiced over release from durance vile," took a horse and buggy without permission, and headed up-country. The report said Calamity, imbibing "bug juice at close intervals and in large quantities," lurched on to Fort Laramie. As General George Custer prepared to ride to his death at the Little Big Horn, Calamity lay nearly destitute at the fort or at a nearby hog ranch.

Calamity's luck turned dramatically upward in the next few weeks. In late June, James Butler "Wild Bill" Hickok led a group of miners and would-be entrepreneurs out of Cheyenne, bound for the Black Hills and hoped-for riches in the new mines. As they passed Fort Laramie, they were persuaded to take several questionable young women along with them to Deadwood, including Calamity—who, it was reported, "was very drunk and was not dressed very well." The best evidence suggests this meeting was the first for Wild Bill and Calamity, with one participant on the journey, Joseph F. "White Eye Jack" Anderson, asserting that Hickok was "not very friendly" to Calamity. But the men agreed to outfit her with an attention-gathering set of new buckskins for their trip into the Black Hills.

In early or mid July, Wild Bill and his companions made a "spectacular entry" into pulsating Deadwood. So memorable was the grand entrance that many years later, old-timers vividly recalled the carnivalesque invasion. Most important for the eventual legend of Calamity Jane, the trip joined her name forever with that of Wild Bill Hickok. No contemporary, however, including Hickok or Calamity, spoke of them as a twosome in those dramatic closing days of Wild Bill's life before his assassination by Jack McCall on August 2, 1876.

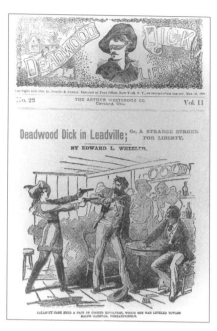

Calamity Jane, dime novel heroine, from the cover of Edward L. Wheeler's Deadwood Dick in Leadville; Or, a Strange Stroke for Liberty *(1879, 1899). (Courtesy of Richard W. Etulain.)*

Heroine of the Dime Novels

Recognized in Wyoming and South Dakota in 1875 and 1876 as something of a social aberration, Calamity Jane was soon transformed into a nationally known popular figure. The travels with General Crook and the extravagant ride into Deadwood with Wild Bill in midsummer 1876 brought her to center stage. The stories and books published about her in the next few years fixed the bright lights of Wild West notoriety directly on her. Those lights rarely dimmed during her later life and have continued to shine brightly in the century since her death.

Calamity's new identity spread quickly after her entrance into Deadwood. Local and eastern newspapermen found her enigmatic and antisocial ways grist for the journalistic mill. One reporter compared her to a vivacious if controversial heroine in a story by Bret Harte. Another brief profile of her appeared in H. N. Maguire's *The Black Hills: An American Wonderland* (1877), a popular travel book previously published serially in a New York paper. Calamity—described as "an original in herself" and as an "uneducated, uncared for" young woman—also was a major presence in T. M. Newson's play *Drama of Life in the Black Hills* (1878).

But it was as a dime-novel heroine that Calamity Jane gained her widest notoriety. From 1878 until the mid-1880s, she appeared in nearly twenty novels of the Deadwood Dick series written by Edward L. Wheeler. In nearly all these brief works, Calamity's character is smothered in the usual claptrap of popular fiction. False identities, disguises, cloying vernacular, and several complex subplots complicate nearly every volume. Although Deadwood Dick, the frontier highwayman and miner, is the central figure, Calamity plays major or supporting roles.

Few of the descriptions of Wheeler's heroine follow the known facts of Calamity's life. Early novels in the series—such as *Deadwood Dick, the Prince of the Road* (1877), and *Deadwood Dick on Deck; or, Calamity Jane, the Heroine of Whoop-up* (1878)—speak of her as from Nevada (probably a mistake based on Calamity's actual residence in the Montana towns of Virginia City and Nevada City). The fictional books have her being seduced by a lecherous Mormon, and arriving in Deadwood, South Dakota, just as the mining camp sprang into existence. Wheeler's novels say that despite being seduced, Calamity endured. Although she dresses like a man, lives an unrestrained life, and has already experienced a "rough and dissipated career," those hardships have not "altogether 'swept away the lines where beauty lingers.'"

Even though Wheeler's novels ventured far from the details of Calamity's early life, he seems on track in some of his characterizations of her. She smokes, swears (offscene and gently, of course), and she rides like a wild wind. Moreover, the fictional Calamity is loyal, sure of herself, strong, and stubborn— all qualities attributed to the historical Calamity. One could not expect, however, that Wheeler would refer to Calamity's alcoholism or promiscuity in his dime novels; those actions would alienate the Victorian sensibilities of his readers.

Wheeler's dime-novel Calamity changes over time. In the first installments of the series, her rambunctiousness and her social marginalization appear in her rough, vernacular speech and her rumpled attire. In this condition she is unworthy of Deadwood Dick, even though she wishes to become his mate—and perhaps his wife. In later novels such as *Deadwood Dick of Deadwood* (1880), *Deadwood Dick's Doom* (1881), and *Deadwood Dick's Disguise* (1882), Calamity's speech is much less crude, her actions less questionable, and she neither smokes nor drinks. Now more socially acceptable, she has become a worthy companion for Deadwood Dick. In fact, they marry in one of the later novels.

All of Wheeler's novels in this series are set in raw frontier settlements such as Deadwood, South Dakota, or Leadville, Colorado. In nonstop action, Calamity, Deadwood Dick, and other lively heroes and heroines frenetically ward off evildoers while trying to protect nascent societies. Arrogant easterners, "savage" Indians, and bloated capitalists—eastern and western—often serve as the convenient villains. In these events, Calamity proves, through her assertive actions, her handling of guns, and her courage, a memorable heroine of a popular genre.

A figure similar to the dime-novel Calamity Jane also appeared in Mrs. William Loring Spencer's *Calamity Jane, A Story of the Black Hills* (1887), the only full-length novel on Calamity before the 1930s. In Spencer's work, Calamity stands out as a social deviant from her first appearances. Crashing a picnic of well-to-do women, Calamity also dresses much differently than the society belles, mocks their pretensions, and looks "more Indian than white." She seems something come in from the wild to represent a yet-uncivilized West. As one character muses, "She had heard of Calamity Jane whose eccentricities were so numerous and daring, so remarkable, that she was suspected to be in every deviltry from robbing trains to playing faro." Still, some of the women in the novel come to value Calamity's courage and loyalty. And when the leading man denounces Calamity as an unworthy visitor to his home, his stock as a sympathetic character falls quickly and precipitously.

By the end of her novel, Spencer has created a much more complex Calamity than appeared in Wheeler's dime novels. The author achieves this complexity by playing on the gender tensions between Calamity's masculine dress and her feminine mannerisms. That duality reverberates from one especially apt description:

Calamity Jane in buckskins; the Wild West woman as performer. (Courtesy of American Heritage Center, University of Wyoming.)

Calamity's "pretty foot and ankle" attract attention as she springs "into her saddle." True, some of the snooty ladies treat her as a social skunk, but the empathetic heroine Meg is drawn to Calamity, like a loving sister. Spencer's Calamity may injure social codes, laws, and community ties, but she appreciates Meg and other women and exhibits love and concern for several characters. Hating/loving her life, this novelistic Calamity displays more ambiguities and complexities than her fictional sisters in Wheeler's dime novels. In Spencer's work, we see some of the inner life of Calamity, through her own admissions and revelations, as well as from the insights of onlookers, the feminine Meg, and crude miners alike.

Calamity's appearances in the widely circulated dime novels dramatically and irreversibly changed her identity. Never again would she be known as Martha Canary, the farmer's daughter from Princeton, Missouri. Through the sensational and popular works of fiction, she had become, by the early 1880s, a frontier hellcat, a Wild West heroine worthy of mention alongside historical figures like Custer, Billy the Kid, Wyatt Earp, and Belle Starr, as well as imagined characters such as Deadwood Dick, Rattlesnake Ned, and Hurricane Nell. In the next two decades, Calamity became increasingly identified as a lively female protagonist of the "yellowback" novels. These continuing

Calamity Jane (Martha Canary) as pioneer woman. (Courtesy of American Heritage Center, University of Wyoming.)

moments of recognition were not always pleasant for her. When journalists or other writers quoted lurid lines about her from dime novels, Calamity usually exploded in anger, labeling the stories and descriptions a pack of lies.

Yet on occasion during the 1880s and 1890s, Calamity seemed inclined to prove the veracity of the wild tales. Meandering in and out of the booming mining, railroad, and agricultural towns of South Dakota, Wyoming, and Montana, Calamity wandered from job to job, unable to find a satisfying occupation or home to end her wanderlust. Her personal life also wobbled. Calamity often spoke of "husbands," but until a recently discovered document proved that she married Wyoming brakeman William Steers in Pocatello, Idaho, in 1888, there was no evidence she ever legally married. That stormy relationship soon ended, as did informal ones before and after.

Ironically, Calamity's falsified but sensational reputation sometimes helped her get work. In 1884, she led a troupe of female entertainers into the snow-bound Idaho hamlet of Murray, and a bit later she joined the touring Hardwick troupe, which financial difficulties soon closed. Calamity's most notable appearance as a Wild West performer came a decade later when she was a featured part of the Kohl-Middleton traveling exhibition. Advertisements for her role reveal how much Calamity had become stereotyped as a female terror of a fabulous frontier. A handbill for Calamity's appearance in Minneapolis depicted her as a western Amazon dressed in ragged buckskins with a knife clenched between her teeth. The caption trumpeted Calamity as THE FAMOUS WOMAN SCOUT OF THE WILD WEST! HEROINE OF A THOUSAND ADVENTURES! TERROR OF EVILDOERS IN THE BLACK HILLS! THE COMRADE OF BUFFALO BILL AND WILD BILL! Nothing in the sensational come-on was true.

Other occurrences added to Calamity's burgeoning reputation as a larger-than-life woman. At the same time as her Kohl-Middleton appearances, perhaps as a lure for that tour, Calamity had a hand in the publication of her pamphlet-length autobiography, *Life and Adventures of Calamity Jane* (probably 1896). The eighteen-page account touted Calamity as an important scout for Generals Custer and Crook; as the captor of Jack McCall, who killed Wild Bill Hickok; and as a notorious stagecoach driver and bullwhacker. None of these assertions can be proven; most seem more puffery than truth. Yet for the remainder of her life, Calamity peddled the autobiography as her life story.

About five years later, in 1901, Calamity reappeared as a Wild West woman, this time in a show in the East. A New York writer, Josephine Brake, came to Montana in order to, she claimed, rescue Calamity from her difficulties—and with the possible additional motive of capitalizing on the reputation of the frontier heroine to help sell Brake's novels. At the Pan-American Exposition in Buffalo, New York, Calamity soon tired of hawking Brake's fiction. She left to join Col. Frederic Cummins's Great Indian Congress, also in Buffalo, where she was billed as a famous western figure. Discontent and alcohol, often a disastrous mixture, quickly unhorsed Calamity. Penniless, the heroine of the Wild West slunk back to the Rockies, courtesy of a return ticket provided by Buffalo Bill Cody.

This public, exhibitionist Calamity Jane of the legendary West rode a far different mount than the mostly private, little-known Martha Canary. The sensational facade of Calamity nearly obscured her personal side. Controversies surrounding the notorious Wild West woman made it difficult to understand what was happening to Martha Canary in the 1880s and 1890s. Yet we do know that she resided for weeks—sometimes months—at a time in Lander and Rawlins, Wyoming, and later in Billings and Livingston, Montana, and in the Black Hills of South Dakota.

She visited her younger sister Lena (or Lannie), who had married a German immigrant, Johnny Borner, and was raising a large family near Lander. She herself became a mother, perhaps of two children. Several Montana newspapers reported that she gave birth to "little Calamity," a son. In the 1880s there is even stronger evidence that she bore a daughter, Jesse, who lived off and on with her mother. Calamity later even indicated that she had become a grandmother.

Calamity seemed unable to break the increasing hold alcohol gained on her life. Rawlins and Livingston newspapers, especially, carried reports of her drunkenness and jailings. There were several reports that Calamity may have been a part-time prostitute. Her relationships with a series of men were erratic and sometimes violent. In Rawlins she was known as Mrs. Mattie King, and next as the wife of William Steers. Then for nearly five years in the 1890s, Calamity seemed largely to disappear, except for two or three minor references to her in newspapers. In her unreliable autobiography, she claimed that she and a man named Clinton Burke operated a boardinghouse, perhaps in Boulder, Colorado. When Burke vanished in the mid-1890s, Calamity took up with Robert Dorsett, the last of her "husbands." Only the relationship with Burke seems to have lasted more than a couple of years.

Alongside these continuing signs of disorder, Calamity also exhibited a clear desire for a less chaotic life. This persisting wish emerges in one revealing incident, when Calamity was interviewed at her home in Deadwood in 1896. When the newspaperwoman spoke with Calamity just before the Kohl-

Middleton tour, she found the housewife Calamity with Clinton Burke and with her daughter Jesse, fretting about her disheveled hair and worried about her unkempt house. Calamity told the journalist that her past was embarrassing and that, most of all, she wanted now to establish a home for her family. Few of her contemporaries understood what the journalist realized on that day in Deadwood: more than anything else, Calamity Jane wished to be a typical wife and mother, like other pioneer women.

The photographs of Calamity reveal a similar distortion of her life. Nearly all stories of Calamity, if illustrated, feature her in buckskins; but of the two dozen or so known photographs of her, only in four or five does she appear in men's dress. All others present her in woman's attire, usually blouses and long skirts, and often with a large hat. Even though aficionados of an American Wild West often portray her as a cross-dressing rabble-rouser, photographic evidence reveals her dressed usually as a typical pioneer woman of the late-nineteenth century.

But the mounting problems that eventually ended Calamity's life are neither unclear nor distorted. After her return from the East in 1901, she seemed increasingly unable to fend off her alcoholism and to keep a job. She spiraled downward, wandering through eastern Montana, ending up in a poorhouse. The end came quickly, following several drinking bouts and illnesses. She died August 1, 1903, in Terry, South Dakota. Three days later she was buried, perhaps at her request, next to Wild Bill Hickok in Mt. Moriah Cemetery in Deadwood.

Searching for Calamity Jane

Long before her death, Martha Canary had been transformed into Calamity Jane. And she has remained, by and large, a Wild West heroine rather than a pioneer woman. Indeed, in a steady stream of magazine articles, movies, dramatic illustrations, and novels, popularizers continue to portray Calamity as a bold, uncouth vixen of the Old West.

This predominant image of Calamity Jane gradually hardened into a recognizable stereotype by the 1930s. But as with other spectacular Old West characters such as General Custer, Billy the Kid, Wild Bill Hickok, and Wyatt Earp, not much appeared on Calamity in the first two decades of the twentieth century. Even though Owen Wister's novel *The Virginian* (1902) and the first important film Western, *The Great Train Robbery* (1903), helped establish the ingredients of the popular western story, biographers and historians wrote many fewer essays and books about Old West characters in this era than they did in the 1920s and 1930s. As a result, the first notable depictions of Calamity Jane as a legendary westerner, following her death, did not appear until after 1920.

The initial nonfiction book about Calamity, Duncan Aikman's *Calamity Jane and the Lady Wildcats* (1927), introduced the romantic Old West image that dominated representations of Calamity from the 1920s through the Doris Day movie *Calamity Jane* in 1953. A journalist inflicted with the sardonic wit of critic H. L. Mencken, Aikman devoted a bit more than a third of his 350-page book to Calamity, along with other provocative sections on Cattle Kate Watson, Belle Starr, Lola Montez, Pearl Hart, Madame Moustache, and other Wild West figures. Supposedly a work of nonfiction, most of its material on Calamity reeked of imagined scenes and what-ifs—even though Aikman interviewed a few residents of Princeton, Missouri, for their distant remembrances of the Canary family of sixty years earlier. His book overflows with sensational details, contrived characterizations, and invented dialogue. Guessing at happenings, as well as at the reasons for these occurrences, Aikman fills in large sections of his biography with speculations, manufactured events, and supposed contacts. He cites few of the known legal documents about Calamity, and the factual material drawn from newspapers and other published accounts could have been condensed into a twenty-five-page essay.

But the Calamity Jane who emerges from Aikman's book fits well with the lively Old West heroes and heroines of the interwar period. His Calamity is a worthy companion for the heroes in journalist Walter Noble Burns's *Saga of Billy the Kid* (1926) and newspaperman Stuart Lake's *Wyatt Earp: Frontier Marshall* (1931). These romantic, overly dramatized protagonists had also been made larger than life and inducted into the pantheon of frontier demigods.

Notable as Aikman's distorted telling of her life story was in shaping the legendary Calamity, it had to share top billing as the molding force with Cecil B. DeMille's extraordinarily popular film *The Plainsman* (1936). DeMille loved spectacular, circuslike, panoramic movies. *The Plainsman* depicts the history of the West as an extravaganza. Opening with President Abraham Lincoln's command that the frontier be cleared of barriers to northern men and families needing land after the Civil War, the movie uses Calamity Jane, Wild Bill Hickok, General George Custer, and Buffalo Bill Cody as western giants smoothing the way for the incoming settlers.

Given DeMille's predilections, Calamity Jane, played by Jean Arthur, must serve as the romantic opposite to Gary Cooper's Wild Bill Hickok. She must also act out the feminine/masculine ambiguity that audiences were coming to expect of her character. If Buffalo Bill and his new wife Louisa symbol-

Jean Arthur's lively, romantic portrayal of Calamity Jane opposite Gary Cooper's Wild Bill Hickok in Cecil B. DeMille's The Plainsman *(1936) did much to establish the positive images of early cinematic Calamity's in Hollywood Westerns. (Courtesy L. Tom Perry Special Collections, Harold B. Lee Library, Brigham Young University, Provo, Utah, #11867.)*

ize a coming civilized West—marriage, pregnancy, acquisition of property, and settling down—Wild Bill and Calamity represent a frontier inimical to civilizing. Frequently, Louisa Cody and Calamity are contrasted as a western lady against a frontier woman not yet a lady.

Throughout the film, Calamity plays a hybrid character. Early on she uses impolite words and descriptions—swearing without swearing. She also drives a stagecoach in a wild, masculine manner and swings a long bullwhip like no other pioneer woman. And she is too forward with Bill, pushing at him, touching and kissing him. Yet her form-fitting buckskins are clean and not unattractive, her hair nicely arranged and never much out of place despite the nonstop action. Perhaps she acts like a man in her bull-whacking and whipping, but she also wants to be a woman, a wife and mother.

One memorable scene in *The Plainsman* reverberates with symbolic meaning and encapsulates DeMille's interpretation of Calamity. Preparing to secure help for soldiers pinned down by Indians, Calamity steps out of the nearly ruined skirt of a stylish dress she had donned earlier in hopes of proving her femininity, and rides for reinforcements in the buckskins worn beneath her dress. Moving back and forth from dress to leather pants, Jean Arthur's Calamity personifies the oxymoronic legend of Calamity that had crystallized by the 1930s. Spunky, perky, and pretty but also assertive and courageous (but not boozy or loose), Calamity plays a romantic, vernacular woman of the frontier who wishes to marry.

It was in another film, *Calamity Jane* (1953) starring Doris Day, that the romantic Calamity came into full flower. This delightful if innocent musical showcases Day's singing talents—and her physical attractiveness. Good-looking, agile, and overflowing with vivaciousness, Day represents the romantic, less gritty Wild West Calamity. There will be no alcohol for her, only "sasparillah"; and her swearing is limited to no worse than her denunciations of recalcitrant miners as a "mangy pack of dirt-scratching beetles" or "slab-sided coyotes." Most of all, the movie appealingly blends romance, adventure, frenetic action, and folksy music.

Revealingly, the film invokes familiar themes about Calamity even as it avoids others. Although in the first scenes Doris Day's Calamity exhibits masculine ways in her dress, speech, and actions, it is love, romance, and marriage that she really wants—and obtains—before the movie ends. And in Sammy Fain's Oscar-winning "Secret Love," whose lyrics reveal that Calamity's "heart is now an open door" and "her love is secret no more," Day displays her love for Wild Bill. The movie omits, however, Calamity's alcoholism and sexual explicitness and makes little use of historical facts, including that Wild Bill died in Deadwood one month after he arrived in 1876. Overall, Day reveals a warm "female" heart, bursting with sentiment, love, and, if necessary, jealousy. Her Calamity is a lively, vivacious frontier woman who fits smoothly into the familiar musical tradition of the depiction of Annie Oakley in *Annie Get Your Gun* (1950).

A series of controversial events transpired in 1941 that shaped several later depictions of Calamity Jane. Jean Hickok McCormick, a shy, petite woman in her sixties, shocked aficionados of western history by announcing that she was the daughter of Calamity and Wild Bill. Adding to the controversy, McCormick claimed to own a diary and letters that Calamity, her mother, had written over the years to her darling "Janey." The national radio program "We the People" featured McCormick, declaring her the real thing. In the decade before her death in 1951, McCormick tried to promote her own story, without much success. But the reputed diary and letters of Calamity were published in pamphlet form and circulated widely.

Two elements ensured the popularity of McCormick's tale about Calamity Jane. So little was available about Calamity that this new source, despite its questionable authenticity, seemed to fill in many satisfying details. Now readers had the personal narrative of one of the country's premier Old West figures, the most notorious of its female characters. McCormick's allegation also attracted attention because it appeared as an appealing mother-daughter story, a narrative line missing from nearly all the largely masculine frontier stories. Without much reflection or new research, biographers, historians, and other writers capitalized on this suspect new information. Some authors made the Calamity-Janey relationship the central feature of their books; others used the ostensible diary and letters to make Calamity a more human and complex figure.

The 1950s, a notable period for western fiction, film, and television shows, spawned three biographies of Calamity Jane. The least successful of the three, Glenn Clairmonte's *Calamity Was the Name for Jane* (1959), also made the most extensive use of McCormick's *Calamity Jane* story. In addition, the author felt free to create conversations including Calamity without substantive sources. Clairmonte's Calamity was a warm, sexual woman troubled with alcoholism. The other biographer who made large use of the reputed diary and letters, Nolie Mumey in *Calamity Jane* (1950), carried out extensive research in newspapers but failed to critically examine these journalistic sources or carefully weigh the evidence for and against McCormick's materials. Mumey devoted about one-third of his 140-page book to the first publication of the diary and letters.

The third and strongest of the three biographies is Roberta B. Sollid's *Calamity Jane: A Study in Historical Criticism* (1958). First prepared as a master's thesis at the University of Montana, Sollid's brief but well-researched book remains the best biography yet published. Sorting through hundreds of newspaper clippings and other obscure sources and interviewing a few persons who knew Calamity, the author provides a balanced—if depressing—portrait of her subject. Although Sollid obviously had not set out to prove previous writers irresponsible sensationalists, her matter-of-fact treatment of Calamity not only undercut earlier biographies but furnished readers with the fuller picture that eluded other writers. Sollid's no-nonsense approach also undermined earlier romantic accounts even as it rejected the McCormick stories as "so out of line with other facts they can be dismissed."

If images of a romantic Calamity Jane dominated fiction, films, and biographies appearing before 1960, a new kind of heroine began to emerge after that time. Clearly, Roberta Sollid's realistic study helped pave the way for the less idealistic treatments of this Old West figure and pioneer woman. Even though many of the more recent interpretations of Calamity have, unfortunately, followed the spurious Jean McCormick account, they have also created a new "gray" Calamity. In doing so, these new gray stories reflect the sociocultural changes transforming the United States since the 1960s. These emerging narratives illustrate, as well, shifting, new views of the American West.

Many of the films and novels about the West appearing since the mid-1960s epitomize a pessimistic mood invading the United States. The buffeting blows of controversy, stress, and change, often associated with an unpopular war in Vietnam, the Watergate controversy in politics, and dramatic shifts in ethnic and gender identities, helped usher in a watershed period in interpretations of the American West. In such movies as *The Wild Bunch* (1969), *Little Big Man* (1970), and the Westerns of Clint Eastwood such as *A Fistful of Dollars* (1964), soldiers, lawmen, and frontier settlers were depicted as violent and immoral Indian haters. In novels like Thomas Berger's *Little Big Man* (1964), Robert Flynn's *North to Yesterday* (1967), and John Seelye's *The Kid* (1972), images of an optimistic, romantic Old West are challenged, reoriented, or destroyed. Not surprisingly, new images of Calamity Jane reflected these shifts in attitudes and popular culture.

Two novels were central to this reimagining of a new gray Calamity after the 1960s. Pete Dexter's *Deadwood* (1986) and Larry McMurtry's *Buffalo Girls* (1990) reinforced earlier realistic accounts of Calamity but simultaneously introduced a mood of black humor missing from previous treatments. Dexter's Calamity smells like the ripe mules and horses she rides. She's unwashed, unloved, and underappreciated, a two-legged screaming eagle bragging of her "husband" Wild Bill Hickok and outdrinking all others, men and vile drunkards included. Calamity is so rancid that a fresh crop of mold goes unnoticed on her neck, and no man pays much attention to her even though fornication and sexual violence rule Deadwood.

McMurtry's Calamity in *Buffalo Girls* illustrates Americans' growing ambiguity about a romantic Old West. Calamity enters the novel puzzled about the disappearance of her frontier and its being embalmed in Buffalo Bill's new phony traveling show, the Wild West. Along with her aging Indian and mountain men acquaintances and her best friend Dora DuFran, a madam and frustrated lover, Calamity is forced to live on the traumatic edge of memory and an uninviting present. By the end of the novel we realize she has conjured an imaginary daughter to whom she writes tearful laments. She also hints at the disappointments she may have suffered as a hermaphrodite.

Similar images of Calamity as an ambivalent, ambiguous heroine appear in more recent films. *Calamity Jane* (1984), a television movie starring Jane Alexander, *Buffalo Girls* (1995), with Angelica Houston as Calamity, and *Wild Bill* (1995), featuring Ellen Barkin as Calamity, display cinematic leading women cut from the same gray cloth as the females of the novels by Dexter and McMurtry.

Based heavily on the purported diary and letters, Jane Alexander's *Calamity* repeatedly tries to control her uncertain destiny in a masculine world. She admits "what I know about wifeing you could stuff in a saddlebag" and on one occasion tells a startled Janey (who does not know the speaker is her mother): "Well, I guess it's the same for us ladies here or there. You either get paid for washing a man's drawers or for pulling them down." Independent, unpolished, and ultimately tragic, Calamity barely holds on in a life full of frustrations. Disappointed in love and motherhood, she nonetheless retains her courage and honor in the face of stinging failures. In her unvarnished and gritty actions, Alexander's Calamity, foreshadowing even more realistic images, illustrates the large distance between her and Doris Day's romantic Calamity of the 1950s.

A decade later in the movie *Buffalo Girls* (1995), the probing treatment of sexuality, gender roles, maternal desires, and a disappearing Old West revealed how far recent interpretations of Calamity Jane have moved from the earlier romantic images. This film also drew extensively on the diary and letters. In several scenes, Calamity and her sweetheart Dora, a madam, are as intimate as the kissing old mountain men. Yet Calamity can traipse around an isolated West with the two trappers, the aging Indian named No Ears, and other men without fear of harassment. Perhaps her ambivalent sexual identity protects her. She writes to Janey in her diary that since "wifeing and whoring" are the only ways of life for an Old West woman, and neither is for her, she dresses and passes like a man. On another occasion she says she's "never really thought of myself as a woman."

Like McMurtry's novel of the same name, the *Buffalo Girls* film uses Calamity as a revealing symbol of a vanishing Wild West. She, the two old mountaineers, and the Indians, No Ears and Sitting Bull, epitomize a frontier passing from the scene and being embalmed in pageantry and showmanship. The Old West must be gone, they agree, because Bill Cody is now dramatizing it throughout the country. When Cody says he wants to make Calamity famous, she retorts "I am famous." After joining his arena show, Calamity tells him "I'm gonna let you make me immortal"—since she's already famous. The film ends as it began, with Calamity riding off into the Rockies. Even if the Old West is dead, she's free to go on.

In the movie *Wild Bill*, Ellen Barkin's Calamity Jane represents womanly concerns also apparent in *Calamity Jane* (1984) and *Buffalo Girls* (1995). She wants Wild Bill to love her but accepts something far less. On occasion, she initiates sexual activity and seems willing to admit that she might be a one-night stand, although she is angry when others mistreat her as a woman.

Calamity is also portrayed as the only nurturer in the heathenish band in Deadwood. Looking after Bill's health, she likewise cares for and cleans up the saloon and helps other needy ones. Some viewers might see her as a whore with a soul, with social conscience in a hell-driven world.

Barkin's Calamity additionally illustrates other late-twentieth-century concerns. For example, she forces Wild Bill to think about the nature of love, men and women, and sexuality—or proves his unwillingness to ponder these important issues. She also worries, by coming on to Bill, whether she's lost her womanliness and become a prostitute. True, Calamity's world is a man's Old West, but she serves as the revealing commentator on gender, class organization, and honor, thereby becoming the most important woman on a masculine frontier. In this film, an ambivalent Calamity seems to represent the complexities of love, sexuality, class, and gender that plagued Americans in the mid-1990s.

By the end of the twentieth century, Calamity Jane figures were appearing in dozens of popular cultural mediums. In addition to starring in fiction and films, she showed up in an increasing numbers of essays, including those by her leading recent biographer, James McLaird. And in the 1970s and afterward, English novelist J. T. Edson turned out more than a dozen novels featuring Calamity as a frontier Amazon, sometimes involved in topless wrestling brawls, but nearly always proving her mettle as a gun woman, rider, entrepreneur, or sex symbol in a chaotic American West. Calamity also starred in an animated television series and was the central subject in various books of poems, essays, or stories. At the turn of the twenty-first century, there was no dearth of interest in Calamity Jane, the Wild West woman.

In the century since the death of Martha Canary, the legendary Calamity Jane has moved through several stages and gradually crystallized into a recognizable figure of popular culture. She has evolved from a woman epitomizing a romantic, untamed Old West. Bruising gender expectations in her actions and dress, Calamity surfaced as a wild woman during her lifetime in hundreds of sensational newspaper stories, reminiscences, and dime novels. Since 1903, journalists, biographers, and filmmakers have followed many facets of the legend they inherited. Films like *The Plainsman* and *Calamity Jane* (1953) rounded off Calamity's rough edges and romanticized her. After the 1940s, several writers and film producers accepted Jean Hickok McCormick's spurious story and embedded a mother-daughter theme in their stories. More recently, novelists like Pete Dexter and Larry McMurtry and films such as *Calamity Jane* (1984) and *Buffalo Girls* (1995) feature a more nuanced figure, not black or white, but gray.

Revealingly, few writers, directors, or actresses portrayed their subject as a young Martha Canary or as an older pioneer woman. But the portrayals may be changing. Earlier, biographer Roberta Sollid, in her pacesetting work, illustrated what form a realistic study of Calamity might take. James McLaird, in a series of valuable essays and in a forthcoming biography, points the way to thorough, factual treatments of Calamity. Even as Hollywood and fictionists seem addicted to Calamity's purported diary and letters as well as to falsehoods about her including a grand love affair with Bill Hickok, several scholars are preparing honest studies of the Martha Canary who became Calamity Jane. This new scholarship will help us to understand the gradual, inexorable invention of this notable Wild West woman.

Sources and Further Reading

Chapter 1—Baby Doe Tabor

Original documents and artifacts relating to Baby Doe Tabor are in the Western History Collection/Genealogy Department of the Denver Public Library, jointly held with the Colorado Historical Society and the Denver Art Museum. Holdings may be searched by using the Internet address http://gowest.coalliance.org. The Colorado State Archives and Health Department, Vital Records Division, holds birth, marriage, divorce, and death records at www.coloradohistory.org. At the same address is the Colorado Genealogy Society, which offers assistance in searching Colorado genealogies; the National Archives Rocky Mountain Region, which houses military service records, papers of federal courts and other agencies in Colorado, and census records for all states; and the Bureau of Land Management, Colorado State Office, which has mining claims, as well as homestead and other land records.

Baby Doe's story has been told many times. Today, the two most reliable sources are Duane A. Smith's well-researched and well-written *Horace Tabor: His Life and the Legend* (Niwot: University Press of Colorado, 1989) and a four-part video presentation produced in 2000, *Leadville's Story of Baby Doe Tabor*, which is characterized by good research and arresting graphics. The video is available from Universal Systems, Inc., P.O. Box 1232, Buena Vista, CO 81211, or email video@coloradovideos.com.

A number of other pamphlets and books have told her story with wide discrepancies in fact and interpretation. These include David Karsner, *Silver Dollar: The Story of the Tabors* (n.p.: n.p., 1932); Caroline Bancroft, *Silver Queen: The Fabulous Story of Baby Doe Tabor* (Boulder, Colo.: Johnson Books, 1950); Gordon Langley Hall, *The Two Lives of Baby Doe* (Philadelphia: Macrae Smith Co., 1962); Theresa O'Brien, *The Bitter Days of Baby Doe Tabor and Memories of the High Country* (n.p.: n.p., 1963); and John Burke, *The Legend of Baby Doe* (Lincoln: University of Nebraska Press, 1974, and Univ. of Nebraska's Bison Books, 1989). Baby Doe is also included in Phyllis Flanders Dorset, *The Story of Colorado's Gold & Silver Rushes* (New York: Barnes & Noble, 1970). Regarding Baby Doe's youngest daughter, consult Evelyn E. Livingston Furman, *Silver Dollar Tabor: The Leaf in the Storm* (Englewood, Colo.: Quality Press, 1982), and Sandra S. Akridge, *The Enigma of Silver Dollar Tabor* (n.p.: n.p., 1985).

For Augusta Tabor, a wide range of pamphlets also exist, with a modicum of agreement among them. Because Augusta kept a journal, gave newspaper interviews, and collected articles about Horace, researchers have access to some "facts," at least as Augusta interpreted events. See, for example, Edgar C. McMehen, *The Tabor Story* (Denver: State Historical Society, 1951); Caroline Bancroft, *Augusta Tabor: Her Side of the Scandal* (Boulder, Colo.: Johnson Books, 1955); Betty Moynihan, *Augusta Tabor: A Pioneering Woman* (Evergreen, Colo.: Cordillera Press, 1988); and Evelyn E. Livingston Furman, *My Search for Augusta Pierce Tabor: Leadville's First Lady* (Denver: Quality Press, 1993).

For Horace Tabor, sources other than Duane Smith's book include Lewis Cass Gandy, *The Tabors: A Footnote of Western History* (New York: Press of the Pioneer, 1934); Sarah J. Burton and Doris B. Smith, *The Tabors* (Leadville, Colo.: Victorian Shop, 1949); Rene L. Coquoz, *The Saga of H. A. W. Tabor* (Boulder, Colo.: Johnson Publishing, 1973); and Ruby G. Williamson, *From Kansas to the Matchless: The Tabor Story, 1857–1880* (Gunnison, Colo.: B & B Printers, 1975).

Discussions of the architecture that Tabor influenced can be found in Charlie H. Johnson Jr., *H. A. W. Tabor and His Leadville Opera House* (Denver: Tower Press, 1980); Evelyn E. Livingston Furman, *The Tabor Opera House: A Captivating History* (Aurora, Colo.: National Writers Press, 1984); and John W. Buchanan and Doris G. Buchanan, *A Story of the Fabulous Windsor Hotel* (Denver: A. B. Hirschfeld Press, 1958). Also helpful in understanding the architecture and other features of early Denver is Stephen J. Leonard and Thomas J. Noel, *Denver: Mining Camp to Metropolis* (Niwot: University Press of Colorado, 1990).

Baby Doe is available in other media as well. In 1956, Douglas Moore's opera *The Ballad of Baby Doe* premiered at the Central City Opera House. One review said it "is not just a great American opera but the Great American Opera." He added that the opera told "a riches-to-rags story," which was "quintessentially American." Today, there is a Baby Doe doll available, whereas the restored Matchless Mine and cabin in Leadville exhibits some of Baby Doe's meager belongings. In addition, Baby Doe Matchless Mine Restaurants are located in Denver and Dallas–Fort Worth, with pseudo-mine decor. Information on all these items and more can be accessed by simply entering the name "Baby Doe Tabor" into any Internet search engine.

Chapter 2—Emily D. West (Morgan)

With the literature on "The Yellow Rose of Texas" being rich in fable and lean on fact, bits of information about her and her times can come from books and letters of better documented characters of the era. Biographies of Stephen F. Austin, the "Father of Texas," give further understanding of the world Emily D. West came to and the woman she traveled with, Lorenzo de Zavala's wife. See, for example, Gregg Cantrell, *Stephen F. Austin: Empresario of Texas* (New Haven: Yale University Press, 1999), and Margaret Swett Henson, *Lorenzo de Zavala: The Pragmatic Idealist* (Fort Worth: Texas Christian University Press, 1996).

Providing historical backdrop are books such as Julien Hyder, *The Land of Beginning Again* (Atlanta: Tupper & Love, 1952); William Ransom Hogan, *The Texas Republic: A Social and Economic History* (Norman: University of Oklahoma Press, 1946); and Paul D. Lack, *The Texas Revolutionary Experience: A Political and Social History, 1835–1836* (College Station: Texas A&M University Press, 1992).

During the western expansion period of the United States, many came to Texas to record their observations. Their accounts include David B. Edward, *The History of Texas, or The Emigrant's, Farmer's & Politician's Guide to the Character, Climate, Soil & Productions of That Country, Geographically Arranged from Personal Observation & Experience* (1836; Austin: Texas State Historical Association, 1990), and James M. Day, *Texas Almanac, 1857–1873: A Compendium of Texas History* (Waco: Texian Press, 1967).

Primary source accounts of the women during Texas's War for Independence, especially during the Runaway Scrape, include "The Reminiscences of Mrs. Dilue Rose Harris," *Quarterly of the Texas State Historical Association* 4 (1900), reprinted in Jo Ella Powell Exley, ed., *Texas Tears and Texas Sunshine: Voices of Frontier Women* (College Station: Texas A&M University Press, 1985).

Texian soldiers' memoirs provide firsthand knowledge of the Battle of San Jacinto from the common soldiers' experience, and what they saw and learned about Santa Anna. These include John J. Linn, *Reminiscences of Fifty Years in Texas* (Austin: State House Press, 1986); William P. Zuber, *My Eighty Years in Texas*, Janis Boyle Mayfield, ed. (Austin: University of Texas Press, 1971); John Holland Jenkins, *Recollections of Early Texas* (memoirs), ed. John Holmes Jenkins III (Austin: University of Texas Press, 1958); and John C. Duvall, *Early Times in Texas, or the Adventures of Jack Dobell*, ed. Mable Major and Rebecca W. Smith (Lincoln: University of Nebraska Press, 1936). An unbound collection, "Memoirs of George Bernard Erath," in the Texas State Archives, Texas State Library in Austin, exhibits both the complaint and weary acceptance of a young and too-wizened common foot soldier standing guard over Santa Anna's opulence and the auction of his goods.

First-person accounts for the Mexican side of the war are the testimonies of participants. For example, consult *Mexican Side of Texas Revolution by the Chief Mexican Participants* (Gen. Antonio Lopez Santa Anna, D. Ramon Martinez, Caro, *secretary to Santa Anna*, Gen. Vicente Filisola, Gen. Jose Urrea, Gen. Jose Maria Tornel, *Secy of War*, comp. P. L. Turner Co. (Dallas: Texas State Library and Archives Commission, 1956).

To understand the thoughts, actions, and justifications of the two main protagonists, Santa Anna and Sam Houston, see their biographies and writings. For example, consult Frank C. Hanighen, *Santa Anna, the Napoleon of the West* (New York: Coward McCann, 1934); Ann Fears Crawford, ed., *The Eagle: The Autobiography of Santa Anna* (Austin: State House Press, 1988); Amelia W. Williams and Eugene C. Barker, eds., *Writings of Sam Houston, 1836*, Vol. 1 (Austin: University of Texas Press, 1938); and Marquis James, *The Raven: A Biography of Sam Houston* (Austin: University of Texas Press, 1929, 1956).

Letters in the Sam Houston Papers and the John Austin Papers, in the Texas State Archives, Austin, are especially revealing. They detail compelling emotions and descriptions and frantic plans to yield a republic in a time when mail was delivered by courier, communications hampered by time.

In other special collections, the writings of officials of the new government provide comprehension of Texas when Emily's stories began, creating a sense of who she might have been. Detailing the New Washington community and association are the James Morgan Papers, Rosenberg Library, Galveston, Texas; letters regarding slavery and the increasing tensions between Mexico and its colonists over this issue and taxes, Stephen F. Austin Papers, S. F. Austin Colony, 1825, University of Texas Archives; Mirabeau Lamar Papers, 1798–1859, for correspondence about the aftermath of the Battle of San Jacinto, Texas State Archives, Austin; and the A. Henry Moss Papers, Archives Division, University of Texas at Austin.

The New Handbook of Texas, 6 vols. (Austin: Texas State Historical Association, 1996), provides excellent, brief synopses of events, places, and people such as James Morgan, Morgan's Point, Lynchburg, Adam Stafford, Anahuac and the Runaway Scrape, San Jacinto, Harrisburg, and New Washington.

Coastal Texas in the 1820s and 1830s is unique in the sea traffic it received, the nature of that traffic, and its population, from pirates to slave smugglers to the first Texas Navy. A review of the following books gives pleasurable reading and information on republic ports such as Galveston, San Jacinto, Morgan's Point, Anahuac, and Velasquez: Richard V. Francavigla,

From Sail to Steam: Four Centuries of Texas Maritime History, 1500–1900 (Austin: University of Texas Press, 1998), and Keith Guthrie, *Texas Forgotten Ports—Vol. II* (Austin: Eakin Press, 1993). Harold Schoen, "The Free Negro in the Republic of Texas," *Southwestern Historical Quarterly* 39 (July 1935, April 1936), details the struggles over slavery, and the freed Negro population in Texas. John E. Weems and Jane Weems, *Dream of Empire* (New York: Barnes & Noble Books, 1976, 1995), and Gary Cartwright, *Galveston: A History of the Island* (Fort Worth: Texas Christian University Press, 1991), visit the legend of the Yellow Rose and her entrance to, and exit from, Texas.

Finally, William C. Pool, *A Historical Atlas of Texas* (Austin: Encino Press, 1975), provides a geographical footprint for the changing political entities of Texas.

Chapter 3—Polly Bemis

Primary sources for this biographical sketch include several published interviews with Polly Bemis, her neighbor's diaries, and oral history interviews with people who knew her. In addition, photographs, census records, deeds, vital statistics, and tax rolls provided other helpful details for both Polly and Charlie Bemis. The first known interview with Polly, a brief one in 1921 by Countess Eleanor Gizycka, appeared in *Field and Stream* 28 (June 1923): 278, and was reprinted in *Idaho Yesterdays* 41 (spring 1997): 20–21. Other interviews ran in Grangeville's *Idaho County Free Press* on August 16 and 23, 1923, and in the *Idaho Daily Statesman* on August 4, 1924. Another article, by Lamont Johnson, containing information he obtained from Polly's nurse, appeared in the *Sunday Oregonian* on November 5, 1933.

Sister M. Alfreda Elsensohn collected most of the available photographs depicting Polly Bemis. She used many of them in her brief biography of Polly, *Idaho County's Most Romantic Character, Polly Bemis* (Cottonwood: Idaho Corporation of Benedictine Sisters, 1978). The photographs are housed at The Historical Museum at St. Gertrude in Cottonwood, Idaho, with copies at the Idaho State Historical Society Library and Archives in Boise. Subsequent authors who have written about Polly Bemis, myself included, owe Sister Alfreda a large debt of gratitude for bringing Polly to our attention.

Several people who knew Polly when they were children provided charming reminiscences. They include Bob Bunting, the late Johnny Carrey, and the late Herb McDowell. Bob Bunting visited Polly in the hospital in 1933. Johnny Carrey's younger sister Gay, now deceased, lived with Polly in Warren for one school term and Johnny spent much of his free time with them. Herb McDowell and his brothers knew Polly in Warren, and Herb interviewed Warren resident

Otis Morris on tape. Notes from, or transcriptions of, these interviews are in my possession. They and other materials will eventually be housed in the University of Idaho's Asian American Comparative Collection, Moscow.

The available documentary sources include census records from 1880 on (except for 1890) and a few contemporary newspaper accounts, all on microfilm at the University of Idaho Library in Moscow. Idaho County records, at the Idaho County Courthouse in Grangeville, detail Charlie Bemis's mining ventures and business dealings; Polly is not mentioned. The records from Polly's court case in 1896 are at the National Archives in Seattle, whereas her marriage certificate and Certificate of Residence are at The Historical Museum at St. Gertrude. From late 1902 on, Polly's everyday life is sometimes disclosed in the small pocket diaries kept by Charlie Shepp, her neighbor across the Salmon River. Photocopies of the diaries are in the University of Idaho Library Special Collections.

No scholarly biography of Polly Bemis has appeared, but mine is in progress. It will also include her husband, Charlie Bemis, whose life I briefly detail in "Charlie Bemis: Idaho's Most Significant Other," *Idaho Yesterdays* 44 (fall 2000): 3–18. The beautifully written and critically acclaimed *Thousand Pieces of Gold*, by Ruthanne Lum McCunn (San Francisco: Design Enterprises of San Francisco, 1981), has been reprinted at least four times since its original publication. This "biographical novel" is based on much that is true, but the fabricated conversations make it more novel than biography. Still, it will fascinate anyone interested in Polly Bemis. The film, *Thousand Pieces of Gold* (1991), fictionalizes Polly's life even more. Despite some inaccuracies not present in the book, it is enjoyable to watch and encourages comparisons between the book, the movie, and Polly's real life. For example, people familiar with either the book or the film are often disappointed to learn that the handsome young Chinese man, Jim, the pack train operator and love interest in the novel and the movie, was one of McCunn's "fictitious characters."

Some of the "pulp fiction" about Polly is quite amusing, particularly the different versions of the poker game story. These include Ladd Hamilton, "How Mr. Bemis Won the Chinese Slave Girl," *Saga* 8 (September 1954): 50–51, 59 (to his credit, Hamilton later wrote "That Famous Poker Game May Never Have Happened," *Lewiston Morning Tribune* [June 14, 1987]: 7A); Lee Ryland, "Redemption of Charley Bemis," *Real West* 5 (March 1962): 12–13, 52–54; Ryland, "The Strange Winnings of Charlie Bemis," *Big West* 1 (December 1967): 32–33, 51–52; and Charles Kelly, "He Won His Wife In a Poker Game," *The Pony Express* 36 (February 1970): 3–5. In a similar vein, book chapters or sections on Polly emphasizing the poker game story include

C. Y. Lee, "China Polly," *Days of the Tong Wars* (New York: Ballantine, 1974), 66–83; Harry Sinclair Drago, "China Polly, the Poker Bride," *Notorious Ladies of the Frontier* (New York: Dodd, Mead, 1969), 151–55; and James D. Horan, "Johnny Bemis and China Polly," *Desperate Women* (New York: G. P. Putnam's Sons, 1952), 310–14.

Historian Benson Tong's book *Unsubmissive Women: Chinese Prostitutes in Nineteenth-Century San Francisco* (Norman: University of Oklahoma Press, 1994) calls Polly "perhaps the most legendary Chinese prostitute outside San Francisco." Others who also perpetuate the myth of Polly as a prostitute include Patricia Hogan, "Bemis, Polly" in *Encyclopedia of the American West* (New York: Simon & Schuster Macmillan, 1996), 1: 134; Wendolyn Spence Holland, *Sun Valley: An Extraordinary History* (Ketchum: The Idaho Press, 1998), 113; F. Ross Peterson, *Idaho, a Bicentennial History* (New York: W. W. Norton and Nashville: American Association for State and Local History, 1976), 59; and Rebecca Stefoff, *Women Pioneers* (New York: Facts on File, 1995), 107–13.

There is a vast literature on Chinese women. Some relevant sources include Denise Chong's fascinating family history, *The Concubine's Children* (New York: Viking, 1994), as well as the scholarly contributions by Maria Jaschok, *Concubines and Bondservants: The Social History of a Chinese Custom* (Hong Kong: Oxford University Press, 1988), and Rubie S. Watson and Patricia Buckley Ebrey, eds., *Marriage and Inequality in Chinese Society* (Berkeley: University of California Press, 1991). For footbinding, see Beverley Jackson's lavishly illustrated *Splendid Slippers: A Thousand Years of an Erotic Tradition* (Berkeley: Ten Speed Press, 1997) and Howard S. Levy, *Chinese Footbinding: The History of a Curious Erotic Custom* (New York: Bell, 1967). For Chinese naming customs, Emma Woo Louie's *Chinese American Names: Tradition and Transition* (Jefferson, No. Carol.: McFarland, 1998) is essential.

For a popular account of the Chinese in Warren, and Polly Bemis, see Sister M. Alfreda Elsensohn, *Idaho Chinese Lore* (Cottonwood: Idaho Corporation of Benedictine Sisters, 1970), 76–88. For Warren in general, including much information on the Chinese in the vicinity, Cheryl Helmers's *Warren Times* (Odessa, Texas: The Author, 1988) is an intriguing labor of love. At first glance, the volume appears to be excerpts from Warren newspapers, but Warren never had a newspaper. The book is actually comprised of articles about Warren that appeared in a wide variety of other sources. For the Salmon River, including Polly and Charlie Bemis, and Charlie Shepp and Pete Klinkhammer, the indispensable classic is Johnny Carrey and Cort Conley, *River of No Return* (Cambridge, Idaho: Backeddy Books, 1978).

As demonstrated, the material about Polly Bemis, and its accuracy, varies widely. A final, unwritten, source is the site of her home and grave on the remote Salmon River, still inaccessible by automobile. Polly lived at this idyllic location for nearly forty years and it is there that one can best recapture the spirit of this remarkable pioneer woman.

Chapter 4—Mattie, Katie, and Ida

In recent years, the literature concerning western prostitution has greatly increased. It remains difficult, however, to find a full-length scholarly biography devoted to a single woman. In general, the subjects did not leave sufficient historical material to make such publication possible. Primary research is best drawn from the local public record. Thus, western newspapers, such as Denver's *Rocky Mountain News*, provide a rich source for information about prostitution, especially when supplemented with data found in court dockets, jail registers, justice of the peace dockets, and cemetery records.

In 1981, Marion Goldman published *Gold Diggers and Silver Miners: Prostitution and Social Life on the Comstock Lode* (Ann Arbor: University of Michigan Press, 1981), a work based on a sociological perspective, which opened western prostitution to serious scholarship. *The City and the Saloon: Denver, 1858–1916* (Lincoln: University of Nebraska Press, 1982), by Thomas J. Noel, although not entirely devoted to the topic of prostitution, included valuable information about the dynamics of the Denver vice world and its relationship to municipal authorities. Noel built on the earlier work of Elliott West, whose *The Saloon on the Rocky Mountain Mining Frontier* (Lincoln: University of Nebraska Press, 1979) explored the importance of a vice district in the building of frontier community. Six years later, Anne M. Butler's *Daughters of Joy, Sisters of Misery: Prostitutes in the American West, 1865–1890* (Urbana: University of Illinois Press, 1985) suggested the regional importance of prostitution in the first historical monograph devoted to the subject. Butler followed with *Gendered Justice in the American West: Women Prisoners in Men's Penitentiaries* (Urbana: University of Illinois Press, 1997), which incorporated much material about the experiences of western prostitutes with the criminal justice system.

Paula Petrik's *No Step Backward: Women and Family on the Rocky Mountain Mining Frontier, Helena, Montana, 1865–1900* (Helena: Montana Historical Society Press, 1987) did much to explore the interaction between middle-class white women and prostitutes in a mining community. Benson Tong's study *Unsubmissive Women: Chinese Prostitutes in Nineteenth-Century San Francisco* (Norman: University of Oklahoma Press, 1994) turned attention to women of color in western prostitution. Less scholarly works that focus on prostitution in Denver include two by Caroline Bancroft, *Six Racy Madams of Colorado* (Boulder, Colo.: Johnson, 1965) and *Denver's Lively Past: From a Wild and Woolly Camp to Queen City of the Plains* (Boulder, Colo.: Johnson, 1971), as well as Clark Secrest's *Hell's Belles: Denver's Brides of the Multitudes* (Aurora, Colo.: Hindsight Historical Publications, 1996). Given the complexity of western prostitution, especially concerning race, much scholarship remains to be written.

Chapter 5—Sadie Orchard

Documents regarding Sarah Creech Orchard are few. A number of copies of them, as well as newspaper clippings and a number of Sadie Orchard's artifacts, are in the Black Range Museum in Hillsboro, New Mexico. Copies of documents, photographs, and articles are also in the Geronimo Spring Museum in Truth or Consequences, New Mexico. Clipping files regarding Kingston, Hillsboro, Silver City, and Black Range prostitutes are in the Silver City Museum, Silver City, New Mexico.

Among other primary documentation is the stagecoach that Sadie reportedly drove—the Mountain Pride with Victorio's picture on each door—which can be seen at the old County Courthouse, Lincoln State Monument, Lincoln, New Mexico. In Hillsboro, Edward Montoya, who still maintains the family residence across from what was the Orchard Hotel, is happy to share his childhood memories of Sadie. Also, James A. McKenna's *Black Range Tales* (Glorieta, New Mexico: Rio Grande Press, 1963) is an account of the way one Black Range miner saw and heard the events of the 1880s and 1890s.

Secondary accounts of Sadie's life tend to pass on myths, one to another. Some are more believable than others, notably Erna Fergusson, *New Mexico: A Pageant of Three Peoples* (New York: Alfred A. Knopf, 1964), 292–94. Others include Thelma Knoles, "Hillsboro—Out of a Hat," *Old West* 5 (summer 1969): 3–7; Jack F. Findlay, "Sadie Was a Character," *Password* 16 (spring 1971): 25–30; the very unreliable Bill Rakocy's *Ghosts of Kingston-Hillsboro, New Mexico* (El Paso, TX: Bravo Press, 1983); Mary'n Rosson, "A Good Old Gal," in Western Writers of America, *The Women Who Made the West* (New York: Avon Books, 1980), 88–103; Mary Frances Beverly, "Sadie Orchard Was a Good Ol' Girl," *New Mexico Museum Magazine* (July 1983): 40–42; and Sandra D. Lynn, "New Mexico's Most Notorious Hotelkeeper," *Windows on the Past: Historic Lodging of New Mexico* (Albuquerque: University of New Mexico Press, 1999), 93–96.

For descriptions of old mining towns and ghost towns in the Black Range area, consult Ralph Looney, *Haunted Highways: The Ghost Towns of New Mexico* (Albuquerque: University of New Mexico Press, 1968); James E. and Barbara H. Sherman, *Ghost Towns and Mining Camps of New Mexico* (Norman: University of Oklahoma Press, 1975); and Philip Varney, *New Mexico's Best Ghost Towns* (Flagstaff, Ariz.: Northland Press, 1981). A feeling for the architecture of the area is given in Susan Berry and Sharman Apt Russell, *Built to Last: An Architectural History of Silver City, New Mexico* (Silver City: Museum Society, 2nd ed., 1995).

Information regarding forts is found in Dale F. Giese, *Forts of New Mexico* (Silver City: Phelps Dodge Corporation, 1991), and an unpublished manuscript in the Silver City Museum by Christina Joslin, *Fort Bayard: A Brief History*, c. 1999.

The Fountain trial is discussed in William S. Keleher, *The Fabulous Frontier: Twelve New Mexico Items* (Albuquerque: University of New Mexico Press, 1962); A. M. Gibson, *The Life and Death of Colonel Albert Jennings Fountain* (Norman: University of Oklahoma Press, 1965); and Leon C. Metz, *Pat Garrett: The Story of a Western Lawman* (Norman: University of Oklahoma Press, 1974).

Chapter 6—Lucille Mulhall

There is no scholarly biography of Lucille Mulhall, although Kathryn Stansbury has done a creditable job in telling the story of this cowgirl in her book *Lucille Mulhall: Wild West Cowgirl*, 2d ed., rev. (Mulhall, Okla.: Homestead Heirlooms Publishing Co., 1992), originally published in 1985 under the title *Lucille Mulhall: Her Family, Her Life, Her Times*. Published twice in limited quantities, the book is now out of print and difficult to obtain. Stansbury dug deeply into the family history, revealing in her second edition information about the parentage of Mildred and Charley Mulhall. I was provided with a copy from the private library of Mulhall resident Dorothy Reseneder, who also lent me a copy of the official souvenir program for the Oklahoma 89'er Celebration, published April 22, 1985, by American Legion Le Bron Post No. 58. In that publication are the articles "Lucille Mulhall," by Fred Olds, and "The Original Cowgirl," by Mildred Mulhall Acton, both of which provided valuable information for this essay.

By far the greatest assistance I received in preparing this chapter came from Martha "Moppy" Fisch of Guthrie, Oklahoma—daughter of Mildred Mulhall Acton, granddaughter of Zack Mulhall and Georgia Smith Mulhall, and niece of Lucille Mulhall. Georgia Mulhall became the official family historian as she clipped items from newspapers across the country when she and her family traveled with their Wild West show. She pasted those clippings into scrapbooks, which are now owned by Martha Fisch. Unfortunately, Georgia sometimes omitted information about the place, date, or publication in which the clippings appeared. The Fisch collection also contains numerous other materials related to the Mulhall family, including show programs and dozens of photographs. Martha Fisch graciously allowed me to view the materials at her home in Guthrie and to copy photographs, newspaper articles, and other documents for publication purposes. While I was researching those materials in February 2001, she also provided me with valuable personal information about her family.

The only other true biography of Lucille Mulhall is *America's First Cowgirl Lucille Mulhall,* by Beth Day (New York: Julian Messner, 1955), but it is seriously flawed. During her research, Day gathered information from both Charley Mulhall and Mildred Mulhall Acton; however, they did not tell her the full and truthful story. For example, they failed to note that Georgia Smith Mulhall did not live on the Mulhall Ranch in Oklahoma, nor did they reveal that Georgia was their mother and not their sister, as had been presented to outsiders throughout their lives.

For further details about Lucille Mulhall, one can turn to more general sources including the chapter, "The World's First Cowgirl Meets the Cherokee Kid," in Michael Wallis's *The Real Wild West: The 101 Ranch and the Creation of the American West* (New York: St. Martin's Press, 1999); "The Story of Lucille," by Fred Olds, in *The War Chief: Oklahoma Westerners* (December 1974); *The Wild West: A History of the Wild West Shows,* by Don Russell (Fort Worth: Amon Carter Museum of Western Art); and *The Cowgirls,* 2d ed., rev. by Joyce Gibson Roach (Denton: University of North Texas Press, 1990).

Chapter 7—Bertha Kaepernik Blancett

The following are helpful publications in learning of Bertha Blancett and her times.

Rodeo in America: Wranglers, Roughstock & Paydirt, by Wayne S. Wooden and Gavin Ehringer (Lawrence: University Press of Kansas, 1996): takes readers behind the chutes and celebrates a great national pastime, revealing the essential character of rodeo today and showing why rodeo retains such a strong hold on the American imagination.

Seeking Pleasure in the Old West, by David Dary (New York: Alfred A. Knopf, 1995): includes the Wild West shows and frontier rodeos and explores how people kept themselves happy in the Old West.

Rodeo Cowboys in the North American Imagination, by Michael Allen (Las Vegas and Reno: University of Nevada Press, 1998): a look at this enduring sport that draws audiences to venues from small western shows to Madison Square Garden.

The Real Wild West: The 101 Ranch and the Creation of the American West, by Michael Wallis (New York: St. Martin's Press, 1999): an exhaustive volume that looks at the founding of the ranch and the performers who worked there and explores the impact the 101 had on creating western myths.

Rodeo: The Suicide Circuit, by Fred Schnell (Chicago: Rand McNally, 1971): the wild men and half-wild animals who participate in this dangerous sport, through words and compelling photography.

Who's Who in Rodeo, by Willard H. Porter (Oklahoma City: Powder River Book Company, for the Rodeo Historical Society and the National Cowboy and Western Heritage Museum, 1983).

Cowgirls of the Rodeo: Pioneer Professional Athletes, by Mary Lou LeCompte (Urbana: University of Illinois Press, 1993, 2000): takes the reader on a smooth ride from the early Wild West shows and the golden age of rodeo in the 1920s, through the decline in the 1940s, to the climb back to the top from 1967 through the 1990s.

Gold Buckle: The Grand Obsession of Rodeo Bull Riders, by Jeff Coplon (San Francisco: Harper Collins West, 1995): how bull riders peak quickly and quit young and how they play out a daily drama with luck, pluck, and human failings.

Greasepaint Matadors: The Unsung Heroes of Rodeo, by Jeanne Joy Hartnagle-Taylor (Loveland, Colo.: Alpine Publishing Company, 1993): a tribute to the rodeo clowns and how they often save lives in the dangerous sport of rodeo.

Belly Full of Bedsprings: The History of Bronc Riding, by Gail Hughbank Woerner (Austin, Texas: Eakin Press, 1998): a chronological history of bronc riding, including the men, women, and animals who left their mark on rodeo.

American Rodeo from Buffalo Bill to Big Business, by Kristine Fredriksson (College Station: Texas A&M University Press, 1985): from the early days of rodeo and Wild West shows to the present, in a well-written, informed style.

The Cowboy Encyclopedia, by Richard W. Slatta (Santa Barbara, Calif.: ABC-CLIO, 1994).

"A Foot in Each World," by Nell Brown Propst, in *True West* (June 1979): the tough side of Bertha Blancett in the arena and the softer, more feminine side away from rodeo competition.

"Bertha Kaepernik," by Nell Brown Propst, in *The Ketchpen* (Rodeo Historical Society at the National Cowboy and Western Heritage Museum, Oklahoma City; winter 1997): a profile of her childhood and rodeo career.

"Rodeo Hall of Fame Adds Bertha Blancett," by Willetta Regan, in the *Porterville Recorder* (Porterville, Calif.; October 30, 1975): a review of Bertha Blancett's life and career.

"Memory Trail," by Foghorn Clancy, in *Hoofs and Horns* (May 1942): a review of Bertha Blancett's life in and out of rodeo.

Biography of Bertha Kaepernik Blancett, compiled for her induction into the Rodeo Hall of Fame (Rodeo Historical Society, the Dickinson Research Center at the National Cowboy and Western Heritage Museum, Oklahoma City; 1975).

"The Women of the Rodeo Road," by Ann Terry Hill, in _Persimmon Hill_ (National Cowboy and Western Heritage Museum, Oklahoma City; winter 1999).

Chapter 8—Cattle Kate

Sources on Cattle Kate are varied and scattered. Ellen L. Watson's grand-nephew, Daniel Brumbaugh, and her niece, Lola Marie Van Wey, graciously provided information and photographs through e-mail and telephone interviews during the preparation of this essay. Kathleen Sun, wife of Tom Sun's grandson, provided an earlier interview in connection with my book _Dreamers and Schemers: Profiles from Carbon County, Wyoming's Past_ (Glendo, Wyo.: High Plains Press, 1999), which contains brief profiles of Ella Watson and Tom Sun.

Primary sources are mainly courthouse records on file at the Carbon County courthouse in Rawlins, Wyoming. Probate information can be found in Ella Watson, Probate File 503, which contains information on Watson and Averell and their homestead filings. The lawsuit filed following her death can be located in Watson v. A. J. Bothwell and John Durbin, 458.

Other courthouse records include the irrigation ditch filings of Averell and Watson; bills of sale recording Ellen Watson's purchase of horses from Arthur G. Williams and her purchase of the LU brand; and her application for citizenship. Averell's mortgages and his notary commission can also be found at the Carbon County courthouse.

The application for Marriage License and the Marriage License itself, May 17, 1886, Fremont County, Wyoming (Territory), are located in Lander, Wyoming. Information on brands was located in the Carbon County Brand Book from 1875 to 1909, housed at the Saratoga Museum in Saratoga, Wyoming. Insights into character and appearance were gleaned from _John H. Fales, Pioneer_, manuscript from David Historical Collection, Casper College Library; and Harry Ward letter, Lake Ranch Stage Station, March 20, 1940, Wyoming State Archives, Division of State Parks and Cultural Resources, Cheyenne, Wyoming.

George W. Hufsmith's _The Wyoming Lynching of Cattle Kate, 1889_ (Glendo, Wyo.: High Plains Press, 1993) provides a differing viewpoint from the tradi-tional tale and gives astute readers a good variety of reference sources. Hufsmith also provides brief profiles of the cattlemen involved in the lynching and probes deeper into some of the mysteries surrounding the coroner's inquests and the grand jury. Duncan Aikman's _Calamity Jane and the Lady_

Wildcats (New York: Henry Holt, 1927) sticks to the traditional version. Ruth Beebe's *Reminiscing Along the Sweetwater* (Casper, Wyo.: House of Printing, 1973) explains much about the history and people of the Sweetwater country.

Newspapers of the time give colorful background. Those consulted for this piece were: *Carbon County Journal*, July 27, August 3, October 26, 1889; *Casper Weekly Mail*, February 15, August 30, 1889; *Cheyenne Daily Sun*, September 2, 1884, June through July and October 1889; *The Wyoming State Journal*, March 28, 1940.

For background on the land acts of the time, see Howard R. Lamar, ed., *The New Encyclopedia of the American West*, (New Haven: Yale University Press, 1998), and britannica.com. T. A. Larson's *History of Wyoming*, 2d. ed., rev. (Lincoln: University of Nebraska Press, 1978) gives excellent background on the Homestead Act and the Desert Land Act as well as the cattle business during the 1880s, water rights information, the severe winter of 1886–1887, and the fencing issue. The story of the Wyoming Stock Growers Association is told in John Rolfe Burroughs's *Guardian of the Grasslands* (Cheyenne: Wyoming Stock Growers Association, 1971), which chronicles the organization's first hundred years.

The Casper College Library Special Collections department also houses a good amount of research materials in the Daniel Y. Meschter Collection, including information on Thomas Watson's homestead and the obituaries of Watson and his wife. Information on single women homesteaders and various statistics can be found in Paula Mae Bauman, "Single Women Homesteaders in Wyoming, 1880–1930" (Master's thesis, University of Wyoming, 1983). For those interested in probing the history of prostitution in the Old West, consult Anne M. Butler's *Daughters of Joy, Sisters of Misery* (Urbana: University of Illinois Press, 1985); Larry K. Brown's *The Hog Ranches of Wyoming* (Glendo, Wyo.: High Plains Press, 1995); and Anne Seagraves's *Soiled Doves* (Hayden, Idaho: Wesanne Publications, 1994).

Chapter 9—Calamity Jane

Readers interested in obtaining the best sources of information on Calamity Jane may find the process frustrating and time-consuming. Although hundreds of essays and several dozen biographies and novels have been written about her, few merit much attention. Most of the significant books, including life stories and works of fiction, are discussed in the text of this book's essay on her. The author has also compiled a near-exhaustive listing of the articles, book chapters, full-length volumes, and films about Calamity Jane. A copy of the bibliography is available from the writer.

Other essays and books about Calamity Jane deserve comment. First, one should begin with the writings of James D. McLaird, professor of history at Dakota Wesleyan University. Now in the final stages of preparing what will be the definitive biography of the subject, McLaird has written several key essays on Calamity Jane. As a start, begin with McLaird's outstanding piece, "Calamity Jane's Diary and Letters: Story of a Fraud," *Montana: The Magazine of Western History* 45 (autumn–winter 1995): 20–35. This article effectively destroys Jean Hickok McCormick's claim to be the daughter of Calamity Jane and Wild Bill Hickok as well as the credibility of the diary and letters she asserted were Calamity's. Another of McLaird's essays, "Calamity Jane and Wild Bill: Myth and Reality," *Journal of the West* 37 (April 1998): 23–32, separates the facts from the distortions in this often overwrought story. The final months of Calamity's tragic life are expertly detailed in McLaird's thoroughly researched "Calamity Jane: The Life and the Legend," *South Dakota History* 24 (spring 1994): 1–18.

Richard W. Etulain also deals with the historical and legendary Calamity Jane in several essays that will become parts of his biography of her. His "Calamity Jane: Creation of a Western Legend: An Afterword," to Roberta Beed Sollid, *Calamity Jane: A Study in Historical Criticism* (1958; Helena: Montana Historical Society Press, 1995), 149–63, briefly traces the varying interpretations, over time, of the subject. His "Calamity Jane: Independent Woman of the Wild West," in Glenda Riley and Richard W. Etulain, eds., *By Grit and Grace: Eleven Women Who Shaped the American West* (Golden, Colo.: Fulcrum Publishing, 1997), 72–92, provides a capsule overview biography, emphasizing Calamity's desire to be a pioneer woman. Appended to that essay is an abbreviated discussion of the major sources on Calamity Jane. A third treatment, in Etulain, *Telling Western Stories: From Buffalo Bill to Larry McMurtry* (Albuquerque: University of New Mexico Press, 1999), 41–51, 158–59, analyzes how powerful myths have over-shadowed the facts of Calamity's story.

Unfortunately, the most recent full-length biography, Stella Foote's *A History of Calamity Jane: Our Country's First Liberated Woman* (New York: Vantage Press, 1996), falls victim to the McCormick distortions and also suffers from other large errors and incorrect information. More useful, although it too accepts the diary and letters as authentic, is the smoothly written chapter on Calamity in Elizabeth Stevenson, *Figures in a Western Landscape* (Baltimore: The Johns Hopkins University Press, 1994).

In the 1940s and 1950s, librarian Clarence Paine produced three valuable sections of a never-completed biography. Two of these essays appear in Chicago Westerners' *Brand Books* (Chicago: Westerners, 1946, 1947), and a third in Roderick Peattie, ed., *The Black Hills* (New York: Vanguard Press, 1952). Also very useful is British writer Andrew Blewitt's fact-filled article in *The English Westerners' Brand Book* 5 (January 1963): 1–9. Of note too is the pamphlet by South Dakota historian J. Leonard Jennewein, *Calamity Jane of the Western Trails* (Rapid City, So. Dak.: Dakota West Books, 1953, 1991).

Until the forthcoming books by McLaird and Etulain appear, biographers and other writers interested in Calamity Jane would do well to mine several major archival collections of material about her. The largest such collections are on deposit in Wyoming at the American Heritage Center in Laramie, the Wyoming State Historical Society in Cheyenne, and the Buffalo Bill Historical Center in Cody; in Montana at the Montana Historical Society in Helena; and in South Dakota at the Center for Western Studies at Augustana College in Sioux Falls, the South Dakota Historical Society in Pierre, and Dakota Wesleyan University in Mitchell. Other important collections on Calamity Jane are at the public libraries of Denver, Billings, Montana, and Deadwood, South Dakota.

Sources and Further Reading for Other Wild Women of the Old West

Sarah Winnemucca

Sarah Winnemucca's own book, *Life among the Piutes [sic]: Their Wrongs and Claims* (Reno: University of Nevada Press, 1994), is critical to understanding her life and thought. She begins with the initial meeting between Piutes and Anglos, then continues on with her thoughts on social morality, wars and their causes, and life at the Malheur Agency in Oregon state.

The most trustworthy and accurate secondary account of Sarah Winnemucca and the Northern Paiutes is Gae Whitney Canfield, *Sarah Winnemucca of the Northern Paiutes* (Norman: University of Oklahoma Press, 1983). Although Canfield's book shys away from analysis, it relates—and puts in order—the facts concerning Winnemucca and her people. Other helpful works are George F. Brimlow, "The Life of Sarah Winnemucca: The Formative Years," *Oregon Historical Quarterly* (June 1952); Mary F. Morrow, *Sarah Winnemucca* (Milwaukee: Raintree Publishers, 1990); Lalla Scott Kamee, *A Paiute Narrative* (Reno: University of Nevada Press, 1966). Sarah is also found in a composite biography by Grace Steele Woodward, Harold P. Howard, and Gae Whitney Canfield, *Three American Indian Women: Pocahontas, Sacajawea, Sarah Winnemucca of the Northern Paiutes* (New York: MJF Books, 1995).

For young readers, Sarah Winnemucca's history is told in Dorothy Nafus Morrison, *Chief Sarah: Sarah Winnemucca's Fight for Indian Rights* (Portland: Oregon Historical Society Press, 1990); Mary Frances Morrow, *Sarah Winnemucca: Paiute Native American Indian Stories* (Milwaukee: Raintree Publishers, 1992), and Ellen Scordato, *Sarah Winnemucca: Northern Paiute Writer and Diplomat* (New York: Chelsea House, 1992).

Prostitutes and Madams

The single best book on prostitution in the American West is Anne M. Butler, *Daughters of Joy, Sisters of Misery: Prostitutes in the American West, 1865–90* (Urbana: University of Illinois Press, 1985). Butler combines a large number of actual cases with analysis. Insightful and scholarly articles include Lucy Cheng Hirata, "Free, Enslaved, and Indentured Workers in Nineteenth Century Chinese Prostitution," *Signs* (fall 1979): 3–29; Mary Murphy, "The Private Lives of Public Women: Prostitution in Butte, Montana, 1878–1917," *Frontiers* (1984): 30-35; Paula Petrik, "Capitalists with Rooms: Prostitution in Helena, Montana, 1865–1900," *Montana* 31 (spring 1981): 28–41 and "Strange Bedfellows: Prostitution, Politicians and Moral Reform in Helena, Montana, 1885–1887," *Montana* (summer 1985): 2–13; and Elliott West, "Scarlet West: The Oldest Profession in the Trans-Mississippi West," *Montana* (spring 1981): 16–27.

For tales of prostitutes and madams, see Caroline Bancroft, *Six Racy Madams of Colorado* (Boulder, Colo.: Johnson Co., 1965); Hillyer Best, *Juliette Bulette and Other Red Light Ladies* (Sparks, Nev.: Western Printing, 1959); Allan G. Bird, *Bordellos of Blair Street: The Story of Silverton, Colorado's Notorious Red Light District* (Grand Rapids, Mich.: The Other Shop, 1987); and H. Gordon Frost, *Gentlemen's Club: The Story of Prostitution in El Paso* (El Paso, Texas: Mangan Books, 1983).

Annie Oakley

Myth-building began with Oakley's first biographer, Courtney Riley Cooper, who combines fact and falsehood in *Annie Oakley: Woman at Arms* (New York: Duffield, 1927), published only a year after Annie's death. Oakley's niece, Annie Fern Campbell Swartwout, offers her own version of Oakley's life in *Missie: An Historical Biography of Annie Oakley* (New York: Macmillan 1954). Walter Havighurst, *Annie Oakley of the Wild West* (New York: Macmillan, 1954) is a fictionalized portrayal of Annie's life that is generally accurate. More thorough and well-researched narratives are found in Isabelle S. Sayer, *The Rifle Queen: Annie Oakley* (Ostrander, Ohio: n.p., 1973) and *Annie Oakley and Buffalo Bill's Wild West* (New York: Dover Publications, 1981).

The two most recent, and accurate, biographies are Shirl Kasper, *Annie Oakley* (Norman: University of Oklahoma Press, 1992), and Glenda Riley, *Annie Oakley: Her Life and Legacy* (Norman: University of Oklahoma Press, 1993). Kasper offers the first authoritative chronology of Oakley's life, while Riley puts Oakley in the context of women's history. Riley also analyzes Annie Oakley's significance in "Annie Oakley: Creating the Cowgirl," in Paul A. Hutton and Roy Ritchie, eds., *Frontier and Region: Essays in Honor of Martin Ridge* (Albuquerque: University of New Mexico Press, 1997), and in Glenda Riley and Richard W. Etulain, eds., *By Grit & Grace: Eleven Women Who Shaped the American West* (Golden, Colo.: Fulcrum Publishing, 1999).

For young readers, Edmund Collier, *The Story of Annie Oakley* (New York: Grosset and Dunlap, 1956), idealizes Oakley as a child of the frontier. Subsequent contributions that kept Annie's story alive for young readers include Shannon Garst, *Annie Oakley* (New York: Julian Messner, 1958; Jan Gleiter and Kathleen Thompson, *Annie Oakley: Great Tales* (Nashville, Tenn.: Ideals Publishing, 1985); Ellen Wilson, *Annie Oakley: Little Sure Shot* (Indianapolis: Bobbs-Merrill, 1958); and Charles P. Graves, *Annie Oakley: The Shooting Star* (Champaign, Ill.: Garrard, 1961); Robert Quakenbush, *Who's That Girl with the Gun? A Story of Annie Oakley* (New York: Prentice-Hall Books for Young Readers, 1988); and Ellen Levine, *Ready, Aim, Fire! The Real Adventures of Annie Oakley* (New York: Scholastic, 1989). Levine adds Annie's husband, Frank Butler, and presents Annie as a role model for contemporary young women.

Cowgirls in general are covered in Joyce Gibson Roach, *The Cowgirls*, rev. ed., (Denton: University of North Texas Press, 1990); Teresa Jordan, *Cowgirls: Women of the American West* (Lincoln: University of Nebraska Press, Bison Books, 1991); and Sarah Wood-Clark, *Beautiful Daring Western Girls: Women of the Wild West Shows*, 2nd ed., (Billings, Mont.: Artcraft Printers, 1991).

Belle Starr

The accounts that set the pattern for inflated Belle Starr interpretations were Alton B. Meyers, *Bella Starr: The Bandit Queen, Or, The Female Jesse James* (New York: Richard K. Fox, 1889), and S. W. Harman, *Hell on the Border* (Fort Smith, Ark.: n.p., 1898). One of the first authors to question the customary stories was the Ozark folklorist Vance Randolph. Publishing under pseudonyms, Randolph released Anton S. Booker, *Wildcats in Petticoats* (Girard, Kansas: Little Blue Books, 1931), 52-63, and William Yancey Shackleford, *Belle Starr, The Bandit Queen* (Girard, Kansas: Haldeman-Julius Publications, 1943). Another writer who combined Belle Starr stories with an occasional accurate date or unique theory was Burton Rascoe, *Belle Starr: The Bandit Queen* (New York: Random House, 1941).

More recently, Carl W. Breihan with Charles A. Rosamond, *The Bandit Belle* (Seattle: Hangman Press, 1970), put the usual legends in a highly readable format for a general audience. Phillip W. Steele's *Starr Tracks: Belle and Pearl Starr* (Gretna, Louisiana: Pelican Publishing Co., 1992) added Pearl's story to that of Belle, and included some family letters.

The only Belle Starr biography worthy of the label is Glenn Shirley's *Belle Starr and Her Times: The Literature, the Facts, and the Legends* (Norman: University of Oklahoma Press, 1982). In addition, Riley offers a more complete analysis of Belle's life in Richard W. Etulain and Glenda Riley, eds., *With Badges & Bullets: Lawmen & Outlaws in the Old West* (Golden, Colo.: Fulcrum Publishing, 1999).

Carl R. Green's and William R. Sanford's *Belle Starr* (Hillside, New Jersey: Enslow Publishing, 1992) offers a highly readable version of Belle Starr's life for young adults.

Contributors

ANNE M. BUTLER is the senior editor of the *Western Historical Quarterly* and a Trustee Professor of History at Utah State University. She has published widely on western women's history and is currently finishing a monograph about the experiences of Roman Catholic sisters in the American West.

RICHARD W. ETULAIN is Professor Emeritus of History at the University of New Mexico. He specializes in the history and literature of the American West and has authored or edited more than forty books. Among his recent volumes are *Telling Western Stories: From Buffalo Bill to Larry McMurtry* (1999), *The Hollywood West* (co-edited with Glenda Riley), *New Mexican Lives* (2002), and *César Chávez: A Brief Biography* (2002). He is at work on a biography of Calamity Jane and a general history of the American West.

CARMEN GOLDTHWAITE writes about the roles of Texas women in history. She is a contributor to *Wild West, True West,* and *Persimmon Hill* magazines and a columnist for the *Fort Worth Star-Telegram.* She is writing the book *Texas Ranch Women* for publication by the University of North Texas Press. She serves on the faculty of Southern Methodist University's School of Creative Writing and teaches a course on Texas women's history for Texas Christian University and the University of Texas at Arlington. Goldthwaite is a member of Western Writers of America and the National Writers Union and is a director of the Society of Professional Journalists.

CANDY MOULTON is the author of nine nonfiction books, including *Everyday Life of American Indians from 1800 to 1900* (2001), *The Writer's Guide to Everyday Life in the Wild West from 1840 to 1900* (1999), *Roadside History of Nebraska* (1997), *Roadside History of Wyoming* (1995), and *Steamboat Legendary Bucking Horse* (1992). She is the editor of the Western Writers of America *Roundup* magazine and the editor of the journal for the Western Outlaw Lawman History Association. With Max Evans she edited *Hot Biscuits: Eighteen Short Stories by Ranching Women and Men* (2002).

GLENDA RILEY is the Alexander M. Bracken Professor of History at Ball State University. She specializes in the history of women in the West. A past-president of the Western History Association, Riley has received numerous other honors and awards, including Fulbright grants to Ireland and Kenya. Her most recent book is *Women and Nature: Saving the "Wild" West* (1999).

M. J. VAN DEVENTER is editor of *Persimmon Hill* magazine, an award-winning quarterly journal on the West, and director of publications for the National Cowboy and Western Heritage Museum in Oklahoma City, Oklahoma. She is also an adjunct professor of journalism at the University of Central Oklahoma. Her articles on the West have appeared in numerous publications, including *Cowboys & Indians, American Cowboy,* and *Southwest Art.* She is author of the books *Western Design* (1995) and *Native American Style* (1999). As a reporter for the *Tulsa Tribune,* she was nominated for a Pulitzer Prize for public service reporting. She was inducted into the Oklahoma Journalism Hall of Fame in 1999.

LORI VAN PELT is a historian and author of the Dreamers and Schemers series profiling Wyoming's colorful historic characters, published by High Plains Press. She writes regularly for the Western Writers of America *Roundup* magazine, *Persimmon Hill,* the *WREN (Wyoming Rural Electric News)* magazine, and the journal for the Western Outlaw and Lawman Association. Van Pelt's historical short fiction appears in *Hot Biscuits* (July 2002), *White Hats* (April 2002), and *American West: Twenty New Stories by the Western Writers of America* (2001); more short fiction will appear in *Black Hats* (April 2003). She is working on a biography of Nellie Tayloe Ross of Wyoming, the nation's first woman governor.

PRISCILLA WEGARS, an independent historian and historical archaeologist specializing in the history and archaeology of Asian Americans in the West, is an affiliate assistant professor in the Department of Sociology/Anthropology/Justice Studies, University of Idaho, Moscow. She is the founder and volunteer curator of the UI's Asian American Comparative Collection, a repository of artifacts and documentary materials. She edited *Hidden Heritage: Historical Archaeology of the Overseas Chinese* (1993), wrote the biography for children, *Polly Bemis: A Chinese American Pioneer* (2002), and is working on biographies of Polly Bemis for young adults and adults. Each summer she leads an excursion to visit Polly Bemis's cabin and grave.

216

Index

Moreland, Isaac, 39

Morgan, Emily D. West, xiv, 29–30; and
Battle of San Jacinto, 37, 38; captured
by Santa Anna, 36–37, 39, 41–43; and de
Zavalas, 33, 34; freedwoman papers, 39,
40; as hotelkeeper, 34–36; and James
Morgan, 29, 30, 31–32; move to Texas,
30–31, 33; return to New York, 39–40.
See also West, Emily D. (wife of
Lorenzo de Zavala), "The Yellow Rose
of Texas" (song)

Morgan, James, 29, 30, 31–32; conflict
with Sam Houston, 39, 41; postwar difficulties, 39; and Texas colonization,
31–32; and Texas independence movement, 34, 35; in war for Texas independence, 36, 39; and "The Yellow Rose of
Texas" (song), 41

Morgan's Point, Texas, 32

Morrell, Dorothy, 140, 143

Morris, Otis, 63

Moulton, Candy, 139

Mountain Pride coach, 104–105, 106

Moustache, Madame, 188

Mulhall Wild West Show, 123, 128, 131;
and Tom Mix, 133; and Will Rogers, 125

Mulhall, Agnes (Bossie), 119, 120, 121,
133

Mulhall, Charles (Charley), 119, 120, 128,
133

Mulhall, Esther Childers, 133

Mulhall, Georgia Smith, 119–120, 133;
daughter Mildred, 133; on Lucille
Mulhall, 122; on Zack and Mary Agnes
Mulhall, 121

Mulhall, Logan, 119, 121

Mulhall, Lucille, xviii, xx, xxi, 118,
133–134, 140, 150; accidents, 132; and
apparent daughter Margaret, 129,
130–131; and Bud Ballew, 130; clothes
and appearance, 125–126; and Congress
of Rough Riders, 122–123; death of, 133;

and death of steer, 132–133; and diminished ranch, 133; drinking, 133; and
Geronimo, 123; Hall of Fame honors,
133; and horses (Governor, et al.),
131–132; and informal competitions,
122; and Interstate and Territorial
Exposition, 123; and J. W. McCormick,
130; at Madison Square Garden,
123–124, 151; marriage to Martin Van
Bergen, 128–129; marriage to Tom
Burnett, 129–130; and Mulhall Wild
West Show, 123, 128, 131; own shows,
131, 133; personality, 120; photos
(action), 119, 122, 125; photos (publicity),
127, 130; ranching background, 118–122,
126, 133–134; relationship with father,
124–125, 128, 130, 133–134; in Rodeo
Hall of Fame, 133; rodeo work, 131; roping champion, 124, 125, 126–128, 131;
schooling, 126; and son William, 129,
130–131; talent as cowgirl, 121–122; and
term cowgirl, 118, 124; terms to describe,
118, 124

Mulhall, Madolyn, 119

Mulhall, Margaret, 129, 130–131

Mulhall, Marmaduke, 119

Mulhall, Mary Agnes, 118, 129, 130, 133;
death of, 133; personality, 119, 120, 121,
126

Mulhall, Mildred (died in infancy), 119

Mulhall, Mildred (The Little Sheriff), 119,
120, 132

Mulhall, Zack, 118, 119–121; Congress of
Rough Riders, 122–123; death of, 133;
and diminished ranch, 130, 133; diverse
activities and success of, 118, 120–121;
Interstate and Territorial Exposition,
123; Mulhall Wild West Show, 123, 128,
131; personality, 119; relationship with
Lucille, 124–125, 128, 130, 133–134

Mulhall, Oklahoma, 121. See also Alfred,
Oklahoma